They All Want to Write

Written English in the Elementary School

— They All Want To Write —

Fourth Edition

Alvina Treut Burrows
Doris C. Jackson
Dorothy O. Saunders

Library Professional Publications
1984

372.6
B 972

First published in 1984 as a Library Professional Publication, an imprint of The Shoe String Press, Inc.
Hamden, Connecticut 06514

Printed in the United States of America

Library of Congress Cataloging in Publication Data

Burrows, Alvina Treut,
    They all want to write.

    Bibliography: p.
    Includes index.
    1. English language—Composition and exercises.
I. Jackson, Doris C.,   . II. Saunders,
Dorothy O.,   . III. Title.
LB1576.B94   1984   372.6'23   84-15470
ISBN 0-208-02042-X
ISBN 0-208-02043-8 (pbk.)

We are grateful to the following for permission to use quotations from their publications:

Doubleday & Company, Inc. (Hughes Mearns, *Creative Youth*)

Harper & Row, Publishers, Inc. ("The Meal" from *Dogs and Dragons, Trees and Dreams* by Karla Kuskin. Copyright © 1962 by Karla Kuskin)

Contents

Introduction to the Fourth Edition

There is current widespread alarm over our dire national need to improve our citizens' command of the English language: the ability to read it (literacy); the ability to speak it with some precision and clarity; and the ability to write it with the same precision and clarity when that is called for, or to project our imaginations and intellects—the essence of ourselves—with verve and flavor, when that is the reason for communicating. Major criticism has focused on the present learning and teaching at the high school level, but those of us who have teaching in our bones from a lifetime of experience, know well that the seeds of this command of language are sown in the elementary grades.

Accordingly, we present this fourth edition of our book, addressed, as it has been since it was first published, to all of the many persons who are concerned that children learn to express themselves in written English in the early years of schooling. Classroom teachers will find here practical help and guidance for day-to-day activities as well as a springboard for their own experimentation; so too, though, will other school personnel, especially school library media specialists, curriculum workers, administrators and supervisors. Teachers and students in college will find it useful, and last, but certainly not least, parents will find in it inspiration to provide the partnership with the schools that is presently being reaffirmed anew as the essential reinforcement for learning.

Our aim is to teach children to write correctly and, at the same time, to learn to enjoy writing so much that they will keep on wanting to do it as long as they live. The techniques we describe are illustrated with many examples of children's writings, and we present effective solutions to the

1

problems of enhancing creativity and originality while maintaining long-term growth in the mastery of language essentials.

As we worked with children, beginning in the thirties, recording and analyzing our findings, we had known of no explicit directions for achieving both excellence in composition and joy in self-expression. Later, we were to find the work of a National Council of Teachers of English commission, described in *An Experience Curriculum in English,* published in 1935, and were pleased to note commission members' support of the beliefs we held as the result of our study. We pay tribute to their work and are gratified to be part of a long and siginificant continuity in studying some of the many dimensions of children's written expression. The commission identified differences between what it called "utilitarian" and "creative" expression, while we used the more everyday terms "practical" and "personal" to distinguish the processes inherent in dealing with communicating external data, as compared with projecting, in writing, the intimately possessed, internal experience.

The first edition of this book was published in 1939. About one hundred children formed the core of our first study, some sixty of whom we taught over a period of four years. The classes were organized as follows:

GROUP I	GROUP II
31 children	30 children
Grades 3 and 4—Saunders	Grades 3 and 4—Jackson
Grades 5 and 6—Burrows	Grades 5 and 6—Ferebee

GROUP III	GROUP IV
31 children	20 children
Grades 3 and 4—Saunders	Grades 1 and 2—Jackson

Since our first four-year experiment we have taught many children in different schools for either one- or two-year periods. We have continued to experiment, to test, and sometimes to discard methods that proved ineffective or which served only to make children dislike writing. We believe that we have found a balanced writing program which shows how to bring forth, step by step, superior results in informational, objective, "practical" composition, as well as in imaginative, subjective "personal" writing. We believe that our way enables children to find pride, self-identity, and joy in both types of communications.

To the earlier editions of our work we have added two new chapters, many new examples, expanded selections of "triggering" stories and verse, and descriptions of procedures not previously reported. One new chapter relates the importance of children's writing to their reading. The immensely significant development of elementary school library media centers, which has occurred since the last edition of our book, has made an enormous improvement in the scope and variety of reading resources available to children. It has also meant the possibility of invaluable assistance to the classroom teacher from the school library media specialist in teaching search skills to children, holding book discussions, and finding books and other materials that are just right for the occasion and for the individual child. The other new chapter samples some of the research done since our earlier experiments—research that fortifies, through new quantitive measures, some of our own conclusions.

Through the years we have grown increasingly aware of our debt to Hughes Mearns. It was he who turned our steps to the new way marked by a signpost which read: "This path leads to a heightened respect for each individual and an abiding faith in his innate power." It is because we followed where Hughes Mearns led that the substance of this book came to be.

A second source of supporting strength lies in the clarity of Suzanne Langer's statement in *Feeling and Form* (Scribner's, 1953). After detailed discussion of the functions of language, she summarizes her observations by saying that all language is used either to convey information or to influence feeling. For this buttressing of our own observation, we wish to acknowledge her philosophical wisdom, which makes the ways we have followed in treating these two functions of language seem more than ever justified.

We want to acknowledge the warm reception given to our work over these many years by teachers, parents, and students of language and teaching methodology. And to the several hundreds of elementary school pupils whose literacy flowered as they talked, read, and wrote; as they painted, studied, and sang; as they played, argued, and grew as persons; we shall be always joyously grateful. We gratefully acknowledge our appreciation to the school systems of Bronxville, New York and Montgomery County, Maryland where we did such happy productive teaching and learned so much that we could share with others.

June D. Ferebee, who worked with us throughout the experiment underlying the first two editions of this book, and who shared in the labor of writing both the first and second editons, died in December 1959. Because of her contribution to these earlier publications and because of her steadfast commitment to beauty, we treasure the association of her name and her spirit with this, the fourth edition of *They All Want To Write.*

A. T. B.
D. C. J.
D. O. S.
February, 1984

3

1

Writing and Growth

*The art of life consists in creating an individual and a
unique self.*
                    Powys, A Philosophy of Solitude

The complete freedom necessary for the life of the creative spirit has
always stood opposed to the methodical acquisition of skills and techniques. Correctness has appeared to be the antithesis of spontaneity. Our
premise has been that a constructive synthesis could be made of these
apparently disparate elements, that a child could indeed become the
minstrel of his own free spirit and a careful scribe as well. To this end we
have recorded our experience.

Long dissatisfied with the results of our teaching of writing, we had
through trial and error discarded at least a little of the empty ritual.
Common belief invited us to experiment more definitely along the lines of
our emerging understanding. Given the happy accident of continuity of
pupil groups we proceeded to test and to clarify our beliefs. These years of
experience and study have led us to believe that we have found ways to
nurture the creative spirit and at the same time to effect power in the use of
writing skills. It appears that the utilitarian and artistic phases of writing are
not mutually antagonistic when the rules of the one and the freedom of the
other are zealously guarded.

BASIC BELIEFS

We believe that writing can play a significant part in a child's development.
If a child is to be an effective, poised individual, he or she must have an
awareness and an appreciation of self-identity and power. Such self-
knowledge comes from frequent opportunities to experiment and to
fumble until out of the effort something is fashioned that the child can

5

perceive as being good. This growth pattern is especially evident when a child is learning to put thoughts on paper. That the product is often crude and clumsy does not matter. It is important only that the child working in his or her own way produces something to which self-approval can be given. The inner satisfaction, the momentary kinship with creative power, gives the child a sense of self-worth and stimulates further effort.

Writing, we believe, serves at least two needs for writer and audience: that of artistic self-expression and that of communicating functional ideas. One is personal, individual, and highly perishable; the other utilitarian, realistic, or intellectual requires the discipline of correct mechanics to be fully useful. The two kinds of writing must be handled differently. Personal writing is sparked and kept alive by complete freedom to experiment and complete assurance of a respectful reception of the product whatever its quality. In contrast to this, the acquisition of form seems intrinsically a function of realistic writing in which other people are concerned. Practical writing springs from relatively constant sources; the need or the authority remains a point of reference against which the product can be checked. The author of practical writing works as a reproducer of known facts, conditions, or ideas presented, to be sure, in the writer's unique fashion. But the material recorded comes from external sources; correction and verification can be required without injury to the individual or the loss of ideas.

Practical writing serves the same purpose for children as for adults. It takes many forms: letters, memos, plans, captions, lists, reports. The child's practical need to explain, remember, or convey ideas makes for receptivity to the teacher's guidance and suggestions. This written product communicates with other people, and it soon becomes evident that if the writer wishes to be clearly understood accurate mechanics are necessary. In this way composition standards take on meaning, and children become more willing to strive to attain them.

In the early grades before children achieve some control over handwriting and spelling, they see their ideas take visible form for sharing by dictating to the teacher. The simple message, perhaps to parents about the date of an approaching program, may be copied only in part by pupils and the rest duplicated or finished by the teacher. As skill is gained less writing is done for the child, who takes on more of the labor of completing a good copy.

In later grades, practical writing reaches correct form by more involved processes. The situation that demands writing is made clear— perhaps a memo for the school bulletin board, a report for a class study, or the program for a class play. In any case, the need is kept vividly before the children as they prepare to do clear expository writing. Information is gathered in the classroom and in the school library media center. It is mulled over, added to, and organized. Children read, discuss, sketch, plan, and write. Rough drafts are corrected individually in a conference with the teacher, which is the very essence of teaching. Reading the rough draft aloud and correcting it is only part of this meeting of minds; encouraging the struggling writer and affirming good points are also essentials of the conference. Making a fine copy of the draft of the report or letter takes time, and the accompanying pride of accomplishment will become part of the children's attitude toward language. Each child needs some special bit of approval: perhaps admiration for neat arrangement and accurate spelling, appreciation of correct punctuation, or praise of the clear statement of the idea and the vividness of expression. The end result of this practical writing should be satisfaction from a job well done that will affect the audience for it as intended.

With *personal* writing, the sources lie almost wholly within the individual, and there is no final authority other than personal taste. Time out to revamp independent clauses may mean loss of the whole idea. More serious, editing story after story may so curb the imagination or so fatigue the uncertain young writer that the desire to write too often turns to dread. Confusion that arises from trying to shape a child's ideas to an adult's conception or pattern has resulted in mimicry or even outright plagiarism. In fact, the same literary designs that teachers would imprint, usually with such deadening consequences, develop more vividly from inner necessity. When children write with the idea of enlisting the attention of an audience from the beginning to the end of a tale, they learn in time to select patterns that give vigor and verve to their writing. To hold even a friendly and accepting audience, a writer must really tell a story. Beginning with a propelling idea, implying just enough probability of outcome to spark listeners' curiosity, opening up several possible ways of working out a solution, and holding suspense until the end—these and other elements are found by actual trial to be effective techniques of story construction. Design thus emerges from the same storyteller-audience situations that were the beginnings of our literary heritage. Writer, storyteller, audience form a whole that operates naturally to strengthen and vitalize written expression. The rules of literary structure have come from just such reality, but they have been crystallized into academic principles that usually leave the young quite ignorant of their functional origin. The real situations that first produced those principles of structure need to be relived again and again by young writers. Continued experience in being sometimes a writer and frequently an avid listener can make an individual so sensitive to

7

elements of story design that he naturally appropriates some of them for his own use. The delight of entertaining an audience with the magic of his own creation is a pleasure to be sought again and again. And satisfaction from such success begets even greater zest for writing.

When the children in our experience came to know that their personal expression was acceptable in the form in which it was presented and would not be tampered with to suit our standards, writing periods were transformed. The impulse to write grew stronger and the volume increased. The children, untroubled by coercion or arbitrary direction, wrote or dictated their ideas for what should be the primary purpose of all creative effort: to please one's self or to entertain others. Children soon catch the delight of using words to paint pictures, or to catch a special mood, to trap the interest of the crowd with the first phrase, to make them laugh.

Mary Ellen dictated this in the third grade:

> Star, what makes you shine
> So bright upon the water
> Making a path for me,
> No one but me?
> A little path
> Just for me!
> I feel like a queen.

After much trial and error it became obvious to us that such subjective expression must not be shaped to fit standards. Our effort was then directed toward building into the child's consciousness a realization of what makes writing good, and the method is that of appreciating the good thing when it appears. The original idea, the fresh invention, the vivid way of saying something is singled out for comment because what is approved determines the direction of growth. This is ordinarily done when the children are sharing their work with one another. As they grow increasingly aware of the elements of good writing, their spontaneous appreciation becomes more discriminating and concrete. The teacher injects guidance unobtrusively so that it does not arouse resistance nor disrupt the spirit of rapport among the children. Even when an epidemic of crudely violent stories or stereotyped plots breaks out, she does not show dismay, knowing that offensive things ignored gradually drop away if there are better things to take their place. It may be opportune for the teacher to read from her collection of stories until attention is diverted and perhaps a counterepidemic is started.

Children need adults to bring them into effective relationship with new materials, new sources of inspiration. Left to themselves without inputs of fresh experience, children are apt to reuse an increasingly thinner content. We found depth of experience to be more productive than a surfeit of experiences, which often resulted only in superficiality and indifference. This is one of the major problems that face teachers today; children, in pure self-preservation, have learned to tune out so much that it becomes difficult to break through even with things they might want to know. The timing of new ventures that open vistas in keeping with the children's developing capacities is never easy. We learned always to keep in mind, however, that the direction of children's growth from dependence to independence is based in large part on the dynamics of their relationship with adults.

The way of working that we describe achieves the aim of making personal writing a happy and spontaneous experience for children. Much of what they write is trivial, but there are flashes of good writing that reveal a startling power. Disarmed by the disguise of fictitious characters and incidents, they divulge secret yearnings and resentments that they would never consciously betray. Grownup behavior is frankly appraised according to its immediate effect upon the children themselves. This is a point of view that adults rarely encounter, because boys and girls, for their own protection, have learned to conceal it. When they are writing out of their innermost selves, however, it is bound to be exposed, and the teacher has to be ready to hear the truth as they see it. Only by accepting real feelings can we get the sincerity and vigor we want to nurture. It is the getting down in one's own language what one thinks or feels that is important. The writer of personal material does not write for the spelling, penmanship, or grammar to be inspected, but to record part of himself to be shared or privately enjoyed.

Practical writing, too, makes its contribution to the balanced growth of writing power. When a child's first contacts with writing are so practical that the results of a written communication are readily observable this kindles a respect for writing as a means to action. The feeling of reality is essential, because a skill that is significant in a child's important affairs has an assured future. The person-to-person directness of utilitarian writing necessitates clarity, the hallmark of fine exposition. Mechanical errors are searched for and corrected. In this objective expression some success is possible for nearly all children. Some of them who cannot lose themselves in flights of invention find great satisfaction in the order and clarity of a well-worded letter or report. Many a youngster feels a first, perhaps an only, power over elusive words by producing an information report proudly referred to as a book. And individuality is just as likley to find expression here and to be further cultivated by such writing experience as by the personal variety.

Standards of attainment, too, are more easily applied in the fields of practical writing than in those imaginative areas where the writer must be his own authority. A child can be more certain that his product is good in the conventional sense. For some children this assurance that they have met accepted standards of arrangement, structure, and punctuation is important and productive of further strength in writing as well as of general self-confidence and security.

Items of mechanics and sentence formation learned in practical writing gradually become matters of common use in the personal writing a child does for his own satisfaction. The fearless honesty of expression exercised in personal writing gives color and conviction to the child's practical writing as well. All these elements of good writing gradually fuse into an enlarged and strengthened writing power as practical and personal writing demonstrate their complementary nature.

As we became aware of children's potentialities for growth in writing, we came to see our own responsibilities more clearly. The more we saw power emerging from the complementary exercise of practical and personal writing, the less we felt the need for pressing children to write. Children's response to their own purposes spurred them to more and better writing. Individual projection to an understanding audience was the basis of wholesome self-realization and a means to stronger, clearer written expression. Our role was to establish those situations that not only allowed for writing but also fostered it and at times required it. Most important of all, we found ourselves responsible for the emotional climate in which creative insights deepened.

Many other teachers have found the techniques described herein to be productive both for the enhancement of creativity and the control of correct form. We believe that there are certain conditions under which these measures work best, and we have attempted to state these as guiding principles.

- Personal writing should not be expected until a child has had a wealth of satisfying experience with oral expression and has gained sufficient physical skill to prevent undue fatigue.
- Each child's ability to express his ideas is distinctly unique and personal. The rate at which this ability grows is likewise individual. Only harm can come from trying to force more mature forms of expression than children show themselves ready to use.
- From the beginning, practical writing must meet high standards of form and organization, which most children accept willingly because their writing serves a genuine use.

- Personal writing needs to fulfill only the child's desires, except upon those extremely rare occasions when correct form is necessary out of consideration for others or when the product is to be permanently preserved.
- It is equally important to accept a child's own form for his personal expression and to help him learn conventional forms for practical writing. Each experience contributes to the other, leading to a natural integration of style and technique as the writer matures.
- Every child writes himself into his product. Style, tempo, phrasing, characterization, choice of subject are exponents of individual personality.
- Since the child can write honestly only what is truly his, time to assimilate experience and information is vitally necessary.
- Involvement in literature contributes immeasurably to rich, adequate expression. Conversely, the effort of trying to write one's own ideas effectively and colorfully heightens sensitivity to good literature.
- Direct sensory experience promotes lively observation and precise, vivid expression. Putting firsthand experience into one's own words helps to avoid plagiarism.
- Children's writing reflects the impact of such mass media as television, radio, comics, and movies, not only in vocabulary but also in tempo and characterization.
- Personal writing serves the need for the release of tensions and for the draining of aggression, fears, and destructive emotions.

The elementary school is as important a site for discovery and development as any high tech center. The growth of the personal entity, though immeasurable as yet by scientific procedures, defies negation. Those who have watched the process *know*. This process remains as mysterious as any original creation upon which human beings have ever speculated. But the manifestations of growth from the limitations of childhood to the full maturity of the articulate adult are discernible though infinitely subtle. Children come slowly into their heritage of written language. It is a privilege to be able to help them do so.

2

Children Begin to Write

The desire for writing grows with writing.
Erasmus, Adagio

For weeks the first grade children had been looking forward to their own picnic. Throughout the winter there had been parties, but every one of them had been planned for others. Now, at the end of the year, the long-promised time had come, and the thought of doing something "just for us" was highly exciting. Naturally, the most important part of a picnic is what there is to eat. When the kinds of sandwiches and fruit were agreed upon, the menu was translated into a store order, which was written on the chalkboard for all to see. Three children were chosen to go to the store and get prices that very day. Since first-grade children could not cross the streets alone when the traffic officer was absent, several sixth-grade boys were asked to go along. Each took a list, copied from the board, to record the prices.

When the shoppers returned to school, the prices were added to the list on the board. The teacher found the total and did the necessary division. Every youngster watched closely to see how much money would need to be brought, and the result was written on a slip of paper to take home.

This, of course, made it official, and the next day every single child brought the money. Important matters are not likely to be forgotten.

Then the same three children who had gone on the morning errand went back to the store and bought the food. They took the same lists again and used them as shopping memoranda. A few others went along to help carry packages. When they returned, everything was ready to begin the preparation of the picnic lunch.

During the process of washing carrots and making sandwiches, a child remarked, "You know, we ought to thank Miss Wetzel's children for taking us to the store."

"A fine idea," we agreed. "They did something very nice for us and we should thank them. Who wants to do it?"

A few volunteered. The letters were written almost immediately and sent to the older children who had been their guides during the morning.

Dear Miss Wetzel's Class,

Thank you for taking our children across the street. If three of our children went alone they would get run over by a car.

Love from
Sam

We doubt that the drawing up of a business contract is more important to an adult than the writing of the grocery order was to these first-graders. The copying had to be exactly right; the success of the picnic depended on it. Through many such concrete experiences children come to know the practical value that writing can have in their own lives and to appreciate why it must be carefully done. Its results are often visible, tangible, or even edible.

BEGINNINGS OF COMPOSITION

In other ways, too, the child discovers that writing is useful in daily living: learning to write one's name or copying a word or phrase from the chalkboard so as to remember to bring lunch money. Here are further suggestions for writing allied to genuine need:

Signs on collections
Lists of children's names and telephone numbers
Lists of birds seen on bird walks
Daily temperature records
Memoranda concerning material to be brought from home for cooking
Captions for pictures or movies
Lists of supplies needed for making a terrarium
Calendars
Greeting cards for holidays and birthdays
Signs to advertise a cookie sale
Invitations or ads for Book Week
Lists of books read

As soon as the written composition of ideas is needed, we talk first about those ideas. The children decide what they want to say, and we write

In October, a first-grade class dictated and Carolyn copied this brief note.

it on the chalkboard so that they may copy it. For example, it may be necessary to tell parents the exact hours of the new afternoon session. One class dictated and the children copied the following message:

We come at 1:00.
We go at 2:30.

Each child proudly carried home the note telling mother something she needed to know.

Copying from the chalkboard is hard work at first. There are always some whose concentration and muscular skill are not sufficiently developed for them to do as much as the others. Encouragement needs to be given to these children so that their first faltering steps in writing will bring them satisfaction. We stand ready to give approval to those who are making a real effort, no matter how meager their accomplishments. Occasionally we do part of the writing, or we excuse certain individuals from the task.

As time goes on, however, we make sure that even the slowest children write enough to grow in independence. Situations frequently arise when only a single copy of a letter is necessary.

To the School Store:
Please bring a large roll of brown paper to our room. We
want to make a big picture. We are in Room 136.

Mrs. Jackson's Class

After the class has composed the message, a child is selected who
needs either the additional practice or the stimulus to do the copying.
Donald was chosen to prepare the order. Having such a responsibility
touched his pride, and he set to work to do the best he could. He could
write at his own slow tempo without the discouragement of being out-
stripped by more capable neighbors working at the same task. Finally, after
considerable labor, he finished the order and delivered it to the school
store. When the paper arrived, Donald obviously felt that he had done a
good job. Satisfactions like this compensate for struggling effort and spur a
child on toward mastery.

Often when writing is finished, the children display their products so
that everyone has a chance to view them. Because children thoroughly
enjoy looking at one another's work, the bulletin board receives careful
inspection. Frequently, we talk with them about the good points in each
paper, commenting upon neat arrangement, careful formation of letters,
and appropriate illustrations. Taking time to enjoy what they have done
offers immediate dividends for their investment of effort.

After many experiences in which the group makes up the message
and the class copies it from the board, the children are ready to compose
individually. There is the usual class discussion to talk over the main points
to be included in their letters, then each dictates a message and the teacher
writes it. The child puts in the date, the greeting, and the close. To make it
more his own, he invariably adds some sort of decoration.

In the daily life at school, there are many opportunities for children to
write messages that are important to them. A child may dictate a note to
mother asking for a smock or one to the science teacher inquiring how to
set up an aquarium. The children help each other to phrase a short letter to
a neighboring group inviting them to inspect the new lighthouse just built
in the classroom, or they help to plan a class note requesting permission to
go on a trip, making copies for mother to sign. Sometimes someone
dictates a letter to father "just for fun"—one that is brief enough to copy
alone and illustrate eloquently.

All possible variations of the telling-dictating-helping-copying procedure occur at this eary age. At the same time the children continue to write the lists, labels, and memoranda that are needed to make their daily living go more smoothly. However, the amount of writing that can be expected in the first school year depends upon the children's emotional stability and their mental and physical maturity. We have found it wiser to expect too little rather than too much. Young children should not be required to write so frequently or at such length that writing becomes a task they dread.

BUILDING STANDARDS

In the notes and letters children write we take pains to stress the value of "something in your letter that is just like you." We begin with the first copied notes by commenting on anything in the decoration that is unique or distinctive, and when letters are independently composed, we transfer attention to the ideas they express. As a child holds up his finished work so that the class can see, we read it aloud, and someone—child or teacher— points out any parts that show the writer had done some personal thinking and feeling about what has been said. Thus in referring to Vicki's thank-you note we commented on the way she described the butter churn, and we called attention to Ruth's quite different reaction. Hearing and seeing one another's work stimulates writing interest and growth.

Very gradually children acquire writing skills, which sooner or later enable them to dispense with the teacher-stenographer. Although they cannot spell all the words they want to use, they ask for the ones they need, and they have the ability to hold a thought while putting it on paper. This transition from dictating and copying to the independent writing of each sentence as it is composed is a big step. Often, in order to preserve the all-important idea of "making it sound like you," we come to a child's aid by writing the final portion from dictation. Countless letters have been saved from commonplace endings by this device.

A letter is corrected by the child and teacher together. In editing at this early stage, the teacher does not tell what to say but questions the intended meaning in such a way that the child tells it. Then the teacher writes what the pupil dictates.

The edited draft may be copied if necessary. Not all writing requires more than one draft, but a child arriving at the middle of the third grade has had a number of experiences in which copying has been essential. This is usually due to the rapid and often untidy writing that results from trying to get ideas down before they are forgotten. Since children recognize the importance of having in "good shape" anything that is to be read by someone else, they accept the job of making a good copy.

Dear   Miss   Greve,
                        Thank   you
for   taking   the   chickens
home.   Did they   get   out
of   the   bath   tub?
                There   is   one
black   one   that   looks   like

he   has   a   flag   on
his   wing.
        How   can   they   sleep
standing   up?   I   should   think
they   would   fall   down.   I   get
so   tired   on   my   feet   that
I   do.   Love   from   Danny.

The personal flavor of this letter was sustained because the child was given the opportunity to dictate the final portion.

19

VARIED OPPORTUNITIES FOR WRITING

Of high value are the situations that lead children to care enough about what they are composing to give it a personal flavor. We believe a child will grow in power in written language if he learns early to respect his individual way of saying things.

Because one third grade found their lockers so small that precious papers were getting crumpled and torn, they welcomed the suggestion of making storage folders for their unfinished work. Since the folders would be kept on a shelf where visitors could easily spot them, it was necessary to indicate that they held material being worked on. Certainly the class did not want "company" to examine them with the notion that their contents were finished samples of writing. Here was a chance to dramatize the fun of "thinking up a title that fits and that belongs only to you." "Of course," it was suggested, "you could call it, 'My Folder of Unfinished Papers.' How do you like that?" Suggesting a title so obviously dull that everyone could disapprove, prevented children from taking the easy, unimaginative way out. The next question, "Has anyone a better idea?" brought no response, and was followed by the suggestion, "Here's one—'Work under Way'; but," it was added quickly, "that's mine. No one else may use it."

Suggestions came slowly at first, and fitting ideas were commended in titles such as "I'm Loaded with Unfinished Work"; "Girl at Work—Do Not Disturb"; and "Approaching the Finish Line." When invention seemed at a standstill, the class moved to a chalkboard demonstration on how to arrange titles for good placement. As each one was written, its capitalization was discussed. Lingering over these details not only produced attractive covers but also permitted the children to know the excitement and challenge of achieving individuality even in performing a uniform class assignment.

When most of the children had thought of titles, all were given cheap newsprint on which to try out spacing, penmanship, and decoration. The teacher gave help or encouragement where needed. Sometimes the class was interrupted to share a pleasing arrangment or a design that carried out the idea conveyed by the title. This often led other children to think of different names or plans for their folders. Since the amount of writing involved was small, anyone could make several trial pages without growing fatigued. Such opportunities for experimentation are of great value because they strengthen a child's feeling of personal responsibility for the quality and the individual character of his or her output and provide a taste of the vitalizing pleasure of working, not for the teacher's approval, but for one's own.

The making of the real folder came at a later period. Each child was given a large piece of colored paper which brought forth pleased comments as it was placed on the desks. The use of this paper was deliberate; it was something to live up to.

With their samples to help them, they tackled this final step soberly. Many decided to use designs that were different from their samples. All these changes were approved after quick experiments had been made on scrap paper to show that the new ideas were satisfactory.

As soon as the covers were completed, they were placed on the bulletin board where they remained for a day before they were put into actual use. The appreciative scrutiny that they received from their makers revealed how much the youngsters cared about what they had done.

Children thoroughly enjoy writing all kinds of advertisements and posters to publicize coming events. It is fun to invent slogans and write copy that will bring buyers to a cookie sale or mothers to a book talk. Here, as in the making of titles for work folders, the emphasis is on thinking, and there is a generous amount of oral exchange. Selecting a few essentials to present dramatically makes for stronger writing than including many trivial items. The writing, when it is finally done, is so limited in quantity that it is possible to exact a high standard of appearance and correctness. Illustration, especially if it reinforces the idea of the poster or the ad, is always encouraged, for it is one more way in which a child may put an individual stamp upon a product. We have found that when children care about what they are doing, they work far harder than any teacher would have the heart to expect.

Even though the sending of letters and notes provides an opportunity to give meaning and purpose to practical writing experiences, it is unwise to use this type of communication too often. If they have to write too many letters, children frequently acquire more distaste for the activity than skill in doing it. So, we have used posters, slogans, and advertisements as invitations and announcements and have reserved letter writing for the special occasions when the warmth of their feeling helps to carry children through the sustained and usually arduous task of composing a good letter.

ORAL LANGUAGE IS BASIC TO WRITING

The foregoing experiences constitute but one phase of the approach to writing. From the first day in school, the children are provided with the opportunity to express their ideas orally. This form of self-expression helps them to grow in the power to state their thoughts with honesty and clarity. In the primary grades, abundant experience in oral expression is more

Does Your Child whine when She or he gets up in the morning?

Come to the Institute.

The New Sarah Lawrence President will Speak to you Mothers and tell you all the problems you need to know.

A P.T.A. Institute offered opportunity for writing an advertisement instead of a letter.

important in the development of ability to write than the actual writing itself. Through discussing plans, telling stories and experiences, and simply chatting with each other, children learn to exchange ideas freely and develop the base for fluent writing.

Always, the important element in this sharing of ideas is the classroom atmosphere in which each child knows that thoughts and feelings will be welcomed. At first some participate very little, but they enjoy listening to others and eventually make contributions of their own.

Some subjects entice all children to take part in group discussions. Experiences during thunderstorms or being in parades, stories about pets, accounts of "the time I had the measles", or "when I went to the circus", reports of dreams—these and many more may start the ball rolling. Informal conversations in which the teacher may take part inevitably draw other children to the scene, and in this atmosphere many an inhibited child talks for the first time in an audience situation.

FIRST REPORTS

Besides encouraging the offhand exchange of ideas, we occasionally inaugurate a class study that is purposefully designed to stimulate inquiry and discussion. This enterprise is an oral one, fitted to the capacities of young children, but it follows the pattern used to guide the preparation for written reporting in later years. First graders can explore a subject in great detail, using such source material as fits their abilities; they work with it long enough to accumulate a supply of facts and to clarify their understandings about them; and they prepare an end product that calls for expression in their own language. Although this book concerns itself primarily with written English, we know that oral reporting in the early grades is a necessary prelude to written reporting in the later ones.

It is essential to start with a congenial subject—some project that will kindle interest quickly and hold it for a considerable length of time. Live things always have an immediate appeal. Through the care and observation of some kind of animal—rabbits, polliwogs, a baby hamster—children learn exciting new facts and taste the satisfaction that comes from realizing that some living thing is dependent upon them. Having something alive in a classroom is not without its problems for the teacher, but it can yield dividends of far-reaching value.

One of our most rewarding ventures was the raising of some baby chickens. The children were so eager that they sat through several sessions of earnest consultation with the science teacher while they planned the right home and food for their guests-to-be. The talk was animated and full of curiosity. These children knew nothing about little chickens except that they were "cute and cuddly," and they had much to learn before they could take the responsibility for their care. Aided by the librarian, the children found needed answers, and enthusiastic discussions rounded out their pursuit.

Please get us
25 lbs. of baby chick mash.
Mrs. Jackson's room
210

A genuine need for writing is illustrated by this order written in a first grade.

At last the day came when a roomy cage was set up at just the right height for viewing and handling, and with much ceremony the children added clean newspaper and food and water and gravel to make it a comfortable and healthful place for chickens to live. The next few minutes were tense with expectancy. Then the door opened and a lusty peeping announced that the chickens had arrived.

Each child served many turns as caretaker, and the responsibility was always carried out with dependability and pride. Every morning the appointed children were on hand early, often before the teacher had arrived, and they set to work at once to clean the cage, remove the babies from the warm box where they had spent the cool spring night, and watch with beaming faces while their little black and yellow charges chirped and ate busily. Always in the before-school time there was a gallery of fascinated observers. Older brothers and sisters, even teachers and mothers, stopped by for a look and on those occasions the first graders were the experts who answered their questions with surprising accuracy and with the confident air of authority.

During class time there was abundant opportunity to talk, to watch, to question, and—most important of all—to enjoy. This was such an absorb-

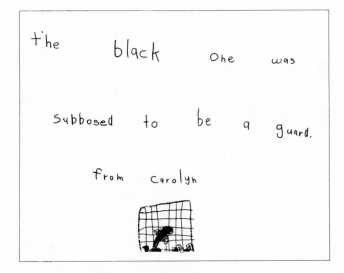

A letter written in connection with the chicken study.

ing interest that there was no need to hunt up things to talk about. It was a stirring and releasing experience that lasted long enough and was sufficiently dramatic to strike below the surface and affect each child so that he cared mightily about what he was learning.

Eventually the chickens became too big for the cage, and our custodian offered to add them to his flock. Parting with their pets was not easy. To help them over this emotional hurdle, we proposed giving a chicken program for the mothers. Again the room was full of bustling excitement: decorating the room, making a frieze, drawing large pictures to illustrate facts, writing invitations to mothers, and finally planning a program in which each child would play a significant role.

On the day of the program, the children sat on the floor so that they could stand easily and face the audience when their turns came. Anne made the speech of welcome and introduced the guests of honor—the chickens, of course. Ruthie was the announcer, holding big cards on which were written the questions previously dictated by the class.

Her voice trembled as she read the first one: "Billy, how do baby chicks get born?" But by the time Billy had explained the hatching process she had gained enough composure to go on. "Penny, why are they so fluffy when they are little?" "Jonathan, when they get a drink why do they stretch their necks when they swallow it?" "Jerry, how do we take care of chickens at night?" "Lloyd, how do chickens chew their food?" "David, why do they have little bumps on the sides of their heads?" And so it went until every child had spoken. The mothers listened intently, as one by one, each child stood up and gave an accurate answer to his question, usually in words quite different from the ones he had used when we had practiced.

Such unmemorized answers are factual reports at the first-grade level. They are the culmination of an undertaking that involved the whole child, both mind and heart, that added to a growing store of knowledge, and that extended language power.

ORAL AND DICTATED STORIES

Just as experiences in oral reporting provide the background for report writing, so telling and dictating original stories eventually lead into story writing. Most little children are interested in this form of self-expression, and with very little encouragement—by merely allowing them time enough for storytelling before an appreciative audience—their stories show gradual but very definite improvement in invention, form, clarification of ideas, content, and individual flavor. Children's dictated stories are far more complex and extended than their meager reading ability can communicate, so the teacher reads the dictated tale to present it effectively. Keeping attention upon story invention is the important goal at this stage.

In one second grade almost every day children signed their names on the chalkboard under the caption: "Who Has a Make-up Story?" At the beginning of the year, day after day, the same five children were the ones who wanted to tell stories, although the whole class enjoyed listening to them. As the weeks went by, new children volunteered, and their stories were received with enthusiasm. The approving remarks made by the class had a definite effect on the stories that followed, although individual gains were often almost imperceptible at the outset. The changes in Kathie's stories illustrate this very gradual growth as well as the amount of mediocre material that must be accepted.

Early in the fall she dictated "The Family of Frogs," to her teacher. In this Kathie portrayed conflict with adults—an idea that runs through all of her stories and that was true in her own daily living. Although there is no evident story pattern, it was probably somewhat connected in her thinking, but moved so rapidly through her mind that she told only the high spots. The story reveals her vivid imagination and suggests a moving picture visualized as she told it. The sentences she used are the immature run-on type.

The Family of Frogs

Once there was a father frog and he was a big father and he had a great big family and he went for a swim. Mother went downtown to buy some groceries and the children were out playing and the baby was inside his cradle. There was an alligator under the cradle and he jumped out. Baby started to cry. The mother came home and she came in and slid down on the floor. There was this pipe that led right out to the water and she slid right down it. But the baby didn't stop crying and one of the children came in. He was too fat and he decided that he needed a glass of milk. So he gave the alligator some milk and then he tried to push him out, but he got much fatter. The alligator's head was just peeping out of the hole. The mother came in through the hole and the alligator's mouth was open and she slid right down his throat. Down in his stomach there was this little house. She opened the door and she looked in. And she saw three ghosts, but the ghosts were friendly and they would not hurt her for the world of alligator's stomach. So they lived happily ever after.

In "The Naughty Little Duck," told less than two weeks later, Kathie limited her idea and developed it more logically. This time she was able to catch in words more of what was going on in her mind. The invention all centers about the duck who did not want his face washed, and she piled up incidents to effect this end.

The Naughty Little Duck

Once there was a little duck. The little duck was an awful funny little duck. One day the little duck went out to visit his grandma. His grandmother asked him if he wanted some ice cream. The little duck said, "Yes." And he went down to the ice-cream store and bought some ice cream. He smeared it all over his face and didn't like to have his face washed so when he got home the grandmother wanted to wash his face. He started to run all through the house and he slid on a rug. It happened to be that they had a vase that stood on the floor, and he slid right on top of the vase and it had some lovely roses in it. He landed on top of it and the water spilled all over the nice rug and the grandmother gave him a shellacking for being such a naughty boy. Then she took him up to the bathroom and she tried to wash his face, but every time she tried to get the wash cloth on he put his head down. He slipped and saw stars so he couldn't feel it and the grandmother put him in the bathtub and she washed his face. When he came out of being knocked out, he ran downstairs and he grabbed his scooter and he scooted home and I think that ever since then he never would buy an ice-cream cone. And he lived happily ever after.

A month later she related "The Family of Pumpkins," which shows remarkable growth in Kathie's ability to construct a well-knit story that works to a most interesting and personal conclusion.

The Family of Pumpkins

Once there lived a very old pumpkin. She had quite a lot of babies. They were very nice. They weren't naughty. One of her pumpkins was pretty. She was the nicest and kindest of all, but the others were jealous, and so she was treated very poor. None of her friends were jealous so she had quite a lot of friends. But her mother didn't think that she should do all the hard work, especially cleaning up the house. So she had the best fun.

"Of all the dirty tricks," said one of her sisters. "We have to do all the hard work while she goes out and plays with all her friends. She has too many friends."

The mother pumpkin said, "She has more manners than you. Until you learn how to behave you'll have to help me."

And so all the children tried to do good work. And pretty soon they had all the best of friends, too. And so they had to leave the mother pumpkin home to do all the hard work.

The last story, "The Fat Old Woman," was given just two months after the first one. Whereas the pattern is not so clear in her mind as the one before, Kathie's power to picture things vividly makes it more alive. The run-on sentence has almost disappeared and has been replaced by more mature types, showing inversion, introductory clauses, and the use of verbals. There is also a pleasing rhythm effected by the balance of long and short sentences.

The Fat Old Woman

Once there lived on old woman. She was very fat, because she ate too much. Whenever anyone would invite her to their home she would say, "Have you got any turkey?" They would say, "No." She would go home. But before she went home she would buy a turkey. When she got home she would eat it. One day when she had come back from her shopping she found her dog gone. He was usually at home. She quickly dropped her turkey on the floor and opened the door and ran down the street. She saw her dog at the corner. Very quickly she went one way while the dog went the other way and they met. The fat old woman thought that she would take him home and she would eat all the turkey herself. She looked on the ground and she saw a run in her stocking. She thought she would go home and sew them, but when she went to get her dog, instead of her getting the dog, the dog got her and ate her up, but it took him a year to eat such a fat lady.

THE CONTRIBUTION OF DRAMATICS

The interaction between story invention and group dramatics merits a thorough analysis and can only be touched upon here. We have found that stories and plays contribute immeasurably to each other. Both stir the imagination of children and help them to grow in confidence and power as they lose themselves in the excitement of being play characters.

By dramatics we do not mean the memorized-line type of play, for it rarely affords any opportunity for the individual to express his creative self.

The Good Witch and the Bad Witch

Scene 1
The good witch is trying to make some magic.

scene 2
The prince came in and showed her some good magic.

scene 3
The prince brings his father the king to the good witch's house.

Scene 4
The prince gets all excited about the bad witch.

Scene 5
The prince and his father and the good witch and her daughter capture the bad witch.

Scene 6
They shake hands and go home.

This copy was used by the announcer of a small group play. The description of the scenes served to make the plot clear to the audience and to remind the players of the forthcoming action.

The plays we do find invaluable are those created by the children themselves dramatizing books or tales of their own making. The dialogue follows a plot line, but the speeches are never written or "learned by heart" and vary considerably with each performance, just as the cast of characters may be adjusted to provide enough parts for all. The children are free to invent and to inject color without the inhibitions that accompany the reciting of memorized speeches and with no congealing fear of

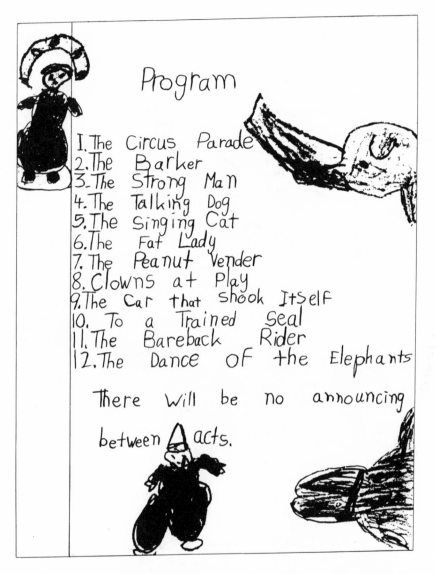

Program

1. The Circus Parade
2. The Barker
3. The Strong Man
4. The Talking Dog
5. The Singing Cat
6. The Fat Lady
7. The Peanut Vender
8. Clowns at Play
9. The Car that shook Itself
10. To a Trained Seal
11. The Bareback Rider
12. The Dance of the Elephants

There will be no announcing between acts.

Preparing a program for his parent's use during a second-grade performance gives a child a reason to write in good form.

forgetting lines. Moreover, these dramatic experiences are an outlet for many youngsters who through the disguise of play characters can reveal hidden facets of their personalities.

GROWTH IN DICTATED STORIES

One way to initiate story dictation is to offer to write down a made-up story that has been of particular interest to the group. This invariably leads to a siege of dictating, with the children enthusiastic long after the teacher has been forced to call "time out" to rest her weary fingers. For a teacher who can type, or take shorthand, these dictating experiences are not so fatiguing and enable a greater number of children to participate.

Little children enjoy dictating stories about pictures they have made. Sometimes a few pieces of manila paper are folded into a booklet that can be filled with pictures, leaving sufficient space for the teacher to write down the story that the pictures illustrate. We have found that in many instances children then make the transition to writing captions under the illustration in these booklets for themselves, asking the teacher to spell needed words or phrases.

One of the essentials of the child's dictating experience is the reading aloud of the product. The teacher takes for granted, that out of great quantities of mediocre output only a little of artistic quality will emerge. Insofar as possible, the teacher reads aloud what is dictated, giving all of it an enthusiastic presentation. She takes pains to emphasize those bits of expression that, because of their originality and freshness of approach, will raise standards and prove inspirational to the others.

This reading should be planned carefully in order to contribute to the children's recognition of vivid expression and of their own ability to create. Very few stories should be read at one time. It is important to choose periods when the children are relaxed and in a receptive mood and not when they are too tired to sit quietly. In a negative atmosphere much that the teacher has been trying to build may be destroyed.

The following are stories told by beginning second-grade children, with comments from the class after the reading.

The Little Piece of Chalk

Once there was a little piece of chalk. He thought he was walking on the sidewalk, but he was walking on the chalkboard. One day he was wandering around the board and he came to a big, big house. It was a doll house. Something was hanging down from one window. It was a big piece of rope. He climbed on the big piece of rope and he ran up into the window. Then he saw the chalkboard again. And he went on the chalkboard and he drew a little girl holding a basket. The little girl walked in the bedroom with her mother. The mother couldn't see the piece of chalk and she wondered how that was drawn.

The mother said, "Well, I can't do anything about it."

So she went out in the kitchen and cooked the dinner. And the little girl went out to play with her friends. When dinner was ready the little girl came in and ate her dinner. After she ate her dinner she went to bed. The next morning she got up and went to school. And they lived happily ever after.

Tommy said, "I like the idea of making a story about a piece of chalk." Peggy's comment was, "I think it was nice where the chalk thought he was walking on a sidewalk, but it was really the bottom of the chalkboard."

Tommy with His New Teddy Bear

Once upon a time there was a little boy named Tommy. Tommy wanted a teddy bear. One day he went out to play. He looked in all the garbage cans. He didn't find any teddy bear. He came home and he asked his mother if they could go to New York. The mother said, "I'll think about it."

So they went to New York. They looked in every store. The mother said she was tired. Tommy said, "Come on, Mother, I want to find a brown teddy bear instead of black ones and white ones." So the mother said, "O.K., we'll walk to the next store."

There was the little brown teddy bear sitting in the window scratching his head. They went in the store. They came out again. Tommy ran all over the town, bumping into everyone with the teddy bear because he was so happy.

Harry thought, "It sounded just cute where Tommy saw 'the little brown teddy bear sitting in the window scratching his head.' "

Ruth like the ending. She said, "Tommy sounded so happy, and it didn't say 'they lived happily ever after.' "

Frank said, "Grace made me see a picture of Tommy when he ran all over town bumping into everyone."

The Little New Pocket

Once there was a little pocket. This little pocket was sewed on a dress and he didn't like it. So this little pocket didn't know who wore this dress. So he planned to go away. And the little girl never went out of the house. All she did was look out the window at the big gray buildings. So all he saw was green and gray, because the dress was green and all he looked at was himself. Of course he had two eyes, a nose and a mouth and two legs and two arms, but he didn't have any teeth because he was a new pocket and the dress was new, too.

He planned to get away so he got off his hook that he was hanging on and tried to get out of the closet, but he couldn't get out of the closet. Finally he tried so much that he got out and looked for the scissor box, but he could not find it because it was moved to another place. He dragged the dress all around. Finally he came to the scissor box and just as he was reaching his hands out of the scissor box with the scissors the little girl came in. He lied down and tried to go to sleep, but he couldn't because he wanted to get away. He went snip, snip, snip, and finally he was loose and he wabbled around the room because he was a little pocket and he couldn't walk very straight. But finally he walked out of the door and he saw this man walking along the hall to this middle-sized box and it was very tall. He wondered what it was because he couldn't think very straight, but finally he knew. "It is an elevator," he said. And he saw a man walking out of another apartment.

The man went into the box and the door shut and it disappeared. So the pocket looked through the cracks and only saw the top and he dropped the handkerchief that the little girl had put in him one day.

He said, "I will be found out. They will see this handkerchief so I must take it."

He took it and he dropped the handkerchief through the bars of the elevator. It stuck in one of the ropes and the elevator got stuck coming up. The pocket squeezed through the bars and sailed down into the ventilator of the elevator. He rolled himself up in a long coil and squeezed through the net. He went sailing right on the man's head and he jumped off and thought he would get the handkerchief. He took the handkerchief out of where it was stuck. The man was in such a hurry to try and fix the elevator that he knocked the lever on. He went sailing up, but the pocket jumped up on the lever and pushed it back and stopped it. Then he pushed it the other way and it went sailing down and he went out of the door and out of another door and was outside.

He felt some drops. He thought it was raining, so he looked

up and said, "Is that a cloud? No, it isn't." And there was the little girl crying. "My, my," said he, "I wonder why she is crying. Oh, I know—because I am lost. I must go right back."

So he went back and took a needle and thread and sewed himself onto the new dress, and he never took scissors and tried to cut himself loose again.

The children loved this one and talked about it at length. They thought it was a different idea. The part about the pocket's seeing only green and gray interested them. They laughed when John said, "He didn't have any teeth because he was a new pocket and the dress was new, too." They liked the ending because "it was not 'living happily ever after' and it ended quickly." And they especially enjoyed the conversation when the pocket thought it was raining.

TRANSITION FROM STORY DICTATING TO WRITING

Eventually the time comes when children desire to take a more active part in the recording of their stories. Usually, in the beginning stages, they dictate a paragraph at a time, copying each in turn until the story is completed. Sometimes they write down the first part of a story and dictate the end of it to the teacher. Finally, they reach the place where they are able to write a story alone, asking only for spelling help.

The transition from a child's dictating to the actual writing of stories is a matter of individual growth. In some instances children take over the writing of utilitarian material before they attempt the independent writing of their story ideas. Probably this is because in utilitarian writing they can go back to sources if an idea is lost, whereas in imaginative writing thoughts follow one another so fast they escape. There is no age limit when dictating becomes taboo. Teachers of older children who allow some opportunities for dictating are amazed at the impetus it gives to all kinds of writing.

In contrast to their dictated stories children's first independent efforts are meager and disjointed. Although the story may be rich and complete in the child's imagination, the thoughts fly so fast that only fragments of them are caught in writing. The teacher, in her reading aloud to the group, must be able to "sell" these first independently written stories so that the writer feels satisfaction from having worked so hard. To do this, she studies the telegraphic style, talking it over with the writer, so that when she reads aloud she can fill in the gaps in order to make the story say what the child wanted it to say.

A third-grade teacher used the following technique for beginning the independent writing of stories: She offered to help four children who had already shown such interest. Siting at a large round table, the teacher wrote needed words on slips of paper just as fast as the children asked for them. This enabled them to turn out a finished piece of work before their energy was exhausted. Reading the stories aloud brought forth several requests by other members of the group for such an opportunity to write. The teacher made it a point to choose only a few for each writing group so that she might give immediate help when it was needed.

THE TEACHER'S ROLE

It is the school's responsibility to help children know the release and delight of personal writing and to acquire pride in meeting the necessary standards of practical writing. To create a setting in which this can occur is a constant challenge to the teacher. She must provide stimulation and variety but protect children from bombardment by so many interests that they become confused and their energies dissipated. The best results are obtained when there is a nice balance between satisfying experiences and time for their assimilation.

Normal growth in writing as in all areas does not proceed in a straight line—but there must be a sense of moving ahead. Development takes place best in a warm and appreciative atmosphere, where children grow in writing power as they mature both mentally and emotionally.

3

Practical Writing

The bond of society consists of reason and speech.
Cicero, De Officiis

Inviting one's parents to a "star party" as a climax to weeks of study of the stars and constellations is a serious responsibility. Hence the third graders worked carefully in writing, correcting, and copying their letters of invitation. The reports that accompanied the conducted tour of the constellations came from much seeing, working, talking, drawing, painting, listening, and planning. Reading, too, was a source of information: the librarian's selection of books of varying difficulty; the teacher's oral reading of books too difficult for the children to read themselves; the reading of star charts and pictures, captions, and labels. But firsthand experiences were the bedrock for this learning. These children looked for planets and constellations in the evening sky; they charted in their notebooks what they had seen. They went to the planetarium to view moving models of the solar system, and to see a film-made procession of the stars showing a whole night's star cycle in a few minutes. They saw and touched specimens of meteorites; they clarified their detailed, concrete experiences through conversation and with many illustrative renditions of what they had learned. Star charts, clearly organized notebooks, and slides would accompany their talks which were planned to show their parent audience how much they had learned about Saturn, Venus, Orion, Aldebaran, and other ear-delighting members of the heavenly regions.

WRITING AND TALKING INTERACT

Because of the labor of handwriting, oral reporting seems most productive for third graders. Writing skills, for all their usefulness in plans, letters,

captions, and explanations, are not elastic enough for the fluency demanded by this age group's swift flow of thought. But segments of the whole cycle of communication inevitably are written; indeed it appears in the star study, as in many another, that writing and talking complement each other. Recorded plans, titles, charts, and notebooks give permanence to the ephemeral spoken word. Illustrations are also part of the solid structure of ideas. They clarify understanding and provide a reliable nucleus for the oral reports. Such visible materials to handle and explain contribute markedly to children's self-confidence by relating language both to the manipulation and to the substance of ideas.

Table of Contents

	Page
Sun	1,2
Beginning of the solar system	3
Solar System	4
Our moon	5
Mars	6
Jupiter	7
Saturn	8
Saturn's rings	9
Comets	10
Meteors	11
Meteorite	12
List of important stars	13
Taurus the bull	14
Orion the hunter	15
Canis Major	16
Lepus the hare	17
Cancer the crab	18
Big and little Dipper	19

A third-grade boy made this table of contents for his star notebook.

Throughout the star study this relation of talking to writing was evident. Daily "star meetings" were held at which facts were gloated over with the joy usually reserved for personal treasures. These informal chats about what the children were finding revealed a deep absorption in factual knowledge. Talking about the many fragments of information not only broadened the children's awareness of the range of man's astronomical knowledge but also led to a sense of the necessity for grouping their many items of information. Questions postponed for future reference were charted so as not to be forgotten. Books needed for special items were often listed. And as the idea took shape that an evening meeting with parents would be the happiest climax for the long study, many plans had to be jotted down; plans as to who would give which topic, and where each part of the program was to be held, since some of it had to be out-of-doors.

Writing made possible the more precise arrangements for the anticipated program. Writing brought about the notebooks that represented a serious organizing effort for these third graders. The well-written table of contents suggests the orderliness that helped to make the copiously illustrated books an effective record.

ORAL REPORTING PRECEDES WRITTEN REPORTING

Learning to make a good oral report must precede the task of preparing a written one. Each gathering of material for oral reports exposes children to the temptation of copying whole sections from reference sources. To lessen the risk of plagiarism we give children many firsthand experiences before they read. Then when they return to books, they already know a great deal about the material they are searching for. This fore knowledge fosters the assimilation of ideas without the helpless feeling of being overwhelmed by new facts one must somehow gather and control.

Children often report their findings in class sessions. They tell interesting facts and ideas that they have discovered in their reading. The mere telling of information lessens the probability of copying or parroting whole pages. Children achieve this independence by talking to their peers and having to make things clear in their own words.

During the first weeks of school in one fourth grade, the real experiences that introduced the oral reporting of children's individual animal studies were prerequisite to the integrity of their later factual writing. As part of a required study of animal adaptation to various climates, the children's own pets and animals living nearby were discussed. Interest in these apparently random fact-finding meetings ran high before a beginning

of organization was attempted. Children were asked, "What are all the different things it's important to know about animals?" With a bit of discussion a chart was made that included

> Appearance
> Food
> Protection
> Enemies
> Where they live
> Their homes

These topics formed the nucleus of further sharing of findings about animals.

Getting facts from people who knew, and from a number of excellent animal pictures, was climaxed by a trip to the zoo. Here the prime questions were: "How do these animals protect themselves?" "What kinds of food do they eat?" "How many babies do they have?" This building of factual background before turning to the printed page equipped the children with meanings for many of the words they were going to meet.

This acquaintance also provided the fourth-grade zoologists with enough contacts for them to begin to select their individual topics. Obviously each child could not report orally or in writing on all the animals that ranged from the small animals near at hand—squirrels, chipmunks, and woodchucks to those of the jungle and forest. Narrowing one's topic is as necessary in elementary-school reporting as in the graduate school. "Take your time to choose the one you want to report on. Look at lots of books to be sure you can find good reading material before you decide. It's better to take time to choose than to change in midstream," they were advised.

SEARCHING FOR MATERIAL

When four or five children had decided upon the animals they wanted to study, the class was given some direct instruction in the use of reference books. First, a trip to the school library media center was in order. The librarian, who had been previously consulted about the need for books about animals, had readied a shelf full of the best ones available. Some were easy, and some would challenge the ablest readers. Contents, indexes, and the arrangement of encyclopedias were examined and their use demonstrated. A dozen books were taken to the classroom for convenient use and sharing; others stayed in the library so that members of other classes could also use them.

Everyone was caught up in the excitement of the search. And, as so

often happens in the quest for material pertinent to a given topic, individuals found as much for their neighbors as for themselves. "Say, you've got to get this book—you're going to need it when you get going on the elephant" was the kind of advice overheard.

As the children found references bearing on their chosen animal they wanted to preserve many of the details for their reports. Some started copying word for word what was in print. The time had come to lay a foundation for later note-taking. The children were each given a half-dozen cards and told to put down the name of any book especially good for their particular animal and the page or pages on which the material was found. "But I'll never remember exactly how many bushels of hay an elephant eats in a day," complained Henry. So facts that had to be precise, like sizes or speeds or weights, were agreed upon as the kinds of notes to take. To copy the exact figures meant also the obligation of citing the name of the book and the page number. This was enough of a chore to check the impulse to copy too many things verbatim. Sketches and diagrams were suggested as being often better ways to get down an idea. It is unlikely that fourth or fifth graders can do other kinds of note-taking without plagiarism. Hence we learned to keep note-taking very simple if done at all.

How much to find out, how many more books to read were questioned one day when the searching and reading were going at full speed. "Look at the chart of things we thought were important to know about animals and see how much you're sure of," they were advised. (See list of topics above). "I know about the bear's appearance pretty well and about his enemies and how he protects himself," said Jon, in such a stocktaking. "I don't know all the places where bears live—there seem to be so many. I'll have to find more about that."

As the children found more of what they were looking for, their eagerness in the quest became more intense. Knowledge added to curiosity. The enthusiasm that springs from working in a company of eager fellow workers became truly electric. A few still feared that they would forget some choice bit of detail, but most were willing to accept the premise that they could find the book and page again from their book card.

During this period of intensive reading two problems arose. As in almost any group of fourth graders, some children found reference reading discouragingly difficult. They needed help, and they needed short periods for concentrated effort. Small groups took turns going to the library for specific information. A notice on the chalkboard invited, "Sign Here for Help," and children needing help wrote their names. The help took many forms. Sometimes it was simply a matter of reaching for the right book and pointing out the appropriate section of its index. Quite often what was

41

needed to help a child to clearer thinking was the teacher's saying "Tell me what you know about the chipmunk's home." Answering such questions often showed where the pupil needed more information. Occasionally the teacher read a paragraph from a difficult reference and explained it. And there were many times when she gave directly the bit of information that an individual was seeking. The other problem was that of fatigue and what the less able readers might do while waiting their turn for help. They were urged to make illustrations for their reports—pictures, an introductory announcement, a surprising statement of size or kind of protection, or a diagram showing, perhaps, claws and pads on a tiger's feet. The children kept in folders the pictorial material that they were getting ready for their oral reports.

NOTE-TAKING IN UPPER GRADES

The most successful approaches to note-taking with upper-grade pupils were found when they became concerned about forgetting data needed in a report whether oral or written, so some periods for special training in note-taking were set aside.

For a whole class or a sizable group of those ready or nearly ready to begin note-taking, available texts in science or social studies were used. In one sixth grade the teacher said, "Let's assume that we are all trying to write reports on fruit growing in New York State. It would be ridiculous for everyone to report on the same topic, but this is just for practice. After we learn how to do it, each person will take notes for his or her own report."

The first step in selection of material for note-taking is to have a clear purpose toward which to work. On this occasion the pupils were asked to skim the selection used for practice work and then formulate orally the three or four topics in the passage that might be worth sharing with classmates. These topics were jotted down in scattered places on the chalkboard. Then the children were asked to read the section again and to try to tell something about each of the important topics jotted down.

"Put your pencils away," the pupils were advised during these readings. "You take more notes with your mind than with your pencil."

After a few samples of telling the important ideas aloud, the students read again, this time to dictate a brief reminder for recording on the chalkboard. Such "memory clues" encase a whole set of ideas. Different children suggested different clues for the same facts, and these were recorded to dramatize the diverse ways in which people work on this complex job. The pupils needed to realize that even when formulating notes on a selection that all had read they could express ideas uniquely. It is in such commonplace learnings, as well as in more colorful ones, that respect for individuality can be enhanced. Independence in expression is the goal rather than a close paraphrasing of what one has read.

Because for children long notes are prone to be imitative as well as time-consuming, brief word clues were the focus. Sometimes the children counted the words used by the author. They found, for example, that one pupil's phrase contained only eleven words: "Insects—greatest pest to orchards—destroy more than frost or storms". Both the detailed treatment of the original version and the economy of notes revealed special values, and children could see the roles played by each form of writing.

After several attempts at oral formulation and dictation, the pupils were ready to try a bit of independent note-taking. They read another paragraph, selected its essential point, and then tried to devise a brief phrase or two that would recall it. While they did this, the teacher was available to give help to those who still needed the step of "saying it aloud." Many wanted to try out their notes orally with the teacher and needed encouragement to sustain rigorous effort.

After two or three sessions of this kind of teaching, some children were ready to go on to taking notes for their individual reports, from which the whole class had been temporarily diverted. Some children needed another lesson focused upon selecting essentials and phrasing them briefly. All needed help when they went back to read various references for their special reports, but they had acquired the basic procedures of skimming, formulating questions, reading and rereading before trying to reduce a long passage to a few brief but revealing phrases. Many refinements remained for later learnings. However, the necessity of clear-cut aims for searching out information and the children's awareness of their obligation to be honest and independent were gratifyingly obvious as they returned to gathering data for their emerging reports.

ORGANIZING AND PRESENTING ORAL REPORTS

After two or three weeks some of the fastest workers declared that they were ready, that there was simply no more to be found about their particular animals. The whole class was assembled to consider how to make an interesting oral report. The children were told that they might start with any topic on their list of things to know about animals. "Begin with the topic you are most interested in yourself," they were advised. "For instance, if you are reporting on the porcupine you might want to begin with his unusual way of protecting himself."

Because children learn much from one another and because first examples in such a situation are influential, it was found expedient to give really detailed help to those who were ready to report. Getting pictures

43

from library files to illustrate certain points was part of the preparation. The first reporters were asked if they needed help on any special part of their work. Perhaps an item of fact had to be checked or a more accurate reference decided upon. But the teacher's main job was that of helping the child to organize his material. "What are you going to tell about first?" was followed by her jotting down on a card the topic to use as a beginning. A sample of the sequence worked out with one fourth-grader is:

Walrus

1. Loose skin and big teeth but real ivory—
   Introduction
2. Where people hunt them and why
   Map
3. The walrus family
   Picture
4. Protection
   Picture
5. Food
6. Future supply of walruses

With this in hand for a guide and with illustrative material arranged in sequence so it could be easily shown, a fourth grade reporter was ready and confident of audience interest.

This individual planning with the teacher took less and less time. As some reports were given in well-ordered sequence, the children became aware of what made a good report. They came to their planning conferences so well-geared to the job that it took only a brief checking to give that sense of certainty for which most fourth graders still look to adults. The careful preparation of content and sequence that each child had made, the sense of group enterprise that had come from the real experiences and from the avid search for materials and sharing of findings, had set the stage for active listening. Discussion after each report indicated that genuine concern had developed for the success of each speaker as well as interest in the subject matter. At the conclusion of a report the audience asked questions that the reporter could answer immediately, or, not knowing, was asked to find answers to report later.

STARTING WRITTEN REPORTS

It is not until the middle of the fourth grade that most of our children showed the maturity necessary for writing extensive, well-stocked, well-organized informational reports. Indeed, even fourth graders can write well only as the climax of a long series of other activities. They must first amass much concrete information; become deeply immersed in the subject matter; and, of course, they must share findings through talking, listening, and illustrating before they can write.

In one class, weeks of study about Vikings had preceded the stage of readiness to write about them. One of the most difficult things about informational writing, even for many grownups, is getting started. This was especially true of the class preparing to write about explorers.

Although these children had devoted much time to the careful reading of reference books, consulted source material, studied pictures, real objects, and other illustrative material, they needed help in finding an organization that would give shape to the mass of information they had accumulated. This presented an opportunity for the economy of class teaching. We brought the group together and asked such questions as, "What are some of the important points you will need to include in writing about Vikings?" After a lengthy discussion, the following topics were agreed upon:

Food
Homes
Places explored
Religion and customs
Famous Vikings
Ships
Sagas

Getting the first thoughts down on paper presents many hurdles. We have found it helpful to ask: "Which of these topics do you know a good deal about?" When Pat said he knew a lot about Viking ships, he was asked to start talking about that subject to the class. Seizing a pencil and paper the teacher momentarily became a scribe. The others watched while she wrote "Ships" at the top of the page and rapidly jotted down his first few enthusiastic sentences as they tumbled out. After a minute or two he was given the chance to read back to the class what was now on paper. Following this demonstration of how one can "talk ideas to paper" the children returned to their places and got set for work. Each was given several pieces of paper. All were elated at having so much paper to start with and relieved to learn that this first draft did not have to be in perfect handwriting but just had to be sufficiently "clean" copy to make editing and recopying as easy as possible. These techniques for putting thoughts on paper seemed to break down the Herculean task into controllable parts.

45

It was quickly decided that the statement of facts must be preceded by something to make a reader take notice immediately. Some children thought that their own feelings about the topic would introduce well what was to come. As is often the case in adult writing, the children wrote their beginnings after they had written the body of their reports. Here are some sample introductions:

About five hundred years before Columbus, the Vikings were tough and bold. They came from Norway, Sweden, and Denmark. The Vikings were the first men to discover America. Back in the year 1000, some people were Vikings and some people weren't. The Vikings were a kind of explorer. They were also fishermen and sometimes pirates.

The Vikings sailed from Norway to Iceland to start a new life because Eric the Red started trouble in Norway. Again Eric started fights so he was expelled from Iceland. He and his men sailed off to the West.

The following report by a fourth grader about a woodchuck contains a great deal of the writer's personality and is a good example of the results obtained by the technique described.

Here Comes the Woodchuck—Big, Fat, and Handsome

Out in the open spaces where there are rocks the wood- chuck builds his home so that the bears and the dogs can't get him. You could find the look-out tower. It is made from the dirt that he has dug out while he was building his home.

A woodchuck's home is a burrow which he digs under stone walls. He spends most of his time eating vegetables like carrots, corn, lettuce and all young vegetables. Farmers do not like it because woodchucks raid their gardens.

If you go over to the woodchuck's home you'd find four to nine babies so that's why every time the farmers shoot one they can't get rid of them because there are so many more than they can shoot.

Their protection is their home mostly. They use their tower to see if any enemies are coming and when they do come, the woodchuck goes in head first and if the enemy comes while their babies are playing outside the woodchuck whistles for them to come in the hole. When the dogs try to get in the hole, the woodchuck just goes out the back door and watches the dog digging away. When the woodchuck is surrounded he'll snap his teeth and claw like a cat.

As experience accumulates, the responsibility for saying clearly what one wishes to report continues to be felt personally. Control of factual data, greater reading power, increasing efficiency in use of library facilities, and longer attention span all contribute to the extension of reporting ability. Other factors also influence this greater strength. Children's intimate and frequent association with a wealth of literature means an inevitable absorption with some of the familiar patterns of folklore and fairy tales, and with some of the form and idiom, rhythm and cadence of our language.

The sheer bulk of prose consumed by our average voracious readers of eight-to-twelve years may partly account for the tendency toward voluminous expression. It also seems true that the respect for accuracy developed by practical writing and the opportunity for freedom in personal expression make children much more sensitive to color, ruggedness, fragile delicacy, or exact phrasing in what they hear. One group of sixth-grade children upon hearing Moti Guj, Mutineer spontaneously picked out many of the elements that make Kipling's style inimitable.

"Oh, read that again, please—where he called him 'warty toad of a dried mud puddle,' " said Alice.

"And read all those other things Deesa called him," urged another. "They're good."

They liked it when Moti Guj swung the baby up in the air in his trunk.

"There's something alike in all Kipling's stories and yet every animal is different. He uses so many big words! If we try to use big words in a story just to use them—well, it sounds queer, that's all."

And again, one snowy winter day when the same group heard:

> A prompt decisive man, no breath
> Our father wasted: "Boys, a path! . . ."
> John Greenleaf Whittier, "Snowbound"

Albert stated, "Oh, boy, I know what kind of man he was! Just two lines to say all that." Whittier's economy of description was not lost upon children who had themselves felt the compulsion to make their characters real. Moreover, this heightened awareness made them infinitely more responsive to the few elements the teacher chose to bring to their attention.

49

These lines of growth are so interwoven with extended reading, personal and practical writing, and genuine literary appreciation, and so tied to the whole business of growing up that it is truly impossible to separate cause from effect. Reading, hearing, telling, listening, and writing become mutually significant. A many-faceted sensitivity emerges through an alchemy difficult to comprehend. But though we do not understand the process, we do know that two of the indispensable elements of this genuine integration are time to assimilate and opportunity to react honestly.

An example of this more facile and extended expression is to be found in a report written by a child of eleven. Though this is an example of practical writing, of reporting information as part of a larger class venture, there is an individual flavor to "many a river has its beginning," "the salmon also have their beginning," or "something like instinct tells them to go back." Carolyn was a spirited child and her interest in the live creature was reflected in the quality of her writing about the journeys and struggles of the live fish. Her description of the canning process is dull by comparison, though the facts are presented in a fashion not greatly inferior to the average adult-written textbook. Carolyn needed checking only on the spelling of "uncertain" and "appearance."

Salmon

In Washington and Oregon on the tops of mountains, many a river has its beginning. These little streams rush madly along, fed by the melting snows of the glaciers. The salmon also have their beginning in that freezing cold climate. Their eggs are orange mixed with a little pink. When the baby salmon hatch they eat almost everything smaller than themselves. (By the way they are only about one-half inch long.) When they grow bigger they finally start downstream to seek their fortunes. When they reach the ocean they live there about three or four years. After this time, something like instinct tells them to go back to the streams where they were hatched. Millions of salmon start up the long, hard journey. Many of the salmon are caught or killed. The ones that escape continue their fight upstream, leaping falls, and etc. When they reach their destination, the male scoops out a hollow in the gravel. Then the female lays her eggs and the male buries them. Then the two salmon float tail downstream and die an uncertain death.

The salmon that are caught are loaded into scows and taken to the cannery. Their heads and fins are cut off, and the eggs removed. The body is passed beneath circular knives. They are cut into the sizes of the cans they are to go into. Then a machine fills them in correctly. The cans pass on a belt to a weighing machine. Two girls in white uniforms refill any can underweight. Then the cans are lacquered because it gives the cans a nice appearance and also because when a ship is loaded with cans of salmon and is going south, it prevents condensation.

The people that are usually employed are either Chinese or Indians.

References

Atwood and Thomas, *North America,* pp. 244–245
Allen, *United States,* p. 253
Pamphlet, *The Salmon*

The cover in which a bit of expository writing appears is of titanic importance to the children. The energy expended in making a cover for an elephant "book" is equal to that devoted to the material itself. Rightly so. For the youngster the product is a total in which size, color, and illustration are inseparable from content. Quite a few grown-up authors confess that they see their future book printed, bound, and standing in majesty upon the library shelf long before the first chapter is completed. As children grow up they take great pride in making by hand more interesting and often more complicated kinds of books. In our experience no other activity gave more zest to growing ability and interest in utilitarian expression.

OPPORTUNITIES FOR BRIEF PRACTICAL WRITING

Caution must be exercised against requiring too much writing even at nine or ten. Better a child write one report containing real substance than several that are mere shadows. There is in most schools a continual need for work that affords practice in the mechanics of sentence formation, writing, and capitalization, such as:

Labels
Keeping one's own reading list,
    month by month
Recording weather and temperature data
Recording feeding and growth of pets
Invitations and messages of all sorts
    to people hard to see in person or too busy to be interrupted
Thank-you notes

Notices about assemblies, journeys,
      school bulletins, playground arrangements
Identification cards for various files
Spelling exercises, both the
      statistically derived lists and "our own" words;
      also dictation exercises
Recording absence and attendance daily
      for the principal and the nurse
Captions for pictures and diagrams
Rules for games
Explanations for bulletin boards
Plans for a party or field trip
Homework assignments

It is highly important that children realize the full significance of practical records. Otherwise, their writing can degenerate into a meaningless chore. Doing useful things well further establishes the pride of workmanship that in itself is an energizing influence.

Writing in response to genuine needs is conducive to ease and high standards in both form and content. The occasional isolated repetition of a few difficult items, plus, in intermediate grades, the use of writing in spelling practice, all contribute to the flow of expression and to improved muscular control.

CLEAR STRUCTURE TO MATCH CLEAR UNDERSTANDING

Though we do not tamper with a child's imaginative or personal creations, certainly direct and thorough teaching is needed in the realm of practical writing.

Much of this writing is read to the class, put into a book, contributed to a group discussion of some larger subject, or, at the more mature levels, is done just to find out how. It is often wise for a child who is weak in this field to read material aloud first to the teacher alone, so they may correct sentence errors together. Usually reading a passage aloud convinces a child that "it says too much" or "it doesn't sound finished." For those who don't see the weakness, the teacher points it out, giving examples of ways to repair the bad spot, but encouraging clarification of statements in the child's own words.

Frequently children come for help before a teacher can assist with the actual writing. Many children feel a need for clarifying an idea before they write it but do not know how. "I want to say that there are three ways of tanning leather," complained Ellen, "but one sounds so much like the other that I can't get them straight. One talks about softening the hide and the other two sound like tanning—you know, to make it wear. I can't make it clear."

Ellen was really asking for help to clarify her understanding of a process. Indeed, without this clear perception, sentence structure is bound to suffer. After she talked it out, writing it was not so mysterious.

Ellen had already half-analyzed her own problem. Another child might only sense a difficulty and will need help to spot the trouble and work out the muddle. This is a slow process, and takes more than a glib prescription. The teacher must consider not only the material the child is writing but also his particular level of maturity, talk over the concrete problem, and provide guidance in straightening out the tangle. Going back to experiment or to reread sources to verify information and then to talk about the matter may heighten understanding. Through conversation the teacher assists a child in clarifying ideas enough to write them, and in making written construction fit the thought. The child will be permanently strengthened by the experience, so that even though costly in time, such guidance is economical in terms of benefit because it makes for increased independence.

Of course the most effective test of clarity comes from the other members of the class. The success of a report is measured by the degree to which it is clear and understandable, or adds to the larger study under way, or illustrates a general notion with concrete detail. These criteria become the children's.

The teacher looks for positive illustrations of clarity, good choice of language, or some accidental use of a superior technique. In class discussions the teacher's comments focus upon how clearly the ideas were developed, how one thought naturally led to the next, how interesting a certain picture was made. The class may ask questions that the reporter cannot answer, and he will be expected to add further detail to the report. This is not a matter of pleasing teachers, many of whom are only too ready to interpret inadequate expressions. Following the reading of a report and the discussion of it, the writer often finds changes that should be made.

Before children begin to write, days, even weeks of observing, analyzing, experimenting, talking, and reading may be necessary. One must know much to say little, if that little is to carry its point home. A great deal of children's nonsentence writing, of repeated "ands," and ambiguous construction is caused by their having to write before they have anything to say or by having to write purely fictitious or sterile exercises. If any adult doubts this, let him try offhand to write an animated lucid exposition of "How To Build a Skyscraper" or "An Interesting Conversation between Two Natives of Tierra del Fuego." No more absurd than dozens we are asked to do in early childhood!

A child needs time to assimilate an experience—whether it is an experiment, trip, reading, or observation—before the ideas gained can become part of his/her own resources. In our experience, writing about yesterday's trip to the museum is sadly unsuccessful. Yesterday's picnic, likewise! Even the most glowing enthusiasm cannot provoke a flow of ideas when the reaction to the experience is too raw to be translated into written form. Time for experience to ripen is as important a phase of the ideas-into-writing cycle as the actual putting of pen to paper. Reflecting, talking, thinking become necessary precursors to the depth of perception that makes clear writing possible. Indeed, even many able children may slip back into nonsentence or otherwise faulty construction when forced to write about what has not been digested and absorbed. The apparent correlation between repeated "ands" and immature mentality adds weight to the belief that a genuine control of ideas is the main condition for adequate writing. *Content begets form.*

ACHIEVING EFFECTIVE ORGANIZATION

Effective organization, characteristic of real intellectuality, is also closely related to thorough understanding. A rich background of ideas is important, but so, too, is the degree to which these ideas have matured within the individual. To let them lie fallow, to sort and resort them, to talk over what has been discovered or read or observed or thought are as necessary a prelude to logical arrangement as is the gathering of factual data. This casual talking over of experience, reporting the results of one's exploration, is a vitally important stage in developing disciplined expression. Here half-understood ideas and vague impressions begin to take form through casual and informal talking about "what we found out" or "what we have done." New questions arise. Relative values emerge. Some clarification and refinement take place from the simple verbalization of ideas. And the fact that talking is so much faster and less strenuous than writing makes such conversational stock taking an economical step toward the eventual refinement of expression. Thus do ideas become an integral part of the person.

A group of eight-year-olds, in planning a star party for the seven-year-olds, realized that many things they'd like to tell (often just because they're so proud to know them) would not fit into a party for younger children.

Seven-year-olds, from the vantage point of being eight, need things made very easy and very clear. This explaining anything to younger children obliges one to be very straightforward and direct, a discipline most valuable to writers of any age. Yes, selection and rejection of data for a specific purpose were beginning to be practiced by these children. Even at the university level, choosing facts relevant to a specific problem continues to be an important type of intellectual exercise.

But of equal importance is that the teacher have awareness of the child's level of development of *orderliness*. This is a very complex matter, differing with every individual, growing with the growing individual; further, it never shows the same earmarks even in two persons brought up in the same general environment, with apparently the same immediate purpose, and with the same I.Q. To a degree, fortunately, a feeling for organization is a part of everyone. Moreover, it appears that the practice of writing purposefully makes a marked contribution to its natural development.

It is very interesting to observe some of the manifestations of a dawning sense of order. Even quite immature children often want to divide a report or a story into "chapters" in an effort to satisfy their need for some sort of dividing line. The concept of "chapter" may seem to be stretching it a bit, but let the young writer divide the offering on, perhaps, the fruit fly into chapters if desired. In short order the child sees that some of the items really belong in another chapter, maybe a new one that should be written about the damage the fly does the world over. This "bundling" of material to put like things together is one of the first stages of logical and coherent writing.

As children mature it is easy to point out, usually following their own discovery of the matter, that within a chapter is a sequence of ideas— smaller divisions within the large one, the basis of paragraphing. That each different idea—each part of the chapter—stands out better if seen in a separate paragraph is about as far as it seems reasonable to go with elementary school children in the debatable matter of paragraph division. Certainly much of the trouble in paragraphing arises from forcing the use of a form before the need for it is understood. The groups under discussion had *experienced* the need for paragraph division for greater clarity. They did not learn it in isolated exercises.

Later on, children become aware of another factor of organization, infinitely more involved than the grouping of like ideas and frequently conspicuous by its absence even in adult writing. This is the active principle in sequential arrangement. The marshaling of functional material toward a real goal signals the beginning of a dynamic organization.

55

A group of fifth graders, for instance, planned to explain the running of an automobile to another group similarly interested. Cogwheels, diagrams, batteries were at hand. Jack told how gas is exploded in the cylinders. Harry expounded upon the gear shift. Peter told how the battery, coil, and generator did their work. After the event was over, the children were talking about it with their teacher. Jim pointed out, "I wouldn't have understood that. You know, we told how each part of the car works, but nobody ever told how they all went together."

The teacher's opportunity was at hand to show that it is necessary in many kinds of explanation to "tie it together as you go along." The class worked out, with little help, a plan showing how they could have done this with their automobile explanations, by tracing power from gasoline to turning wheels.

A live organization, propellent and galvanic, of ideas that "hang together" is difficult to achieve, even for adults. Still, in reflecting upon the automobile report, the genesis of this mature mental faculty was being used. The children had the experience before they could understand the reason for vitalizing their organization. Having sensed the need they could see what to do about it in a concrete setting. These boys had worked from a wealth of content for weeks, had organized their learning for a purpose real and significant to themselves, had analyzed their talks according to how clearly they had told the story. With further similar experience they will all be well on the way toward exercising relatedness, an intellectual function often developed only by the highly gifted.

As we patiently encourage the slowly increasing power of organization, it becomes clear that whatever plan a child follows in a piece of writing it must be his own. Help may be received, but only after its need is felt. Following someone else's scheme of sequence is a purely external procedure of no help and is perhaps damaging to the individual. The writer does not then *learn to organize*, but rather to imitate some other person's mental processes, to juggle words. As given in one dictionary, the meaning of the word "organize" is "to give life or being to; . . . to cause to unite or work together in orderly fashion; . . . to endow with life." (*The Winston Dictionary*, College Edition, 1957, p. 684.) One is not organizing thought when one is fitting data into another person's scheme.

The fostering of an individual's organizing ability takes time, but because the process exercises innate faculties, it precludes long sessions spent on made-up exercises.

After extended reading, study, talking over, note-taking, and more talking over, Elaine, in sixth grade, made the following plan for her report on wheat:

I. Planting and growing winter wheat
II. Where it grows best
III. Its value to the country
IV. How it is shipped and stored

The last item, that of storage and shipment, was the teacher's suggestion but easily accepted as part of the job when Elaine saw its significance. After having read her account to the class, and although satisfied with its acceptance by the group, the writer noted that she might have discussed the value of wheat to the country last of all, because shipping really "came right along after growing," but value and costs were something quite different and would be a better ending. Thus do experience and guidance interact.

Winter Wheat

Winter wheat is usually planted in September with a drill. It grows several inches high and then droops. It does not die but simply rests for the winter. It begins to grow again in the spring. Its color changes from green to golden yellow. Fields of wheat look like golden sand with a patch of green grass here and there with the wind gently blowing the wheat back and forth.

In late June or July the wheat is harvested. The harvesting machines have a thresher machine combined with them. The thresher has a little wagon that is attached at the side to catch the wheat as it comes from the thresher. . . .

Only about one sixth of this report has been reproduced here because of lack of space. Maps and graphs added to Elaine's three typewritten pages.

EXPERIENCE REPORTS

Children do yet another type of reporting which, though it uses actual experience or factual data or both, takes on some of the quality of imaginative stories. This is the kind of report that Bill wrote about his beloved dog, Brandy, using both incident and characteristics that made his pet come alive on paper. His warmth of feeling and the details he chose charmed his audience. Such experience "stories" bridge the gap between practical and personal writing showing the relationships as well as the distinctions between factual and fanciful aspects of life and literature.

Report on a Pet

The dog that I'm going to tell you about is a boxer. She appears to be a very ferocious looking dog on the outside. She is a very homely dog. Every time the garbage men come around she is missing. When you kick at her she makes a very terrible sound and bites you very lightly. When you walk in the door she will bark her head off. She is very fat because everybody feeds her.

Brandy, my dog, only has two enemies . . . all cats, including our cat and one dog, another boxer. The boxer knocked my father off his crutches once and Brandy was there when it happened. She has hated that dog ever since.

This scavenger lives all over the place. Actually she has only one home that loves her as much as we do. I mean our house. People feed her bones and she takes them from other dogs even when she has a bone stashed away every place you can think of. We used to feed her a whole can of dog food, but now we have seen what it has done to her, we only feed her a half a can.

Brandy can't have any babies because she was spayed. I wish she was not spayed, but my father and mother don't think so. They are glad. They don't want puppies.

Brandy's voice is a whimper. When she gets up enough wind to bark, she does it. Her protection in some cases is her bark. After she knows she has done something wrong, she puts her paw out and looks so cute that you could hug her. Another protection is her teeth. She shows her teeth when she is mad.

My dog has a special habit. When you pet her just before her back leg, she will pick up her right leg and try to scratch where you are petting. When a cat comes her way, Brandy's hair stands up on end and it looks like she has had a Mohican hair cut.

Brandy has four feet as most other dogs do. I don't know how she does it, but she keeps all four feet in step. She can run faster than I can in spite of all her weight and four feet to handle.

Brandy may not have a use to you, but she has a very good use to us as a watch dog. Her use to me is that she makes me feel happy when I'm sad . . . she has such a crazy mixed-up face.

ENGLISH ESSENTIALS

Even under the best known conditions—vitality of purpose, richness of background, confidence in the group and the teacher, much satisfaction in knowing "how much better we can do than a year ago"—a few common danger signals in the mastery of technicalities should be watched for.

Clarity of expression seems often to be endangered by "thens," "whens," and "ands" used incorrectly. Susan reread her three sentences, omitting "then" to see if she could feel the "then idea" better without saying it.

Before:

Then the blossom begins to come out. The plants are then two or three feet high. The blossom is first white, then shell pink, rose-pink, and red. Then the petals fall.

After:

The plants are two or three feet high. The blossom is first white, later shell pink, rose-pink, and last red. Then the petals fall.

Another frequent pitfall is the lengthy but incomplete sentence. When, in the process of growing up, the more able children naturally begin to use complex and compound sentences, such errors occur. A long dependent clause like the following often passes unnoticed. Ruth did not tell what "the switch on the line" did or what happened to it: "The switch on the line which was usually open where slow freights had to be side-tracked to let express trains pass." Having Ruth reread her lines aloud to see what happened to the switch made her see how "where" caused confusion, and that she needed to finish the sentence. "Who," "where," "which," and "then" might come to be viewed with caution by the children themselves.

At times it is economical to isolate special ills of writing, observe them closely in one or several class periods, and work on them directly. The ever-present nuisance of showing possession is sometimes abated by a dictated exercise such as the following:

We played "Snatch-Club" with Mrs. Brown's class at noon today. We had two teams and so did they. Jack's team played first and Mary's second. Our opponents were quick and well-organized. They wasted no time forgetting their numbers. We won one game and so did they.

> Jack's books
> a girl's coat
> their balls
> their bats

The difficulty illustrated had shown up in previous work and many were aware of it. The teacher has to underscore the problem, clarify it as concretely as she can, and then provide simple practice exercises to work on. Language texts, of course, furnish some helpful ones. A week or two later the genuine writing needs of a group of ten-year-olds may require the same items. Many will remember, but others will not. (Indeed all through high school and college "others" will not. Even in adult writing, mechanics need continued attention.)

The following notice was written for an assembly two weeks after the exercise on possessives. It made use of the forms that had been isolated for practice:

Assembly Notice

All children will please take their regular seats for assembly on Wednesday, February 10th. Miss Wright's class will give a play from the story, "Jane's Father."

For these and other more difficult items of English form, some specific drill seems necessary for almost all children. Correct use of apostrophes, punctuation of conversation, spelling of "its" and "their," for example, need to be spotlighted even after much use in a child's writing. Comparatively little of such practice is needed, fortunately, when children from the first grade on have held high standards of practical writing, and items of form have been supplied or checked by the teacher and pupils when needed. Such skills can become more nearly habitual after much correct use in concrete situations. After the habit of writing with fluency and with a sense of security and satisfaction has been established, these technicalities can be assimilated more readily into a growing fabric of purposeful written expression, either personal or utilitarian in nature.

No real barrier exists, of course, between practical writing and personal expressions termed "creative." Indeed *practical* writing can also be *creative,* and some transfer really occurs from the techniques practiced in utilitarian writing to the joyous artistic outpouring written for its own sake. From the beginning the need for clarity has set standards high but possible of attainment for each child. Continued, this has become a discipline, strengthened often by the approval of fine work, by the encouragement of obvious improvement, and on rare occasions by negation. The reality and often the dramatic quality of this approach is perhaps the strongest factor in the carry-over of standards from the practical to the more subjective and more personal writing of stories and lyrical expressions. When almost all of the large group of sixth-grade boys and girls volunteer to rewrite or retype a story to satisfy their own standards, the identification of the individual with the job has been clearly felt. The children have made a real integration between two distinct but related functions of writing, between themselves and the fruits of their labor.

4

Personal Writing

There is no art to writing but having something to say.
Robert Frost, The Washington Post

Most of us remember all too vividly the ordeal of "composition." No matter how zealous we may have been in filling private notebooks, we approached the task at school with distaste, if not with dread; and the anemic accounts produced on assignment were a far cry from the adventures we made up for ourselves when our imaginations ran free. At school we wrote to please the teacher; at home we labored solely for the joy of using our creative power.

Those secret stories that many children write for their personal pleasure or for that of a few special friends are usually crude, extravagent and childish, but invariably they have life. Moreover, because their creation is prompted by an inner urge rather than by an external compulsion, marked changes occur in the thinking and feeling of the young writers. This eagerness to write for one's own satisfaction or for a trusted and appreciative audience does many things for children. It stirs and stretches their imagination, it develops a sense of ease in handling language, and it encourages the desire to make words say what they want them to say. So in our classrooms we have tried to approximate the conditions under which children write spontaneously for their own fun and satisfaction. The stories they write are read aloud for mutual entertainment, and no direct attempts are made to correct or improve them. Interest is centered on writing more and more stories for when children write copiously and with interest they make surprising gains in language power.

HOW STORY WRITING IS INITIATED

The question arises, "How is story writing begun in the first place? When a teacher is faced with a new class, how does she go about stirring this

61

storytelling power into life?" Our way has been simple as well as happy and fruitful. It is based on the fact that making up stories is not only a natural impulse but also a contagious one.

During the early days of a new term we use short periods—"rest periods" they are sometimes called—for gathering the group about us and sharing stories other children have written. The occasion is for immediate enjoyment, but the necessary groundwork for future growth is also being laid. We are establishing the habit of appreciative listening and stirring in the children the desire to make stories of their own. Children, for example, might be introduced to the Bear family and then hear John's story about bathing the cat.

It was early afternoon on a winter Saturday and Bo was calling his cat. "Here, kitty, kitty. Come, Kitty."

His cat appeared, its black fur stained with mud from the melting snow. Ulp! No cat could be that dirty.

"Oh, Bo," called Mrs. Bear, "you'll have to wash your cat next week," but when Mrs. Bear saw the cat she quickly changed her mind. "Er—well, on second thought, you'd better wash it now."

"Now, Mother?"

"Yes, now."

"Well, all right."

Five minutes later Bo had the tub filled with scalding water. "I guess the cat would rather have it hot than cold," he mumbled. Carefully he picked up the cat by its tail. A howl rent the air, but Bo still held on. Slowly he dipped the cat in the water after putting half a box of dishwashing soap in.

"Yeo-o-o-ow". The cat wriggled loose and fell struggling into the water. Covered with suds she jumped out, spilling suds all over the bathroom.

"Darn you," shouted Bo, throwing a drinking glass at the fleeing cat. Crash! The glass flew into the next room where unfortunately Mrs. Bear was entertaining the principal of Bo's school.

"Help!" Then the principal came out very red and with the glass wedged very firmly on his long nose. "Goodbye, Mrs. Bear, and I must say that I never saw such a—"

The principal's sentence was cut short by the cat, who was still trying to escape from Bo. Bo tackled the cat, or he thought he did, but the cat climbed the principal. Bo missed him and hit the glass on the principal's nose.

A little while later when they had gotten untangled—wack—crash—bam! Poor Bo! And all that night Bo had to stand up in bed.

This episode is so full of action and vividly told details that children can readily picture it in their imaginations. Quite likely they will make under-their-breath remarks about Bo's stupidity or the "poor cat," and some adventurous child is sure to laugh aloud at the predicament of the principal. We laugh, too, because it *is* a ridiculous sight. Besides, we always like to read some stories in which children are aggressively clever, and adults can be tolerantly laughed at; such stories dissolve the fiber of resistance and are convincing proof to children that they dare to write freely without fear of the teacher's displeasure.

The impulsive reactions during the reading will be followed, no doubt, by more comments at the end. The mood we are trying to induce is a relaxed, companionable one with sufficient leisure to visualize the story and savor it to its full.

Since nothing stifles creative effort so quickly as adverse criticism, whether voiced or merely felt, we allow only appreciative comments in the story-sharing time. The tendency to pick flaws is checked in this beginning period when the children are listening to stories from the teacher's stockpile (see story supplement). To this end a few poor ones are always read. At the first negative remark we stop to discuss why we expect only approving comments or none at all. Our point is that if anyone takes the time and effort to write a story for our pleasure, we cannot be so ungracious as to pick it to pieces; and the children, through airing their own experiences, reveal how faultfinding takes the heart out of any activity. The exclusion of negative criticism is an absolute *must* for any successful program of creative writing.

The short periods of reading stories for enjoyment are continued until two things happen: the children begin to show signs that they are ready to write stories of their own, and the pattern of acceptance is so firmly set that even the most humble effort will escape condemnation.

This whole process of initiation is of great importance. Every fall, whether the group is a new or a familiar one, a third grade or a sixth, we go through these same steps. It is essentially a warming-up process; the group has to be drawn into the rapport necessary to happy, easy writing, and the individual's own desire to write must be tempted to the point of action. With some groups two or three weeks suffice; for others the preparation moves slowly through a month or more, and there are occasional groups that require a whole semester of stimulation before writing gets under way.

Finally, when the time seems ripe, it is suggested that the children begin writing stories. The invitation is intentionally casual, and the way to respond is made easy. A time is provided for those who wish to write, and the others are allowed to turn to some self-chosen quiet work. The nonwriters may do such things as read or draw pictures of story incidents, work on arithmetic or spelling, finish up some uncompleted task. No stigma is attached to not writing, but acclaim is given to those who make the venture. With the occasional ones who are eager to try but who lack ideas, we visit a little, hoping to make a suggestion that will set their pencils going. If after a short conference no story plans are forthcoming, we counsel waiting until another day. A child who has no characters in mind, is free to use any from stories we have been reading. *Whereas we once thought of an incident as the necessary starting point of a story, we now realize that many young writers invent with ease and originality when they begin with characters and let them act out their experiences on paper.* To help children create characters of their own, we may use a more direct approach. We read several stories with different characters and call attention to their names and the things they did. Then we suggest that the children make up some of their own. We might ask such questions as, "What did your Rack Raccoon do when his mother's back was turned? Is he the pest of the neighborhood? Who is the tattle tale in the family?"

As the other children get excited about their own inventions, we might say, "Grab your pencils and make your characters act on paper." Not all children are ready for this, but they can make pictures and name their characters. The teacher writes on the chalkboard the words needed by the writers. Soon she takes a few minutes to visit the ones who are drawing pictures and asks questions about them. Sometimes she writes a sentence or two as a child answers.

Stories do not even have to have titles. Starting with a title is often a limiting or inhibiting experience. Writers need the freedom that allows thoughts to wander as they will. To help a child feel more daring we sometimes remark, "You can never be really sure how a story is going to turn out; so it's an adventure for you, too. If you want to name it, that can be the final touch before you share it with the class." Many children forego titles entirely. When they finish one story they often lose themselves in creating another. At the peak of writing excitement, ideas often come with a rush.

This whole procedure may sound careless, but we have found that it bears good results. The first concern is to free a child so that he can reveal his thinking and feeling through writing, without concern for neatness or correctness. True personal writing wells up from the subconscious, and unless the items that require conscious efforts are minimized, they can easily bar the way.

READING THE FIRST STORIES

It is a red-letter day when the first stories are finished, and a sense of achievement pervades the sharing time. For the halting or the fearful or those whose voices do not carry, we read their efforts, having gone over them with the authors beforehand to make sure we can present them well. The more able or secure children usually choose to read their own. We put away distractions and sit comfortably in order to listen with ease. At first, we thought it strange that the children somehow moved closer and closer together as we went from one story to another. Later we understood this as the urge to be near the storyreader as part of the joyous communication of spirit generated by story creation.

During the reading period the teacher gives herself wholeheartedly to even the simplest story; listening as naturally and eagerly as she likes the class to listen to her. The story takes over completely. By some curious form of osmosis this spirit of attentive listening spreads throughout the group. It is courteous listening, but more than that, it is creative listening, which works magically upon the children to release their native gifts and to build up their confidence. Even sophisticated adults are exhilarated and prodded by the feel of a responsive audience, and children, who are extremely sensitive to emotional climates, react more strongly still.

No early story is passed by without some sort of favorable notice. If no child volunteers an appreciative comment, the teacher can do so. We *never* ask, "How could this story be improved?" In the most meager effort something can be found to enjoy: a hint of lively action or picture-making detail, a touch of invention, a curious name, or a glimmer of humor. Later in the year comments are often by-passed, but in the beginning they are important because they point up the elements that make all stories entertaining and alive. Moreover, they help to make the first storywriting experiences happy ones so that even a hesitant writer will want to try again.

WHAT CHILDREN WRITE ABOUT

What do children write about when they write just for fun? Why, about themselves, of course. To be sure, they are not aware that this is what they are doing. They think they are making up adventures of an imaginary hero or a mischievous bear. But in reality, when they become absorbed in telling about Uncle Rufftuff or the Bossy King, it is their experiences—their own thinking and feeling—that they unconsciously reveal.

When children begin to write because it is fun, they do not choose the topics that are often doled out as the easy ones based on immediate experience: A Summer Adventure, My Dog, My Trip to the Farm. They rarely write openly about themselves or about happenings that are recent and therefore freshly in mind. The reason is plain. If they write about themselves, they cannot write well about anything that has not yet become a part of those selves. Only when the experiences have had time to sink into deeper levels of a child's consciousness and there be intermingled with the residue of other experiences and other meanings, do they become the stuff from which imaginings and interpretations are fashioned.

As they grow in writing experience they draw more and more from this reservoir of emotions and ideas, through the alchemy of imagination transmuting them into stories and poems. The world portrayed in this writing is essentially a child's intuitive creation—a most satisfactory world, indeed, in which the actual-familiar and the wished-for are happily blended. It is rarely peopled with everyday characters, and is not limited to pedestrian reality. Animals or half-fairy-tale beings take on the attributes of humans, while at the same time they accomplish with ease what is ordinarily impossible. It is an upside-down world as well, in which the child, not the adult, is the person of importance, dominating each situation by means of magic, shrewd intelligence, or merely a slingshot.

More than this concerning the substance of children's writing we cannot say. It is true that when they write without restraint, they write about themselves, but even now, with added confidence stemming from increased knowledge of child development, we are not satisfied with our understanding of what those selves are really like. We do know that they are very different from adults in their desires, sense of values, and points of view; and also that they change markedly in the various stages of growth. Realizing this we are slow to take exception to ideas that at first glance seem discourteous or crude. They may not appear so to a child, and we try not to curb the fun of writing by quibbling over differences inherent in our points of view.

When a few youngsters have grown excited about a group of lively characters or a new pattern of writing, their enthusiasm spreads through-out the group until most of the class gets caught up in the story-making activity. The fact that a familiar thread runs through their stories seems to add to the children's interest and to free their creative power. Writing comes more abundantly and is of better-than-usual quality. Under such impetus some children produce the only spontaneous writing they ever do.

One fall a group of nine- and ten-year-olds came upon a simple story of the adventures of five little bears.* The next day an original five-bear

---

*Sterling North wrote several stories about the little bears which appeared in the children's magazine *Child Life* in the thirties. They were a real inspiration to the children who "took off" from them to write many new stories about bears with additional characters of their own.

story appeared, and immediately the contagion began to spread. Every child wrote at least two or three stories about the bears and one boy wrote more than twenty-five. Although they used essentially the same characters and frequently the same type of mischievous incident, their tales were remarkably varied, both in content and style. Curiously enough, too, of the large number of stories written that year the bear stories were outstandingly the best. Here is one of them; others appear elsewhere in the book.

A Bear Story

"Children," said Mother, "you are going to take lessons in language."

"How many do we have to take?" asked Pug.

"Four," said Mother, "Greek, Latin, German, French—now that I think of it you should have Spanish and, of course, English."

Mother had studied language and wanted the little bears to, but Father disagreed with her. He had gone away for a year, and Mother jumped at the chance.

"You shouldn't have to take them all at once, but you have a year and I won't make you go to school."

Just then they saw Father coming up the walk. "I am going to tell Father unless you promise that we won't have to take languages and you'll promise to take us to the movies ten times each month and let us go swimming every day this month," said Pug.

"All right. Don't tell him."

Father opened the door. "I forgot my suitcase," he said. "The boat doesn't sail for an hour."

The invention of characters can be a difficult step for children, and newly created ones often produce in their writing the formality and self-consciousness that one feels with strangers. But if children have characters at hand—old friends with whom they have laughed and adventured—they find it relatively easy to use them as vehicles of their imaginings. Recalling the great story cycles of heroes such as Robin Hood, King Arthur, and our own Paul Bunyan, we realize that the community use of popular heroes has long been the storyteller's privilege and practice.

Furthermore, if these familiar characters are a compound of realism and fancy they make invention easier still. Although such beings may behave like humans, they are not bound by ordinary limitations and standards. This allows the child's story people to wander at will between the real world and the unreal, combining the magical and the commonplace, and acting in ways that children dream of but dare not emulate.

In our classes the roguish bears—Eenie, Teenie, Tiny, Bo, and Pug—have long given lively impetus to story writing. From time to time we have suggested that someone devise a new set of characters, and occasionally a child has done so. Dixie had her Otter Family—Big, Middle-Size, and Small. When the baby came she named it Tiny. John invented the Great Chimino, and Donald wrote many stories about Droopy, the Little Aeroplane. But by and large, few newcomers have challenged the popularity of the bears. That does not mean, however, that there has been no invention of character, for in the guise of friends, enemies, and relations there have been many colorful additions to the original five until now the group of Bear characters make up a sizable clan. There have been the baby Daisy May, Uncle Upper Bumper, Eenie's boon companion Roy Bear, Teenie's girl friend, and a host of cousins and playmates. When children have a set of old characters as a nucleus, they seem able to invent new ones readily enough whenever the need arises.

The tales about such imaginary, childlike creatures are unusual in their fresh originality. This fact shines out more clearly when they are contrasted with the realistic stories that children sometimes attempt. In concocting a horse or dog story, a child commonly apes the situation, the vocabulary, and even the cadences of the animal fiction he reads. Almost never is there anything in his tale that bears the stamp of the author—no personal insight, no natural awkwardness of expression, no humor. A similar lack of inventiveness and personal flavor generally marks stories about everyday people. Ordinary characters rarely touch the wellsprings of imagination or humor, but fall instead into dull, conventional molds. It is the half-fanciful characters that set invention working and reveal most clearly what a child actually thinks and feels.

ENCOURAGING ORIGINALITY

Writing is a heart-warming delight when children are sure of an eager acceptance of their stories. Although many children like to write in an almost fierce privacy, they usually look for an audience as soon as they have finished. After all, stories are invented to be told to others. The joy of devising a story is only half realized until the tale is shared, and the delight of creation is reinforced by the pleasure of appreciation.

Younger children know of our interest in stories because of their previous happy experiences with dictating and telling them. It is quite natural, then, that they should bring their first stories to us. The word "bring" is worthy of note. We do not collect stories; we do not demand that they be handed in on a given date or as finished; we do not even *ask* to read them; we wait until the children, quite of their own accord, bring them to us.

The teacher is definitely in the role of recipient. And it is a *story* that is offered, not an exercise in composition or punctuation or spelling. A story is offered—it would be absurd to talk of periods or paragraphs, of spelling or neat writing. Those matters are taken care of in practical writing. Here is a tale woven out of this child's unique experience, feeling, and imagination. To the writer the story is satisfactory and complete. We accept it eagerly, just as it is, without suggestion for change or improvement.

This is not always easy, for the desire to show how to make the story better is a deep-rooted one. We may feel that it could be improved by developing this idea or cutting out that one, but we also know that if it is to be the *child's*, it must be left in just the form which at the moment seems good to the writer.

Here is a story written by Peggy when she was barely nine, exactly as she wrote it.

Grandmother's Skirt

Once there lives an old laddy with gray hair, dubble toes and a very sweet hart but she allways fell down because her peticoat was allways hanging. She lived all alown way way on the tip top of a great big hill one of her hobies was baking pies blueberry chery and apple were her very best. The only one in all the world that she loved was her own grandbaby who hardly ever came to see her. Today however she was in her living room and when a nock came at the door. She jumped and ran to see who was coming, she opund the door and to her serprize no one was there she was all setled down again when another nock came. Again she went to the door and there she saw her grandbaby whose mother had got run over she had taken lots of monny so she could live with her grandmother and they bilt a new house and were very happy. After that the grandbaby allways held up her grandmothers peticoat and she never fell

Now, it would be easy to criticize this. "What does baking pies have to do with the story? You haven't explained why there wasn't someone there the first time she heard a knock. Why not leave that part out? Whatever are 'dubble toes'? You need a lot of periods and capitals and your spelling is a disgrace."

Of course from the point of view of a nine-year-old, food is always a splendid thing to have in a story, "serprizes" never fail to interest, "dubble toes" sound fascinating, and periods and spelling do not affect a story anyway! So perhaps the very changes that, from an adult point of view, would strengthen the tale, would really spoil it entirely for a nine-year-old audience and would most surely have spoiled it for Peggy.

We read the story eagerly, ignoring the spelling and punctuation. We admired the amazing idea of "dubble toes" and pointed out that probably no one ever before had thought of writing a story with a hanging petticoat. We commended the way the story came full circle, beginning with the petticoat and ending with it. Peggy beamed and volunteered that she had "a lot more ideas for stories even better than this." The story was read to the class, who added their approval.

Perhaps if we had criticized "Grandmother's Skirt" or any of the dozen mediocre tales that followed Peggy might never have written this delightful story. For ease of reading we have corrected spelling and punctuation.

The House That Echoed

Once there was a sweet old lady who lived all alone with her parrot in a huge, big house with 143 rooms. She might have been a happy lady but she wasn't because whenever she said anything she heard an echo. There were echoes in every room. When she said, "Good morning, Polly," she heard high and whispery, "Good morning, Polly." *(The echo was always written very small.)*

When the parrot said, "Polly wants a cracker," the little old lady would hear, "Cracker, cracker, cracker," echoing all over the house.

She was determined to stop the echoes and to live happily ever after. She sent for some men to come out from the city to put hangings on all the walls of the 143 rooms. (New hangings had just been put in our music room at school to deaden the reverberations there.)

But when the men had gone she said, "Well, now *that's* fixed." And all through the house she heard, "fixed, fixed, fixed."

"What shall I do?" cried the sweet old lady. "I know. I'll open the windows and doors and then the echoes will slip outdoors." So she opened and opened all the windows and all the doors in the 143 rooms.

"*Now* I won't be bothered any more," she said with a sigh, settling down.

"Any more, any more, any more," whispered the echoes.

"Oh, oh, oh," cried the little old lady and she ran out of doors into the woods. She walked and walked trying to think what to do next about the echoes when suddenly she heard an awful crying. She ran through the woods and found a whole lot of children, 439 children, all sitting in the woods, crying.

"Goodness gracious," said the little old lady. "What are you crying about?"

"We used to live in an orphan (sic) but it burned down," said a boy.

"Well, blow your noses and come home with me," said the little old lady.

So they did and all those children filled the house so full of noise because of pillow fights and not wanting to wash, especially the boys, and asking where things were, that there wasn't any room for echoes at all. And the old lady was happy. So were the children.

The following story is typical of the kind of thing we have learned to accept as cordially as we did "The House that Echoed," overlooking the weak, confused plot, but calling attention to the spark of real insight—in this case, the quick characterization in the first four sentences.

In a bee castle there lived a cross old queen bee. She kept every bee over-busy. The king was kindhearted. He couldn't bear the queen himself. Soon he decided to get the "S" band. This was a band of stingers, stingers and selfish. The queen had many more ladies than the king had men. She forced the ladies to fight.

In two weeks, in our time, the queen got a rose with an invitation written on it. It said as follows: "You are invited to fight the King's 'S' band. Bee-bee." (The bee-bee meant answer soon.) The queen was expecting this and answered back, "Yes."

When the day came there was a carpet of bees' wings they lost during the fight. There was a bee called Octar. He was a "selfish." He was the king of the "selfish."

When the battle was over he was the only dead. Guess who won.

We read this story to the children with sufficient vigor to support the feeble plot. Nancy was happy that everyone liked her picture of the king and queen—and started another story. By accepting this halting tale without criticism we kept the way open for her further writing.

Inevitably there is an occasional tale so utterly hopeless that one's heart sinks before the eager anticipation of the writer.

The Cat Sleep

One day the cat said. I am ging to sleep. gone to sleep. She went to sleep. By the time I went to sleep I heard a noise. So I went to the bed and I look there and them. I went to the chair and I look there and them. Boo?

P s ti si a Mouse

the end

Certainly this is a challenge to ingenuity. How can one present such a story as this in a way that will give the child his bright moment of delight? The teacher chose to read it at the very beginning of the reading period, summoning every ounce of dramatic ability she had to give importance to the tale. She turned to beam on the child, saying, "O, Johnny, our very first riddle story. What fun!" And then before the children could sense the obvious inadequacies, she rushed on to the next story. Johnny went on writing and each succeeding tale required less agility of his teacher.

Sometimes the offerings are actually offensive to the teacher's taste, but these, too, are received without adverse comment. This can take considerable forbearance, for children can be very thorough in establishing the tone of a story. Stories about messes are disgustingly detailed and these, by the way, are always very humorous (to the children); war stories involve endless gruesome killings; and many tales are practically dripping with blood. We have learned to ignore the qualms we may have and to listen to these distressing themes, if not with enthusiasm, then at least with courteous attention. This excerpt from "Red Duke" is a sampling of an epidemic of "tough" stories that swept a fifth grade.

"So you three mugs thought you'd squeal on Red Duke, eh? Well, there ain't anyone never squealed on Red Duke that really lived to tell about it," said Red Duke, breathing hard.

"Aw, let's kill the dirty squealers and get it over with," said Jake with his finger on his trigger.

"Shut your mouth, I'm running this gang," said Red Duke. "I'll rub these boys out when I'm ready, see?" He glared at the trembling men. "Now you lily-livered yellow dogs, how much does Black Mike know?"

This one was followed up with the truthful comment that the rough language and vigorous action are admirably suited to the characters. Older children inevitably recognize their teacher's personal likes and dislikes, but by that time their confidence in her genuine interest in every story is well-established. A sixth grader offered his repulsive war story to us with the easy remark, "This isn't the kind of story you like, but I knew you would read it. I think it's super."

There are stories, too, that verge on impertinence. These are always about imaginary beings who, of course, are not bound by the usual rules of decorum. Though it may rankle to hear a teacher labeled Miss Pasty-puss or to see one of our own foibles humorously portrayed, this is not a personal attack; it is a natural and mild outburst against adults for the sense of inferiority they make youngsters feel. It is merely a safe outlet.

All children yearn at times "to put grownups in their place," and if they write freely, their hidden emotions are bound to show through. So we listen undisturbed to these revealing stories because we know that only by accepting ideas as they are offered can we cultivate the sincerity and fearlessness so essential to originality.

Being sure of the teacher's friendly concern adds immeasurably to the joy of writing a story. Children are often eager to read the first part of a tale to her; indeed we have known many who come with shining eyes to show each new paragraph. Still more often youngsters look up from their writing to say, "Just *wait* 'til you read this one." "You'll be crazy about *this* part." It is easy to tell by the tingle in the voice that every sentence has added zest because of the prospect of sharing it with an appreciative friend—added zest and added power, too, for joy releases power just as surely as uncertainty or fear restricts it.

PRESENTATION TO THE CLASS

Delightful as the enthusiastic acceptance by the teacher is, the truly exciting experience is the presentation of one's story to the class. A few children may wish to keep their stories "secret," and we respect their wishes even when it means that over a period of years we see but a small fraction of their personal writing. Occasionally, although a child enjoys sharing his story with the teacher, he may hesitate to present it to the group. Usually the temptation, "I know the class would enjoy your story, especially the part where . . . May I read it to them?" is too strong to resist. However, if he truly does not want the story read, we never insist.

Toward the end of third or the beginning of fourth grade, children begin to take over the presentation of their own stories. In order to achieve the best possible results, the preparation for this is carefully done. When a story is finished the young writer goes off to a quiet corner or out into the hall to practice reading aloud. The discovery of words that have been omitted or meaning that is not clear, can lead to the insertion of a few words or phrases. This is the time, too, when the perfect title may pop into the writer's head, although as we have said the naming of a story is not necessary. Occasionally a child will invent a new ending for a story as it is read to the class; this, too, we welcome warmly.

We do not underestimate the importance of setting the stage for this sharing occasion. Paying attention to such details as a comfortable seating arrangement so that the reader does not have to strain to be heard or the others to listen, and choosing a time when the class is in a relaxed mood make possible the full satisfaction to be derived from these experiences. These satisfactions in turn produce the impetus that carries story writing on.

VALUE OF ORAL PRESENTATION

The frequent periods of reading and listening are a vital part of the writing process. There is no greater spur to writing than the keen delight of watching one's story "catch" an audience, unless perhaps it is the heart-warming approval that follows the reading. A nine-year-old may sit rigid with happiness or twist excitedly while her story is being read; and then in a sudden burst of sheer joy make the announcement, "I'm going to write more stories. My next one will be even better'n this one. I bet I write a hundred stories." And often an older child, though more self-contained, is no less moved by the pleasure of accomplishment. Donna, in the absorbing excitment of her reading, used to wriggle herself halfway across the room, and sometimes she grew so pleased she laughed aloud.

Although the children are urged to present their own stories simply because they enjoy doing so, we have discovered three important values that were not foreseen. Oral reading itself has improved. Many children who have spoken in dull, halting tones when reading from books, have read their own stories in an easy, lively fashion. This gain has remained, in part at least, upon the return to book reading. Improvement in writing style is a second by-product. Because of the abundance of reading and listening, the tongue and ear have learned to work together for more pleasing sounds, so that the reiterated "and" or "then," the clumsy connective, and the monotonous sentence pattern gradually disappear. Sentences change in length and tempo to fit the changing pace of a story. And lastly, the children make headway in recognizing where sentences begin and end. The scribbled papers may lack capitals and periods and some of the constructions may be rather involved, but children never fail to read their stories correctly. The ear seems to know without question where to stop and start again.

But far more significant than the gains in English language power is the effect upon the personality of the child. There is something deeply rewarding in the feeling that accompanies the reading of one's own story to a group. Because there in black and white is the idea that until now has been an intriguing but invisible part of self, the glow of success is a peculiarly personal and vitalizing one. The child has identified with the protagonist of the tale, and accepts the approval accorded the hero. For a brief time the child is not subject to the limits set by adults, but a being with omnipotent power who moves characters about at will. In this dual role of hero and manipulator the writer/reader stands among peers as a clever and capable person. Such an experience cannot but add to a child's sense of stature and security.

BLOCKS TO WRITING

Once well initiated, story writing usually continues under its own momentum providing nothing is done to check it. With shy and self-conscious children a very little thing may disturb their confidence and thus shut off the flow of ideas. Praise or blame can be equally devastating. The former, if excessive, may oppress the sensitive child with the fear that the performance can never be equalled; the latter may but strengthen a conviction of worthlessness. For this reason evaluation is avoided and interest is kept directed to the way the story affects the audience. "Wasn't that part funny or exciting? Couldn't you close your eyes and see him coming bumpity-bump down the stairs?"

Sometimes our teacher overeagerness trips us. We have caught ourselves saying, "That's a wonderful story. Now why don't you . . ." *It never works.* The child seems to feel that what comes naturally is not right, and promptly puts it aside. It is like the human-touched egg to which the bird will not return. Such an error makes us realize anew that at this stage our concern lies not so much in the specific product as in the sincerity and ongoingness of the writing process.

We have come more and more to treat each story as a thing to be relished and laid aside, while we turn with expectation toward new stories. When attention is fixed upon a single narrative a child may come to regard it as a standard or model and try to imitate what has already been done. Others whose writing is not equally lauded may lose faith in their own creations. In a few unfortunate instances certain gifted children have been told their stories were good enough to be published. Immediately self-consciousness set in, and there was a quick falling off in the freshness and vigor of their writing. It is growth that we want—growth that involves the cultivation of spontaneity, the strengthening of the individual voice, and the habit of writing not for commendation, but for the satisfaction it affords. Therefore we rarely gather stories into more or less permanent booklets nor select "best" stories for school publications. Such activities tend to halt rather than to stimulate growth in writing power. It seems better for children to find their reward in the joy of new creation rather than in the preserving and revering of what they have already done.

We have already talked about the block to creative effort of overconcern with the clerical aspects. Imagination is a demanding master; it refuses to operate freely when attention is shared with anything else. Since an elementary-school child has as yet attained but a small measure of control over the details of English mechanics and form, he must be relieved of responsibility for them if he is to create joyfully and well. Spelling, too, can hamper the flow of ideas, so we promptly give the spelling of any words the children ask for, no matter how simple, because in the excitement of creation many actually forget how to spell even everyday words. No time is used for filing or looking up words in a spelling notebook; good ideas are often lost through such delay. As Julie remarked one day, "I just can't keep up with my ideas." And Allen, who is almost a year younger, finds transcription such an ordeal that only every fourth or fifth sentence gets on paper and words get left out, although he achieves an exciting story even in this fashion.

Once there was a monkey. He was called Minnie, the Monk. One day he was taking a walk through the woods. Then he saw a fire and then he call the fire department. Then he heard a siren. Then he saw the fire truck.

"I rang the bell."

"Where is the fire?"

"This way." (Of course he forgot.) He led them on a wild goose chase.

One fireman said, "You are going to caught."

"Bang! Bang! Bang!" goes the judge's hammer.

"You are going jail."

"But, but, but, but, but, but, but, but, but, but."

"Shut off your motor boat."

"I saw the fire."

"Well, where is it?"

"I'll find it."

"Come on boys," says one fireman. "Come on, little monkey."

"Okay, okay, I'm coming." (The fire was right out on the back lawn.)

When Minnie stepped out he saw.
He said, "Fire!"
The firemen ran to the engines.

Indeed, unless we mitigate as much as possible the travail of story writing, the child will not only write fewer stories but shorter, duller ones as well. It is for this reason that we have confined our teaching of mechanics to utilitarian writing in which the child is not so emotionally involved. *In personal writing there are never any requirements of form or standards of correctness.*

But the school is not the only influence that can curtail a child's expression. Sometimes the home is at fault. Tom, who had been writing freely and happily for some time, came to school one day with the troubled announcement, "My mother doesn't think much of the five bears." By now many children in the group had been writing about the bears, who had become real and beloved characters. The disparaging remark of Tom's mother, therefore, discredited for him not only his latest story but also the writing of the other children. Tom wrote no more stories that year.

Another child who had begun to write freely was slowed down to a marked degree when his mother belittled his brief but delightful stories by saying, "You're too big to be writing such simple things. When I was your age I could write compositions several pages long." (Grownups, even when acting in good faith, tend to glorify their own childhood accomplishments.) Pressure to meet an imposed but shadowy standard undermines a child's confidence in his own power and so confuses him that writing ceases to be gratifying and becomes instead a labored effort to satisfy a demand he does not comprehend but feels obligated to meet.

Unquestionably, the stories created by a child's own urge to write are more crude and ragged than the tidy compositions of earlier generations. At the same time they are more sincere and they exhibit a far more generous use of good techniques of English expression. The period of elementary-school life is primarily one of development through experience and exploration. Crystallizing forms too soon only limits the possibilities of growth. Our object in story writing is to cultivate a sense of joy and power in the activity itself, and we feel that external evaluation intended to improve the creative products of this activity should wait for a later period of near-adulthood. Until the desire to write is firmly established, correction and criticism can halt the whole process.

This explains why, in certain cases, a divergence of opinion between school and home poses a considerable problem. We have had some successes and some dreadful failures in trying to explain our point of view to parents. When discussing the language program in parents' meetings we mention how differently we approach the two types of writing. We send home evidences of practical writing which were required to be accurately done, but every effort is made to keep the freely written stories in our own hands. As we observe the later records of children whom we have taught, we are more and more convinced that the stress we lay on respecting one's own thoughts and expressing them in one's own way pays off.

There are always a few children who rarely, if ever, attempt imaginative writing. For them, we must depend on practical writing, which should be required of all the children, to reveal their growing ability to put ideas into words. In reports and articles we take pains to commend any gleam of style or touch of unique or vivid expression that may appear. Beyond this we feel an obligation to search for and find other avenues through which their imaginations can develop. It is essential that all children have some way of expressing what is peculiarly theirs. Perhaps in music, rhythms, or dramatics, in sports, the arts, or the sciences, they will realize the delight of producing something uniquely their own and will feel the spur to further effort that each attempt at creation brings.

Certainly to try to force children to "write for pleasure" dams the whole stream of writing, *both* practical and personal. However, once in a rare, rare while we do try to help the uninspired to catch the excitement of storytelling. Our usual way is to make the occasion, when the mood seems right, to gossip about one of our familiar story characters. We all may invent funny things he did when he was little or propose possible future escapades. When ideas begin coming we may say, "Oh, these are good! For the next fifteen minutes let's write them down as fast as we can." Sometimes we write, too; sometimes we move about the room to give a needed lift to the timid or apathetic. The literary results of such an experience are usually of small value but often some sluggish minds are stirred or a few of the diffident discover that they, too, have ideas. But this kind of mass stimulation is charily used.

HOW CHILDREN WRITE

The infinite variety of human nature is nowhere more apparent than in the diverse and sometimes devious ways that children follow in putting thoughts on paper. Some can write in the midst of swirling activity, while others find the presence of even one other person a deterrent. Some love notebooks and the snugness of pages between covers; other choose the freeness of single sheets. Some think out all of a story in advance; others work from the most trivial starting point and know only what is going to happen next. Some write best in solitude; others like to write occasionally with a partner.

This desire to write a story with another child at first caused us real concern. Only reluctantly did we consent to try it out. After experimenting for more than a year, we became convinced that a child who sometimes wants to write with a friend, perhaps in a classroom corner or some other protected spot, is fortified by the experience. One child who had produced very little distinctive writing made up a complicated mystery with two other children. Afterwards he turned quite naturally to writing alone again, and his humorous account of the difficulties of moving from a house to a town apartment was a decided improvement over any previous solo writing.

Without exception we have been pleasantly surprised by the quality and sparkle of stories written by pairs or trios. Our fear that in such team enterprises one worked and the other loafed has been completely dispelled. Indeed, it appears that here as elsewhere, ideas grow in the company of ideas.

Some children work slowly, laboriously, choosing each word and achieving economy of expression. Others write quickly and with a flourish, dashing off a story as fast as a pencil can go. Still other children write a bit, erase, rewrite, cross out, start over, and out of an assortment of scribbled scraps fashion an appealing story that delights the group. Any inclination to change a child's own way of writing should be firmly checked.

THE UNFINISHED STORY

Not every story reaches the stage of completion necessary for reading aloud. Many times a child abandons a story half finished, and rightly so. Invention is at best a fickle power. A child may start a story in a fine burst of enthusiasm only to find that the idea does not work out; the adventure that had begun so gaily comes to a standstill in disappointment. An argument could be made that children be required to finish a story before starting another. Upon a few occasions we, with an eye to character building, have followed this policy and regretted it. Almost without exception the children have tied trite conclusions to their often delightful beginnings. Nothing has been gained but a salute to perseverance, and much has been lost. The forced completion has made storytelling a disagreeable experience; only a singularly courageous child again attempts a venture that might so suddenly turn into painful drudgery. The teacher is left with the serious problem of overcoming a child's distaste for writing.

There are many times when a story is best left half-finished. Often the beginning is so engaging that it is difficult to accept the child's verdict, "I don't like it anymore." "I don't know how to end it." "I have a better idea now." Here, for example, is Ann's story. It starts in a pleasing manner, but it is easy to detect the spot where her invention faltered.

79

Once upon a time there lived a great big hen. She had laid some eggs. She was just going to sit on them when she saw a big fat worm. "Well," she thought, "this will be my last time I go off my nest. One little worm won't hurt."

But sly Mr. Fox was close by in the brambles. "My two dear children like eggs. I think I will get them some," he said. So he went home half-walking and half-running. He told his children how long it had been since they had some nice, soft-boiled eggs.

"May I have that ball, the little one you were playing with yesterday?"

"Here it is," said one of the foxes. "But you have spoiled our little ball."

"Do you want eggs?" said the fox. "Do you want to play a joke on Mrs. Hen?"

"Yes," was the reply.

"Now," he said, "which one of you wants to go to the beach with me?" They all did so Mr. Fox took them all.

When they got to the beach Mr. Fox told them to wait on the sand. Then he took the rubber ball and went down to the ocean and filled it with sea water. He then took his children home to bed. The next day he got up bright and early and again hid in the bushes near Mrs. Hen's house. Now Mrs. Hen saw. . . .

Ann said, "I'm sick of this story—it's flopped." We agreed. Better to drop the story there, having had the fun of inventing Mrs. Hen and sly Fox than to drag it to a lifeless close. We accepted Ann's verdict quietly and read with enjoyment what she had written. Thus we kept the way open for future stories, many of which reached a satisfactory conclusion.

At other times it is obvious that a youngster has written a part of a story just for the fun of using a word or a phrase that has excited his imagination. Having used the bewitching phrase, he has no further interest in the story and is content to drop it. Here is a nine-year-old's unfinished tale plainly written just to use a fascinating word.

The king was in an awful rage. "Where is my wise counsellor?" he shouted.

"Here I am, your majesty," said the wise counsellor, bowing until his beard touched the floor.

"Well, don't I have the biggest castle in all the world?" said the king.

"Indubitably, your majesty," said the wise counsellor, bowing until his beard touched the floor.

"And don't I have the largest army in the world?"

"Indubitably, your majesty."

"And don't I have the most golden treasure in all the world?"

"Indubitably, your majesty."

"Then why don't I have. . ."

Again, a story may be laid aside merely because a newly discovered idea is so tempting that a child loses interest in a current plot. We allow the shift to the fresh idea since we know that the satisfaction of reading a whole story will help offset a tendency to skip endlessly from one unfinished tale to another. The child who regularly abandons stories, almost without exception, fails to complete work of other kinds as well. The basic problem can be better handled in areas involving objective materials than in this realm of highly personal ideas.

We have learned to value that first quick surge of a story idea and to hide our disappointment when a promising beginning is forsaken. Occasionally a child returns to an unfinished story and completes it, but more often forgets it in the onrush of new ideas. Nevertheless, we urge children to save these beginnings because there might be in them a name, a character, or a bit of action for a new story.

Probably one of the most common reasons for not completing a story is the simple and seemingly unavoidable factor of physical fatigue. Again and again we have seen a child tire of his or her story just because the labor of getting the words on paper was too onerous. When it is possible to relieve this impasse by writing for the child from dictation, interest does not flag. But this course is seldom feasible.

We do not know to what extent this element of physical fatigue curbs a child's outpouring of ideas. We do know that Debby, who wrote with average facility for a nine-year-old, spent five writing periods on a long but never-finished story and then turned to a shorter one. Her loss of interest in the first was probably due to fatigue induced by the effort of trying to write in pace with her swift imagination. We have watched children who write slowly develop terse, telegraphic styles in order to transfer their ideas to paper without too great an expenditure of energy. Others have said, "I have a story idea, but I just thought I would rest this period." Still others have written part of a story and then, as their hands grew weary, asked to tell the balance. Some have attached abrupt and trite endings to their tales, saying in explanation, "I know the ending's not so good but I got tired writing." This whole matter of fatigue is one aspect of writing about which we are especially curious for we feel it has not yet been adequately examined or dealt with.

TEACHING TECHNIQUES

Abundance of writing is our initial goal. Only by writing and writing and writing do the channels open for true thinking and feeling to come through. We make of our story writing a kind of playtime—play in the valid sense of doing something with one's whole heart—and we do all we can to keep alive the spirit of adventure and fun. As a result we get quantities of stories, many of which are poor and all of which could be improved. Yet we waste no time in remaking the poor ones nor in dwelling overlong on the few that hold promise. Like the lumbermen around their campfire guffawing over a new Paul Bunyan yarn or the eager crowd transported by a minstrel into knightly feats of derring-do, we ask only to be excited or amused. Self-consciousness drops away when attention is focused on the enchantment of the story and not upon its shortcomings.

The more they write, the more they must bestir their minds for new ideas. Invention is indeed the primary activity of creative power. It is the *quality* in stories for which we watch most eagerly and are quick to acclaim: "That was a different idea." "What a surprise to have Mother Bear . . ." "You could have ended your story there, but instead you invented another happening. That's good." By question and comment we direct attention to the new, the individual, the unexpected. We try to forestall a rehash of current television fare, to encourage children to write out of their own musings and reactions. When they do that, there is always at least a touch of the unique and the unusual.

During the reading periods we watch for such storytelling techniques as may appear and try to make the children aware of them also. After a particularly tempting beginning we may stop the reader just long enough for the listeners to realize how much they want him to go on. We do not urge the use of such elements as good beginnings, details of characterization, moments of suspense. When children are writing with affectionate interest these things begin to appear of their own accord, and this is especially true if they have been mentioned approvingly in other stories. Naturally the effective techniques appear first in the stories of the more imaginative children, but in time others gradually absorb and use them. Each child seems to take over the elements that fit the maturity of his or her own thinking; hence these elements are a part of the fabric of the story and not something superficially added because of the teacher's urging.

Even in matters of vocabulary we no longer stress the use of colorful words. Instead our emphasis is on clear and true imagining; for when a child lives a story vividly in his mind, the fitting words seem miraculously to appear. We appreciate the words for the effect they have upon us. We see "the little bears squirming in their hot collars"; we hear Pug when he "growled in his toughest voice." There is no special virtue in long words, new words, or bookish words. A word is good only if it tells exactly what the author had in mind.

But far more potent than our guidance, is the subtle communication between the reader and the audience. The pleased sigh that follows a good beginning says more clearly than any words, *"Now we're off to a good start."* The sharp intake of breath, the irrepressible giggle, the sudden stillness that comes from tense expectancy, all tell the reader what grips and moves the listeners. These flashes of success work powerfully to illuminate and foster sound narrative techniques because they are part and parcel of the moments when a story is working its magic in the hearts and minds of those who receive it. Thus against the natural reaction of responsive listeners the children shape and test their story-making power.

Sometimes it is possible to trace to the reading and appreciation of one story the adoption of a specific technique by many of the class. In an eight/nine-year-old group, three quarters of the stories ended with the comfortable and hackneyed assurance, "And they (he, she) lived happily ever after." The other quarter took the hero safely home, gave him his supper, and left him in bed. But Mary's story was different.

A Caught Fish

Once there was a little boy. His name was Bob. He was six years old. He decided to go fishing. So he dug some angleworms and got his pole and went to a lake. He fished and fished and fished. With angleworms. But he didn't catch anything and he got discouraged. Suddenly a gull flew over his head. The gull squawked and Bob looked up and the gull dropped a fish he was carrying home. Bob caught the fish in his hands. "Well," he said, "at least I can say I caught a fish."

When the teacher finished reading there was a quick outburst of enthusiasm for the swift and dramatic ending:

"Oh, Mary, you stopped right at the place for laughing."

"Well, he *did* catch a fish and that's that."

"In this story the last part is the best of all."

So the story was immediately reread with special emphasis given to the ending.

Although no further discussion of this technique took place, the stock endings soon began to disappear as the children experimented with other conclusions. Two or three wrote obvious imitations of Mary's tale in an effort to capture for themselves the warm approval that had been accorded her. And warm approval they received though not for the imitation, which the children dismissed with "The end sounds like Mary's story," but for some phrase or situation that was fresh and genuine. Others adapted the technique to fit and strengthen their own styles. Here are the last bits of three stories written shortly after Mary's.

The prince came tiredly around the curve of the world back again to his own home and there in the garden with flowers all around it was the golden crown just where he had dropped it.

He went down a long black hall and came to a great door. He pushed and pushed. It finally creaked open. He found himself in *another* big room. "My," he thought, "I'll never get out of here." Just then he saw a window with a water pipe going by it. He quickly rushed to the window, slid down the pipe and was safe at last.

Buttercup Wilkins slowly licked the jam from her face and paws. She carefully closed the door of the jam closet and wearing a smile at the edge of her whiskers she slipped past all the mean chattering cats whose noses were so uppity they did not even see her.

Mary's story alone does not account for this development, but Mary's story *plus* the lively appreciation of it was directly responsible for the experimentation that followed. When children listen constructively to both story and comment, thus identifying themselves with the very warp and woof of the tale and its reception, they become increasingly imbued with what makes writing effective, and inevitably this learning is reflected in their own stories. Appreciative listening sharpens the urge for more writing and deepens the insight necessary for better writing. Indeed, listening, like writing and reading, is an indispensable arc of a productive circle.

ENRICHING ACTIVITIES

Not only do we encourage abundant writing, but we strive to enrich that inner consciousness from which personal expression springs. At odd moments we take time to savor the *qualities* of things: the stinging drive of rain, the first faint mist of green upon the trees, the muffled sound of footsteps upon a snowy day. We take time, too, to recognize the graphic truth of those spontaneous comments that children often make about what they touch or hear or see. We tell what we see in clouds or fog, what we hear in wind or rain, what we feel when walking on soft grass or crunchy pebbles. Often we note on the chalkboard the colorful or metaphoric phrases the children suggest. "Crunchy as potato chips" or "gossipy whispering" they may say about the sounds of walking in dry autumn leaves, for example. Then we erase these descriptive terms that so delighted us lest any child feel obliged to use them in a story or poem. The only residue we hope for from this exercise is the conviction that one searches for the word or phrase that says exactly what one sees or feels. Seeking to fit first-hand sensory experience into words often results in vivid expression.

At times apart from writing periods we share with the children some of the beauty, wonder, laughter, ruggedness, and vigor that we have found in literature. No medium is its equal for stretching and strengthening the imagination. The atmosphere for our reading is one of warmth and companionship. Here, too, when the action of a story grows lively, we may close our eyes to see it better; or we may say together some familiar lines of poetry because we like their meaning or their sound. Nowadays, when through movies, comics, and television children are exposed to so much that is commonplace, artificial, and vulgar, we feel a double obligation to give them satisfying experiences in books; else how will many of them ever know the magic and the rhythm and the power of their mother tongue? Such reading is never consciously compared with the children's own efforts, but we are confident that through their rapt listening much is absorbed that will add to the inner store from which the child creator draws.

GAINING CONTROL OF SKILLS

Will there be any improvement in skills if children write just for the joy of creating a tale? The answer is an unqualified affirmative. In both mechanics and style, the ability of these children at fifth- and sixth-grade levels definitely surpassed that of any other groups we had ever had. We had anticipated growth in the techniques of storytelling, but we were frankly surprised when after a lapse of weeks or even months, depending on the individual child, the aspects of punctuation, paragraphing, capitalization, and spelling taught through practical writing began to appear in their stories. Even such stumbling blocks as apostrophes and quotation marks, first encountered in utilitarian writing and then explained and checked in that field over a period of time, began to be used voluntarily in personal writing. We have, we believe, developed an acceptable degree of power over mechanics by teaching forms in practical writing and waiting for their inevitable adoption in personal writing.

5

Children's Verse

Tell me, where is fancy bred,
Or in the heart, or in the head?
How begot, how nourished?
                    William Shakespeare,
                    The Merchant of Venice

To a young child life is new and full of flavor, to be reached out to and encompassed with all the senses. Because acquaintance with language is new also, the child's use of it tends of be original, and frequently, so vivid and rhythmical that it verges on poetry.

Unfortunately, many adults seize upon such expression to quote as amusing or quaint or to make over into a more familiar pattern by saying, "Oh, you mean . . ." All too soon a child begins to discount this natural, unique mode of expression and to substitute for it the empty, ready-made phrases that adults put into mouth and mind. The lesson learned early is that commonplace words and ideas protect one's own thoughts and feelings against being laughed at or criticized. We believe that this leads into having commonplace thoughts and feelings as well. The fresh insight, the vivid emotion, the sensitive awareness wither away, and the original quality of thought, as well as spoken language, begins to disappear. So it is that children lose touch with the deep core of their own individuality. Happily, this contact can be restored—at least in part. They can be led again to savor experiences more poignantly and to enjoy telling their reactions to them. Although their comments may not be formal poetry, they are the stuff of which poetry is made.

STIMULATING INTEREST IN POETRY

Natural phenomena seem to lend themselves readily to the adventure of poetry telling. We all are affected consciously or subconsciously by stars, night, changes in the seasons, the winter's cold, the color of autumn, but experience of them is not timeworn to children.

Perhaps, when there is heavy fog or when the first frost covers the ground, we talk about it together in class, and the children are encouraged to put into words their awareness of the phenomena. They react keenly to the quiet of fog, the sheen of a frost-covered lawn, the clink of icy branches, the crunch of snow under foot. Looking at these out-of-door happenings closely often establishes a mood in which they tap hidden resources of thought and feeling.

One windy morning the children came in drenched by an unexpected storm. They were so excited by the experience that they were talking breathlessly about what it was like. Each child seemed to be searching for the exact words to describe how it affected him. The teacher said, "Let me write down what you're saying about the storm. It may paint a picture or be a make-believe idea or tell something you wonder about. You don't have to say much—just a few words that really fit. You'll have to keep very quiet inside so that you won't forget your thoughts."

A quiet, expectant waiting gradually gave place to open delight as they took turns telling their ideas. The teacher wrote fast to capture their thoughts. Here are some of their responses to the storm which we read later.

> The wind has a shape like the waves.

> It is pushing through the trees
> It has holes in it so it can get
>   by the branches.

> The wind is rustling through the grasses
> It is whistling down the valleys.

> The wind is sweeping through the town
> It is resting on the housetops.

> The wind sounds like a boat
> Leaving the dock.

> It is raining needles
> Because it pricks you—
> It's like a porcupine
> Rubbing against you.

Clouds open up
And swiftly little drops come down.

The rain touches the blades of grass
And they bend with the heavy load.

I think that the sky and ground
Look like they were twins—
The puddles look like the grey sky
And they look so much alike
That I think that it's hard
To tell them from each other.

Often we have stimulated our classes to poetic effort by reading to them from our collection of child-made poems. Hearing the ideas of other children, our pupils gain courage to tell their own thoughts and feelings. Of course, an abundance of great poetry is read, too. However, much care is taken in selecting verse to read when the children are trying to express their own ideas; it is too easy for them to copy or to be overawed and to feel that their thoughts are not good enough to share with others. We choose verse that is free in style rather than rhymed or strongly patterned. A child's ear often is so captured by rhyming that the meaning is missed, and in trying to make poems the child forgets what he or she wanted to say and concentrates on the jingle.

Whether we read from children's poetic offerings or from the writings of accomplished poets, we keep the reading periods short. They take place when the class is relaxed and comfortable. During the reading we mention a part that "sounded different" or was "a new way of talking" about rain, or snow, or fog, or that used picture words. Only a little reading and talking are done. Ten minutes when the group is really listening are a better investment than a longer stretch when they are not so receptive.

POETRY AND MAKE-BELIEVE

In choosing poems, like the following, we take advantage of children's fresh and dramatic views of the natural world.

Morning is when the sun
Wakes up.
He yawns
And turns his lantern on

He wakes up all the birds
And other animals, too.
I surely would hate to be the sun
Getting up so early
In the morning.
I've never gotten up before him.
I wonder how he knows
What time it is.
I guess the moon comes in
And stops to wake him up
Before he goes on
To night again.

The moon must get tired
Of his business
Because on rainy nights
He never comes out.
That must mean
He's taking a snooze
Under the white clouds.
The stars crowd in with him—
He goes rolling out
Because he has no room.
After he rolls out
He mumbles to himself,
"How greedy those little stars are—
They can rest all the time
When I have to sit
Up in my throne
And shine upon the earth."

The wind comes down
In braids;
It comes down
Twirling around
On the clouds
When they're low.
The rain comes down
In splatters.

I like to watch the wind go by—
It must get out of breath.

I wonder how it floats
And ruffles
And makes all that noise
Many times at night
It wakes me up
With all its tumbling.

The cars are rolling along the snow-dressed road
Looking like black bugs—softly, softly—
Horns honk in the grey mist—softly,softly—
As the snow drifts down
Softly, softly.

Darkness creeps along
As if it were going to pounce upon you.
On rainy days he steals the sun.
The clouds come floating by—
The darkness must run its fastest
To get to the other side of the world.

When the silver raindrops
Softly patter on the earth
It sounds like small feet running along,
And the trees hold out their arms
To catch the gleaming.

PICTURES IN POETRY

Children also enjoy poems that paint vivid pictures. The following have
some intensity of feeling in their central idea or use language with special
color and pattern. All of the poems have some individuality of vision or
play of language that lifts them above prose.

Where does the dark go?
I don't know.
It may go down the well
And have the wind pull it up in buckets.
Or it may go down the chimney to hide,
And then when he thinks
The day has been enough
He creeps out.
All of a sudden

Before you know it,
It's dark.
I do wonder where the dark goes.

Pansies nod their faces in the breeze,
Gossiping the news of a new little baby
That was born.
He has a velvet face, all yellow with violet,
And his mother is so proud.
That's the gossip that goes around
When a new pansy baby is born.

We've got a Japanese cherry tree
That grows in our back yard.
It glows with pink
And makes a background
For all the other things—
Like a candle in the corner.

The wind is dashing
Through the trees;
It knocks the poor little leaves
Off their hinges
And chases them down
To the ground.
And then the mean old wind
Whisks them into the fire
Where they burn
Into black crumbly ashes.

FEARS AND SECRET LONGINGS

Some of the poems we read are those that little children tell when they are
not afraid of being laughed at or misunderstood. Even though these
expressions may have little intrinsic poetic worth, they sometimes have
therapeutic value. Often they are dictated by shy, insecure children, who,
through the telling, gain faith in themselves. Many times, however, they
express insights in forms quite transcending in artistry the feelings behind
the poems.

Whenever I'm in trouble
And talk to myself out loud,

The trees nod their heads to and fro—
They know what is troubling me;
They hold out their arms
As if to make a bed for me.

I've always hated little children
Younger than me
Because they have
Such funny ideas.
They always want
To play with dolls and things.
That isn't a bit like me—
I always like to pretend
I'm a mother
And can drive a car.
I wish they were like me—
Sometimes at least.

Home's left behind when I go away traveling.
All my dolls as children may come with me,
But still my house is left behind.
My dogs and animals all may come,
But home is left behind.

At night when I go to bed
You never would know
What's going inside my mind;
But it's nice to think
About all sorts of things
That nobody would know about
Except yourself.
I think and think
And when I wake up
In the morning
You would never know
That I thought about
Those things.
And I even don't know;
But the next night
I try to remember
And keep the same adventure.

WONDER IN CHILDREN'S VERSE

Children's poetic expression emerges from a variety of everyday things and from their looking at the familiar with curiosity and wonder. Often they question what adults see as quite ordinary and wonder what lies beneath the surface of life. Great size or strength as well as the diminutive and weak impress children. The affection for animals sustains them, and humor often finds its way into their perception of the world around them. Feelings about these experiences come through in their attempts at poetry.

I always wondered
If cocoons were butterflies,
I always wondered
How they creep out of their shells,
I always wondered
How they creep along
I never could see their feet.
I think they do very well
For their age and how small they are.
I wonder how they learned how to fly—
I think they taught themselves.
Sometimes I wonder if I could fly
As well as they could.

Feathers tickle!
Why don't they tickle the hen?
They're on his back
So I think they should tickle him—
They tickle *me.*

I often stay at the end of the beach
To look at the sea.
The water comes in
And takes the tiny grains of sand
From my castle
And carries them all away.
Where do they go?
Do they see fish?
Or even a whale?
I wonder.

I wonder why birds
Sing so beautifully.
Maybe it's because they practice,
Or maybe it's because
They were born to know how.

INDIVIDUAL DICTATION OF POETRY

Sometime—early or late—during the reading of poems, children begin making poems of their own. Since the ideas are often fleeting, they may be lost before a child can write them down. Therefore, provision must be made for them to be dictated.

At the outset of a poetry-making period, time is taken to get the group in tune. A few carefully selected poems are read to create an appropriate mood, and a little talk helps to get started. Something like this may be said: "Telling a poem is like painting a picture, only it's painting with words. It's as if you were standing by pots of paint and splashing the color on a paper with rapid strokes before the picture could leave your mind. When you tell a poem you plunge right in, and with just a few words you give a picture, or a feeling, or a make-believe reason for something." Then, at another time, "Poems sometimes tell your hidden feelings. Try telling about your wonderings or your secret wishes."

For a few very shy youngsters the following comments seem to open the way: "Making up poems is like water flowing from a spring that has been choked up. First it is muddy, but after it has flowed for a while, the water bubbles out clear and sparkling. You'll find that it's exciting to tell poems. You never know when you are going to get something you'll especially like. So you have to keep on letting them pour out."

We often suggest: "A good time to think of poetry ideas is at night just before you go to sleep when you have that comfortable drowsy feeling."

By stressing the fact that poetry is a quick way of saying something—"Poems don't need all the words that are put into stories; you just hit the high spots"—children are helped to make the transition from the detailed wordiness of a story to the essencelike quality of poetic expression.

The room setting is extremely important. The children and the teacher, too, should feel free from pressure. Quietness and a minimum of movement are two essentials. Before dictation begins, the children are helped to start activities on which they can work alone. Painting or crayoning a picture, modeling with clay, or weaving, keep the hands busy and at the same time permit the child's mind to follow any course it chooses. Not all are active. Some find that sitting in a quiet corner, or looking out of the window helps them reach that dreamy state in which their thoughts take on the feeling of poetry.

The teacher usually sits at a table beside the one who is dictating. Because the presence of another is often confusing, each child comes up alone to tell a poem. Others with poems to tell can raise their hands, so the teacher can jot down their names and call them in turn.

At the close of a poetry dictation period, at least one contribution from each child who has participated is read by the teacher. When all of the poems have been read, the children tell which parts made them see pictures or were new ways of telling something that is true. Interestingly enough, it is the worthwhile things they mention. The mediocre expressions have not made enough impression to be remembered.

To free children so that they can reveal themselves is a matter that calls for patience and faith on the part of the teacher. She listens carefully for each hint of the individual voice and welcomes it warmly, no matter how crude it may be. Indeed, the crude expression often tells of superior things to come. The glib or sentimental phrases are a far cry from the honest, unaffected responses of the real child.

Of course, the opening-up process takes time and at first yields only meager results. But slowly, as children gain the courage to be themselves, there is deepening sensitivity coupled with growing ease of communication, until eventually many attain the power to reveal themselves in language that is fitting and poetic.

From the beginning the emphasis is on letting children respond easily and naturally to experience. There has to be time for "moodling" if they are to discover that "down underneath" they have thoughts to surprise and please them. We avoid showing undue concern about the words they use, for we know that when ideas and feelings are welling up spontaneously the right words to express them will come. We may comment casually on the fact that such words as "pretty," "nice," "beautiful," "lovely" tell little, but never in connection with an individual's specific work. On the other hand, we point out how clearly one can hear the sound of the wind when Lois says, "It wakes me up with all its tumbling"; or can see the blowing storm clouds when John says, "The clouds are mad, they are bursting with madness." We share our delight in Bob's vivid image of the Japanese cherry tree, which "glows with pink and makes a background for all the other things—like a candle in the corner."

POETRY WITH YOUNG CHILDREN

It is fascinating to discover that even very young children take pleasure in dictating their poetry ideas. The following groups of poems, told by six- and seven-year-olds, illustrate the growth in self-expression that occurred over a two-year period. A few of their first attempts are given to show how very simple were the beginnings of this poetry dictation.

> Leaves, I love you
> When you are colored.

> Sunshine, sunshine,
> I wish you would sunshine
> All through the spring.

> Come little snowflake,
> Come little snowflake,
> Soon it will be
> Good time to play.

These were dictated later in the first and second grades:

> Little tree
> Standing still
> He sees everybody
> Standing still.

> Sunshine, I like you.
> Would you come for a big while
> Because I want to make a picture of you?
> I shall color the sky
> Just as yellow as you are.

> Puff, puff—
> The trains go
> Up the tracks and down the tracks,
> Carry people and baggage
> Up the tracks and down the tracks,
> All the day through—
> Puff, puff.

When I'm in New York
All I see is crowds—
Some going in theaters
Some going down the street
Some going in offices.
In the night
I see elevator lights:
The buildings light up,
They look like fireflies
Anchored in the air.

Little birdie,
Every winter do you go down south?
'Cuz Mommie's going down
In the great big car;
If you stay on top of it
You can fly tomorrow morning.

GROUP POETRY DICTATION

Many experiences lend themselves to group dictation of poetry ideas. Sometimes they have to do with anticipation of a holiday such as Thanksgiving or Christmas. Often an outdoor adventure—scuffling through autumn leaves, catching the first snowflakes on mittened hands, examining the miracle of springtime during a walk in the park—inspires children to make observations and comments that are colorful and frequently poetic.

Sometimes the teacher works with only a few individuals, sometimes with the entire class. When the children are in the appropriate mood, they stimulate each other to tell ideas in the very special way that reflects inner thinking and feeling. Sitting in a group near the teacher, one child at a time gives thoughts or impressions about what has been seen or felt. The teacher records them as quickly as she can. Later she may work with the class or a small group selecting the thoughts that have true color and individual flavor, eliminating repetitions, and arranging ideas in a pleasing sequence.

Sometimes each child makes a copy of the group poem in careful handwriting, and with a suitable "decoration" it becomes a gift for a parent or a special friend. Frequently this type of poem lends itself to choral speaking, which the class or a small group can present to an audience.

Toy Makers' Chant

We are the toy makers
Tip, tap, tap!
We are the toy makers
Tip, tap, tap!

Hammering, cutting, painting, and inventing
We are the toy makers
Tip, tap, tap!

Sawing, sawing,—buzz, buzz, buzz
Polishing, polishing—smooth, smooth, smooth
Snipping, sewing—pricking our thumbs
OUCH!
Shaping and shining
We make our toys.
There will be happy faces with big broad smiles
When children get our toys for Christmas.

Some Thoughts About Spring

When Spring comes
The sun takes its place
As a comforter to the world.
It sends its hot rays
And makes a blanket
Around the cool earth.

The ground feels soft again,
There are fairy rings on the grass,
Crocuses are popping out of their beds—
Little fairies dressed in yellow.

Spring has a happy thought
Of seeing flowers and leaves sprout;
Mother Nature is painting the grass and trees
Green again;
And when we walk in the rain
We can smell the spring coming.

Spring makes us think
That summer is on its way,
With the busy times
When all the animals
Are feeding their young,

And the birds
Are on their nests.
We trust spring—
That it will bring us
Warmth and happiness;
We feel free
When spring is here.

Dictated by a fourth-grade class

TRANSITION FROM DICTATING TO WRITING VERSE

In the primary grades the teacher must act as the recorder to catch children's philosophical musings and poetry ideas. As children grow older, a transition period allows many to spell and write well enough to capture at least some of the highlights of their individual reactions in written form. Armed with these notes, a child may refer to them when dictating to the teacher. Always we encourage the individual to enlarge upon what has been written. The jottings help to capture thoughts that came in a rush or expressions that sprang from within.

As the teacher writes from dictation, the child's rhythm of talking indicates what should be included in each line. It is gratifying to hear the way children's poetic language falls naturally into patterns that fit the individual and what is to be conveyed.

INDEPENDENT WRITING OF POETRY IN LATER GRADES

Some of our pupils continue to write poetry throughout the elementary grades and on into high school years. By far the majority, however, increase their writing of stories and reports rather than verse in the late elementary school.

Even with a great deal of stimulation to write their own, most of our older children did very little, though they maintained their zest for listening to adult-made verse. Rather than require attempts at verse writing, we continued to hold open the door to poetic experimentation, to welcome it when it came, and to search for reasons for an apparently natural diminution of lyrical expression. The causes lie, we have come to believe, in the increasing pressures from areas of subject matter and skill mastery and from a heightening interest in the overt and factual standards that seem a normal part of children's orientation in the years of preadolescence. Perhaps, too, there is a deep-seated need to protect oneself from exposing the more intensely subjective facets of personality, a period for gathering of inner strength for the later demands of adolescence when, given a conducive environment, the writing of verse again appears to flower. The children who continued to write poetry, for the most part, have shown the more mature control of imagery and form that one would expect from individuals with so strong a commitment to their own subjective responses.

For ventures into group composition our technique has generally been to set the stage by talking quite casually about the subject at hand, while inviting comments that would give unique and true impressions sensed by individuals. We have not expected, nor have we gotten, universally productive responses, but we have always had a majority of children contribute actively. Many others participated quietly though not passively. We have made it possible for those few who could not become honestly involved to turn to other quiet work.

Usually a session of this kind of dictation of verse has resulted in the chalkboard's being filled, with more lines spilling over to chart paper or a convenient notebook. Then came the task of selection and arrangement by a committee. Ordinarily this has been better when left until next day, but at times it has been imperative to clear the boards the same day. One plan has the advantage of perspective; the other of momentum. In either case, the committee has always found some alternatives about which to consult the teacher and the class. At times, oddly enough, the very children who could not, or would not, get into the current of expression when ideas were flowing were the most helpful at the editing-polishing stage.

POETRY IN THE PERSPECTIVE OF THE CLASSROOM

In a busy schoolroom poetry making does not go on without interruption. Because it requires an atmosphere singularly free from pressures it usually cannot flourish when children are engrossed in other types of class activity, such as preparing a play or following a strong science or social studies interest. But in the unhurried periods that afford a sense of leisure and repose, poetry making can come into its own. After dictation gets under way it ought to be continued for at least a week or two even at the cost of considerable readjustment of the daily schedule. Poetry making is essentially an uncovering process, and the truly personal thoughts and feelings are often slow to emerge. However, as children begin to realize the satisfaction that comes from voicing their own ideas, they unconsciously permit more and more of their deeper selves to be revealed. Often they become so captivated by the experience that they appear before school begins in the morning or stay on after dismissal to have their poems written down or to show what they have written.

Even the best child poems contain only a line or two of unusual beauty or individual sparkle, and in an effort to create a more perfect whole a teacher may feel tempted to weed out ordinary expressions or to build up worthwhile bits, but the temptation is to be resisted. A child is bound to suffer loss of confidence when a teacher makes suggestions for the improvement of a poem, or adds a few words to smooth over what she considers to be the rough spots. Much of the satisfaction that children derive from poetry making comes when their offerings are read aloud to the class. It is this sharing that seems to insure the continuance of the experience. When a poem is especially colorful or original in its expression of truth, it receives appreciative comments from the others, but it is never unduly featured. Once it has been shared with the group, its maker seems to forget about it. Instead of mulling over what has been done, he turns instinctively to new effort.

6

Individual Growth in Writing: Case Studies

If we are to achieve a richer culture, rich in human potentialities, we must recognize the whole gamut of human personalities and so weave a less arbitrary social fabric, one in which each human gift will find a fitting place.

Margaret Mead, from The South Seas

Case studies of real children, ranging in ability from average to highly gifted, present a clearer picture of growth than any amount of generalized description. Selections of their writing, both personal and practical, reveal some of the basic trends of maturation and learning that take place in the elementary school years. From these samplings it is evident that each child lends his unique quality to his writing when he is allowed to do so, and that this uniqueness is effective style. The obligation to learn correct forms in practical writing and the manner in which children can and do apply these forms in personal writing are shown as each child develops. And conversely, it appears that children color their utilitarian writing with that delightful individuality fostered by their free and copious expression of imagination and invention.

These cases reveal the growth of ten different personalities. Could we present a hundred of those we have worked with, the result would be a hundred personalities, each as different from the others as those presented here. We have sought, therefore, to select the ones that give a true cross section of the children we have studied. All these children were of average or superior ability, but even weaker children showed visible growth.

In some cases we have included only one year's work; in others we have sampled a period of four years of effort and development. A more exact picture could, of course, be sketched if more cases appeared, since each child grows in his own particular way. Each child was unique at the beginning of our study; naturally they were even more different as time went on, for age always increases divergences of ability. No groups with whom we have used more conventional methods have approached the degree of control shown by these children over accepted English essentials of form, structure, and organization. It has become our conviction that every writing experience, lived joyfully and richly, contributes to the maximum development of writing power.

KATIE IN SECOND GRADE

Katie arrived in our second grade with a report from her previous school describing her as "cheerful, willing and well-behaved, an average student." This was, indeed, a reasonably accurate picture of Katie who would be picked out of the group not because she had any special ability or disability, but because she was so pleasantly "average." She did what was asked of her without comment but with a cheerful concentration of her competence. She rarely compared her achievement with that of other children, seeming to be satisfied with the knowledge that she had done her best. Although she did not volunteer for classroom responsibilities, she was always ready to do her share of whatever the class was undertaking and, because she was a careful worker, she was often chosen to be a member of a small group to work on a special project. In class discussions, she listened attentively, responding with her eyes rather than her voice, although here, too, if a specific response were asked, she would have an opinion to express. As she moved through her days one had to seek ways to give Katie the joy of being important.

Early in the fall when Katie wore a new dress, the teacher took time to make her the center of attention while all admired its lovely colors. Perhaps because she had thus been brought to the attention of the children, at storytelling time that afternoon the class asked Katie to tell a story. She had previously been only an appreciative listener but now, urged by the children, she told, with some reluctance her first story. It is here reconstructed from notes the teacher made of this important first step.

> Once there was a little girl and her mother. They didn't have any money. So they had to go out and look everywhere, but they couldn't find any. Then the little girl saw a box under a bush, and she looked in and there was a *lot* of money—one thousand sixty-seven gold dollars! So they took it to the store and got all the things they wanted.

It bothered neither Katie nor her audience that this tale was almost a duplication of the story told by the child who preceded her. The one new element she had introduced, "One thousand sixty-seven gold dollars," caught the children's fancy, and Katie squirmed with delight as they talked about this fantastic sum.

A few days later when someone recalled the massive sum of money, a child asked Katie if she had another story. As in other situations Katie responded to a request. This time the story was her own and gave the first indication of the slightly impish humor that was to mark many of her tales.

> Once there was a little kitten named White Paws because, of course, he *had* white paws. Well, one day he jumped on the desk and knocked a bottle of ink on the floor. And he walked all around in the ink and all over the carpet. So they had to call him Black Paws, and he had to stay outside after that.

Katie just glowed when appreciative laughter acknowledged the "good joke" about the kitten's name and at the end of the period asked when the next storytelling time would be. She no longer needed the prod of a request to start off on a story. Sometimes what she told was merely a new variation of a story told by another, but at other times she drew entirely on her own invention. Usually there was the mark of her own special light humor.

The practical writing required in the early months of second grade (lists, memos, brief notes) Katie did both amiably and capably. This sort of writing, which requires coordination of mind and muscle just to produce the necessary words, often finds its individual distinction only in the decoration children love to add. Katie's embellishments were simple and neat. As the physical act of handwriting became less arduous and children could be concerned with what they were saying, Katie's writing began to reflect something of the special touch which marked her stories.

Her note of appreciation to a mother who provided a Halloween party for the class follows:

Dear Mrs. Burns,
> Thank you for giving us a party. You tricked us with a yummy treat.
>
> Love, Katie

Some time after Halloween when children were dictating stories, Katie, pulling her chair beside the teacher, listened to two or three stories. When the teacher asked if she would like to dictate, too, Katie immediately began her tale of an orange jack-o'-lantern. It is interesting to observe that each time Katie was ready to take a new step forward, the way had to be opened for her with a request or suggestion.

Once upon a time there was a little orange who lived in a store with lots and lots of other oranges. Right then it was Halloween and this little orange saw all the children and their mothers coming in that store and buying pumpkins for Halloween, for jack-o'-lanterns, of course. Well, this little orange wished someone would buy Him for a jack-o'-lantern. He was very little and didn't know any better. So, well, the other oranges told him he was silly but he didn't care except that he cried because no one bought him for a jack-o'-lantern. Well, when Halloween night came, all the pumpkins had been sold, but *still* the little orange wanted to be a jack-o'-lantern. And you know what happened? A fairy came in that store looking for a jack-o'-lantern to scare baby ghosts with and she saw this little orange crying so she said, "Why do you cry like that?"

And this little orange said he wanted to be a jack-o'-lantern and you know what? That fairy said, "You are the very thing I have been wanting. I'll make you into a jack-o'-lantern just my size, and we will scare baby ghosts and everything." So she took him home and they lived happy ever after.

This tale, with its well-maintained story line is so far removed from Katie's first feeble attempt at storytelling, that one might anticipate continued accelerated growth. However, it represented a high level of achievement, which Katie did not attain again for some time. Although she continued to tell stories, many were similar to her earlier efforts. And when at Christmas, the class became interested in giving plays, a general lull in storytelling took place.

After Christmas, there were occasions for short notes that Katie particularly enjoyed since she could write just what she wanted. Her pleasure in this writing is quite obvious.

Dear Miss Moore's Class,
Thank you for inviting us to your machine program. I enjoyed it very much. I liked the pulley and the song you sang. The mural of the machines was really something to see.
Your friend,
Katie

Dear Sarah Lou,
Too bad you are sick. We got our goldfish. They look pretty surprised to be here.
Love,
Katie

Later when the class was studying weather, several children dictated poetry ideas about wind, rain, or snow. Although this activity was not uncommon in the class, Katie had never taken part in it, but once again she edged herself near the teacher, listened to others dictate, and then responded quickly to the teacher's asking if she had a poem to dictate. It was something of a surprise that her first effort should prove to be so effective.

> Lightning
> Who made you?
> Did some great giant
> Write you with a flashing pen?
> Did he?

Once again Katie seemed astonished she had produced something that could enchant the other children. She quickly announced that she had "lots more poetry ideas" and in the next days dictated several. Some of these were as trite as:

> The wind blows through the trees
> It makes a good breeze

But another really sounded like Katie at her best:

> The world is like a bakery shop window.
> Soft white frosting
> Is on top of everything.
> Don't try to eat the cake, though!

However, she seemed disinterested in poetry after this brief period and dictated nothing until late spring when she came in from the playground early one morning to ask the teacher to write down her poem.

> Run little squirrel, run.
> Run across the yard.
> Don't look back
> At the big black dog.
> He can't *ever* catch you.
> But run, little squirrel,
> Run, run, run!

At Easter time, storytelling became again an important activity of the class. When Katie joined in, it was obvious she had only the start of a story in mind, but she began with a sparkling assurance that had been lacking in the fall. Her tales were marked by long repetitious dialogues but usually she managed to stick to her story line and bring about some sort of logical conclusion.

> Once upon a time the Easter Bunny and his helpers were dyeing eggs and they ran out of pink dye. Now, of course, every Easter basket has to have some pink eggs but the Bunny didn't know what to do. He sent his helpers to the store to get more dye, but there wasn't any.
> "Well, get some," said the Bunny.
> "We can't. There isn't any."
> "Well, get some anyway."
> "We can't."
> "Yes, you can."
> "No, we can't."
> "Yes, you can."
> [This was repeated several times while the children laughed.]
> "Well," said the Bunny, "I know one thing we can do. We can take our red socks and cook them up in some water and that will make a good red dye and then we can put more water in and make it pink."
> "Good idea."
> "O.K. Take off your socks."
> So they made some red-sock soup and then dyed the eggs, and every Easter basket had some pink eggs in it and no one knew that they were really dyed with red socks.

During the spring the amount of practical writing done by the children increased slowly as their mastery of handwriting and spelling skills made them more independent. However, only two children in this class attempted to write stories although several asked to finish in secret a story which they had dictated in large part. Katie used this technique of dictating part and writing the rest to surprise her teacher with the end of this story.

> Once there was a squinch bug which can squinch down so small that human people can't even see it. That's why it is called a Squinch Bug. Well, one day this little squinch bug was walking along the edge of the teacher's desk and it saw her glasses so it tugged and pulled and pushed and shoved those glasses until they were right *under* a paper. The teacher wanted to read to the children, but she can't find her glasses anywhere. So everyone starts to look and the squinch bug sits and laughs because no one

looks under the paper because the teacher keeps patting the corner of the desk and saying "I *know* I put them right here."

Well, after a while the teacher *accidentally* happens to knock off the paper and she said, "There are my glasses. My goodness, how did they get *under* that paper?"

The squinch bug laughed and the teacher heard and she said, "Did you do that?"

The squinch bug said, "Yes. Ha. Ha! Joke on you."

And the teacher said, "Just wait till I get you," and she was going to swat that bug but . . .

[The balance of the story was written by Katie. Spelling and punctuation have been corrected to make for easier reading.]

. . . the squinch bug quickly made himself very small. First the teacher could hardly see him even with her glasses and then she couldn't see him at all. So she swatted the place where she thought he was, but he had gone away to think up other tricks for her.

When the teacher read the story to the group and the children had fun identifying the teacher in the tale, Katie announced that the story had a name, "Too Small To See But Not Too Small To Play Tricks" and added that it was her best story—so far.

For Katie second grade had been a year of sampling various activities. She had felt a happy satisfaction in her adequacy in practical writing, and in the field of personal expression she had experienced a warm reception for everything she offered. She had also known the special delight of finding just the right words for a fleeting "poetry idea" and of telling a story that charmed her listeners. Katie, one of the great number of so-called "average children," upon occasion moved from her limited but adequate way of working into vivid expression of her own ideas. Her explorations led her to travel the road with happy expectations and new courage.

GEORGE IN FOURTH GRADE

George entered our school in fourth grade, a sensitive, slightly built lad whose need of friendship was apparent from the first day. With keen interests in science that he was always ready to express, he frequently irritated some of the less intellectual children who felt that he was trying to show off. Actually, this was not the case. It was only that George's enthusiasm for precise knowledge spilled over into his eagerness to be a part of class discussions. In contrast to this strength, he was weak in the

Famous People

One famous person was Eric the Red. He was known for his red-hot temper. He was thrown out of Norway and Iceland for killing some men. Then he sailed farther west and discovered Greenland. It really wasn't green. Eric just said it was green to get people to go to it and live there with him.

Customs

The Vikings would raid islands to get thralls, food, clothes, and women. Some of these islands were the Shetlands, the Faroes, and others near England. They would raid Ireland and other big countries, too, such as England and France.
P.S. Thralls are slaves that they had captured.

Norse Gods

When Vikings roamed there were beliefs that there were a lot of gods. One was the god of thunder called Thor. He had a big hammer that he would throw into a cloud and the hammer would make thunder and the hammer would come back to him eager to go again. Another god was Odin. He was king of the gods. There was a belief that if the god of the land saw a dragon's head on a boat there would be bad luck. Another belief was that the dragon's head protected the Norseman from the dangers of the sea.

Sagas

One saga is about Leif Ericson. He found North America. There are two sagas about how he found this continent. One is that he was caught in a storm and discovered it by accident. Another is that he heard of this land and set out to explore it.
P.S. A saga is a story passed down from father to son by telling it.

The finished copy of this quite lengthy report was carefully proofread, illustrated, bound in heavy colored paper, and taken home for a present. George's account of his parents' enthusiasm for the gift reinforced the deep satisfaction that had attended the completion of this book.

Writing reports of factual data continued to delight George. Quite on his own responsibility, he wrote a report on the John Glenn orbit, catching the dramatic flavor of much that was going on at that time on television

112

and radio. One day when the children were asked what they would choose for a "choice period" George replied, "I'm going to write some more on my report about John Glenn. I've got him as far as the third orbit now." The spontaneity of his comment was evidence of the pleasure he derived from thus recording his own knowledge.

In early spring, the class was actively engaged in a study of the solar system. Again, during group discussions, George showed delight in sharing newly found facts. After several weeks of class work, each child selected a planet about which he was to become an "expert." George was the first to say he wanted to start writing his report. His enthusiasm for the work had been manifested for days in his choosing to read more reference material than was generally required. The impulse to gather accurate data and to write it in a manner that others would enjoy carried him through six closely written pages of rough-draft writing. For a nine-year-old, his finished report showed a considerable knowledge of the facts then known about Mars, and a sense of personal concern that gives vitality of style to his writing.

The following excerpts from a few of George's topics indicate this range and accuracy of information as well as clarity in presenting it. The form is often childlike, but the extent of his mastery shows through the occasional immaturities of expression.

Mars

Introduction

I would like to tell you about the planet Mars, the planet of mystery, the planet of colors. I think that Mars is one of the planets that causes a lot of interesting questions. Mars is the mystery planet in our solar system—even though it is a close neighbor we don't know much about it yet. Now I have the pleasure of introducing Mars.

Some people think that there is life on Mars because they think the lines on Mars are canals full of water. But most people think the lines are plants and there are no people on Mars.

Tycho Brahe in the sixteenth century made the first observations of Mars. Tycho was a Danish astronomer who liked astronomy very much . . . Astronomers think that there are great sandy waste lands on Mars. One mystery is what causes the color to change. Scientists think it's because of the seasons but we can't be sure. The reason we have so many mysteries about Mars is because we can't get a good picture of it. The air around the earth blurs our seeing it clearly.

George did not return to story writing. He was content to put his individual stamp on the practical writing he enjoyed so much. However, there was one exception. When a wave of enthusiasm for poetry writing caught the fancy of most of the children in the spring of fourth grade, George had a try at that, too.

The Universe

The universe, the universe
Full of gases
Full of meteors
Would you like to be going
In a rocket
From planet to planet?
I would!
Would you?

The effort is not rich either in imagery or individual flavor. Even though attempting a poetic form, George dealt with an intellectual idea somewhat as he might have in report writing. Apparently he still needed to feel that he was in complete control of facts, but at least he showed a willingness to play with words and to permit some of his wishes to shine through.

In practical writing George gained the confidence that released his superior powers and brought increasing satisfactions and enrichment into his life. Not only in writing was this evident but also in his relationship with his classmates. George had come into his own. Now the give-and-take of play and teasing fell into perspective. Fortified by his success in holding his classmates' interest when he read his distinctive informational reports, he took recourse less frequently in hurt feelings or excessive retaliation. And now the tone of the nickname "Old Georgie" used hurtfully in the fall, had changed to one of affection for "good old Georgie."

ELLEN IN THIRD GRADE

Whereas a few children in third grade begin early in the year to write stories in a richly fanciful manner, in our experience a much larger number delay this stage of writing until they have achieved considerable assurance in spelling and handwriting. Not until January of her third-grade year, did Ellen volunteer a story on paper although before this time she had done the practical writing tasks generally required of her class.

Whatever the origin of this postponement in Ellen's case, she quite made up for it in the volume of material she wrote in the latter half of third

114

grade. Both practical and personal writing showed a spurt of growth in this five-month period. Much of her writing was mediocre in quality, but a gradual progression in imaginative detail and in mood can be observed. As she gained confidence in projecting her own feelings in her stories, they took on some of the characteristics for which Ellen herself was so much loved by her classmates. She had a gift for unobtrusively setting things right for other people. When tensions mounted in some minor conflict among the children, it was Ellen who would quietly suggest a way out of the impasse. Her desire to forestall people's getting hurt amounted to a real compassion seldom observed in children. Ellen not only felt goodwill toward her companions; she took time to express it even in the hurry and pressure of everyday classroom life. Yet little hint of this inner loveliness comes through in the first story she wrote.

The Secret Cop

Once there was a boy named Peter, but everybody called him Pete. One day, Pete was playing with his little sister, Sue. Mother said that he had to take care of his little sister while she was going to see a lady. Sue wanted to play dolls so *he* had to play.

All of a sudden he heard a big noise at the museum. So he ran to see what it was. He grabbed his little sister's hand and ran. He saw some men coming out of the building with some guns, so he hid behind a tree. He wanted to go after them because he was a secret cop. So he hid. He walked and walked. Soon he saw the men go into a cave. His little sister stumbled on a gun that one of the men had dropped, so he picked it up and went in. He told him to drop his guns and he picked them up. Then he called the police when he got home with the men.

Two days after this first experiment in controlling characters on paper, Ellen wrote another story. Sustained by the friendly reception accorded her tale of capturing the museum thief, she wrote a pleasant little story in which she personified two cars who found good drivers and friendly homes. Note the light touch given to the attraction between the cars and the balance effected in the parting between Speedy and the "lady car." Ellen illustrated this story with a crayoned drawing in which the two cars actually seemed to smile even though they had no facial features. Her picture showed both cars standing in front of a blue house, facing each other in a driveway surrounded by sunny green fields, bright flowers, and strong green trees.

Speedy

This took place in a small town named Smallville where cars were made. One day the men were working on little Speedy. The next day they were all through. It was a beautiful day. The sun was out. Then a man came around to see all of the beautiful new cars. He saw Speedy. Then the man went over to the other man and gave him something. Speedy did not know what was going on. Then he got in Speedy. Speedy did not like the man to get in him.

He turned on the motor, Brr—rr—rr. Br—rr—rr, and off he went, out into the world. On the way at a red light, he met a truck. Speedy started to talk to the truck.

The truck said, "Don't bother me, Little Car. I have work to do. Run along."

The light was now green. He somehow turned the corner. He saw a beautiful lady car. The man parked near the lady car. They said, "Hi." Then the man came. Speedy did not [know] what to do. Also a lady came out. The lady got in the other car and the man got in Speedy. Soon the two cars went off. Then Speedy put on his blinker and went into a beautiful driveway.

Although she read the above story aloud with proper deference to sentence endings and in an altogether clear and understandable manner, her punctuation and spelling were full of errors. It was not until much more writing of stories gave her the necessary confidence in her own imagination, not until purposeful correction of rough drafts of reports and letters resulted in correct practical writing of which she was justly proud, that she asserted control over spelling and punctuation. In later grades she attained a very creditable balance between ideas and correctness, but throughout the third grade her accuracy in matters of form remained very low.

Several days later Ellen wrote a story about a crocodile that reflects the age-old interest in the person who cries too much or who cannot cry or laugh at all. Ellen's handling of this theme was characteristically immature, but she showed courage in trying a new kind of invention where feelings are not quite so sunny as in the story of Speedy.

Crocodile

Once there was a crocodile who had the "crying giddies." His name is Tye. He was always crying. Tye never stopped crying. One day he was going to the lake. When he looked into the lake in two minutes the lake would overflow. One day he went to the doctor. He gave him medicine and some pills. Now Tye could never cry, and when he felt sad he still could not cry.

The crocodile story brought to a close the cycle of story writing that had so pleased Ellen during January. It had been her first venture into the realm of written expression, and it had provided her with rich satisfaction. In the weeks that followed, Ellen continued steady progress in academic areas. She was a good little mathematician with a sure sense of how to go about the work and with obvious pleasure in being sure she was right.

In the late winter the class carried out a science study of the human body. Ellen chose to report on "The Heart, The Eye, and The Bones." The wording was very clear and direct: "The heart isn't like a Valentine heart," and "Your heart is almost the same size as your fist."

The treatment of the eye and the bones was in much the same hard-working vein, showing an honest attempt to be clear and accurate.

The pride engendered by this experience provided a firm foundation for the beginning of Ellen's next big step in practical writing. The report that follows was the culmination of a long-term study of Indian life in which the class had its first systematic individual guidance in gathering data, selecting important matter to include, writing a rough draft, and editing it with the teacher. Many facets of this process had been learned during the preceding few months, as for example, in planning and writing letters and editing them before copying and mailing. But the longer task of gathering information, reading and rereading for specific information, plus the sequential steps of organizing material around important topics was a big stretch for these children nearing the end of the third grade.

The following topics were included in the class outline, and Ellen wrote copiously on each one. She arranged her topics in a sequence that pleased her:

> Indian food
> Education
> Weapons and utensils
> Clothing
> Indian homes

An excerpt from only the last topic is included here.

Homes

The Lenni-Lenapes' wigwams were like upside down bowls. First the Indians bent over trees called saplings and made a frame. These they covered with bark. Then the women made grass mats to put over the wigwams so that when it rained the

117

water would roll right off the house. For the door, usually a skin of an animal was used.

Inside for beds, the "wilden" would have furs. In the top of the wigwam would be a hole for the smoke so that they could have a fire in the house.

Ellen concluded this account so rich in visual details with some mention of how she would feel about smoke in a wigwam. The complete report totaled five rather closely written pages. The length as well as the content were a matter of pride to Ellen. Copied from corrected first drafts in "best handwriting," mounted on heavy paper, copiously illustrated, and bound in book form, the report became a worthy gift to her family. After completing this long writing job, Ellen enjoyed other pursuits for a time— and then in May she again turned to the pleasures of story writing.

The first in this group concerns a boy who on his way home from school found a motor that he could use in a rocket he was building. Ellen's rather lengthy introduction casts the story in the familiar framework of a dream and then starts the action.

So that night he had a dream about the moon. He went up, up, up. Zoom, up more he went. Now he saw the little, little earth. Soon he was on the moon. It was summer on the moon. Little people were running all around putting little moon cakes in one big bag. Now Pat was standing on a big moon cake. Two little moon men went up to Pat and were squeaking and pushed at Pat's feet. Pat was a little afraid so he jumped off the moon cake. The little men ran back to the bag and put it in and ten little people had guns and were all ready to shoot him when he woke up. He ran to the rocket and threw it out the window and went back to bed and that was the end of his rocket.

The class enjoyed the novel idea of "moon cakes," the vigor of the action including the disposal of the rocket, and even the return to quiet sleep. Though a story of limited imagination, it did show a bit of originality. Ellen had the satisfaction of manipulating characters and shaping events as she chose. Curiously, the leading role never becomes quite real in this fast-moving tale. It is obvious that Ellen is experimenting with plot, not with characterization.

A direct contrast to this earlier emphasis on action is to be seen in the next story, which Ellen wrote later the same day. Although the plot here is slim, there is a clear effort to build more of a person in Mr. Pink-Eyes. It is here that Ellen's kindliness shines through again as it did in some of her earlier stories. Both characters achieve the cozy living arrangements that seemed so meaningful to Ellen herself.

> Once there was a man named Pink-Eyes. He always said he was seeing pink elephants. One day, the circus came to town. It passed by Mr. Pink-Eyes' house. In the parade were three pink elephants. Mr. Pink-Eyes' eyes popped out of his head and fell on the floor. He picked up his eyes and put them in his head. One of the elephants came to the window. Mr. Pink-Eyes was afraid, but he patted the elephant and said, "Go away." But the elephant did not go away. He liked Mr. Pink-Eyes, so the two lived together and Mr. Pink-Eyes was never afraid of an elephant again.

Three weeks later, Ellen wrote her last story of the year, fittingly entitled, "How Nice Are You?" A more fluent style and more rhythmic phrasing are at once apparent. So, too, was the much better handwriting on the original. Although it was devoid of punctuation, Ellen read it aloud with appropriate terminal inflections, showing that she had fashioned it with her "inner ear" alert to accustomed patterns of English sentence melody. Perhaps of even greater significance, is the fact that this last story of the year is better rounded as to plot and lacks such unattractive, though childlike, elements as Mr. Pink-Eyes' dropping his eyes on the floor! Here we have characterization and incident moving along in proportion to each other and playing complementary roles.

How Nice Are You?

> Once upon a time there was a little dog named Pups. Poor little Pups had no home to stay in. No home at all! One day, Pups was walking around. Soon he saw five little mice running around him.
> "Hello," said Pups.
> "Hello. Do you know who we are?"
> "No."
> "We are mice."
> "Oh!"
> "And we are here to help you because you are so nice to mice. And we want to help very much. Will you give us a piece of your hair?"
> So Pups pulled out a piece of hair.
> "Thank you. Now say, 'one-two-three.' "

So Pups said, "One-two-three" and [there was] a big house in front of Pup's eyes.

"For me?"

"Yes," said the five mice together. "For you."

"Thank you very much," said Pups.

"Thank you," said the biggest mouse, "for all the things you have done for mice."

And all five mice went away and Pups never saw the mice again.

The End

It is obvious that in this last story in third grade Ellen projected much of herself through her generous little characters. Her freedom in revealing their kindness through fast-moving conversation other than just generalizing about their good intent is admirable. The children loved the "mouse talk" and both the storyteller and audience enjoyed the novelty of a dog's being nice to mice. Though the faint echo of an old fable is to be heard, the theme is handled with some originality. It was the bigger animal who started the cycle of kindness which returned eventually to him, just as Ellen herself was often a moving spirit in a cycle of generous behavior that encircled her and her many good friends.

RUTH, GRADES THREE THROUGH SIX

Ruth entered our school at third grade and came into a group notable for its espirit de corps. The children welcomed her warmly, but were at the same time abashed by her shyness. She was naturally a bit awkward, a stranger to a group that had known one another for at least two years. There was a kind of glow about her, however, that made her easily accepted without the teacher's needing to promote friendships but an unusual timidity as well, to which a number of circumstances had contributed. This diffidence limited the effectiveness of her abilities, which, though not at all outstanding, were adequate for normal growth. She needed constant assurance of her power to enter into the various activities of the group and even to cope with routine tasks.

During the first half of the third grade the children continued storytelling and dictating. Though she had always been an appreciative listener, it was not until after Christmas that Ruth ventured to tell a short story. When, near the end of the year, a few of the children began to write, Ruth, after frequent assurances that "it would be all right," wrote the following stiff and meager tale.

120

Tale of a Monkey

Once upon a time in a jungle lived a monkey. He had a lot of friends. This little monkey always played tricks. One day all the little monkeys were playing under a palm tree but one. He threw down a coconut. All the little monkeys looked up and ran away.

It was Ruth's first and was therefore important, as all first stories are important, but this one especially because of her timidity. Her feeble attempt was courteously accepted by the group. This along with her delight in seeing her own story on paper proved so tempting that in spite of her fear of failure Ruth was eager to try again. Because writing had once been fun, her practical writing also began to show improvement, and she worked with zest at most of the tasks that up to that time had been burdensome. Another year of growth, continued building of self-confidence, and further experience in writing with satisfaction began to free her from her fears. The following story written at nine years gives evidence of developing ease and fluency, in marked contrast to the awkward poverty of the "Tale of a Monkey." In her typically uncertain way Ruth asked for many corrections while writing.

When I was a Little Girl

When I was a little girl I didn't like to go to bed. One night Mother had a dinner party. I thought I would listen to what they said. So when they went into dinner, I sneaked into the living room and hid behind the couch. I waited and waited till finally they came in. Some people sat on the couch and talked. They had long dresses on. Pretty soon they started dancing. I had never seen anything so funny in my life. Pretty soon I started laughing. Everybody got scared. I felt awfully bad and crouched down. Everybody asked where the sound came from. Someone said, "Over there." Daddy looked behind the couch and saw me. He yelled, "You bad girl, don't you do that any more." And I never did.

By reading the story with all the dramatic power she could summon, the teacher saw to it that Ruth had the satisfaction of an audience's spontaneous approval. Even though the story had not sufficient merit to be read again to the class, it had served its purpose in keeping alive Ruth's desire to write. At the same time, the experience in telling a story had done much for Ruth's growth in fluency of expression. Obviously the first sentence sets the stage quite directly for the action of the story. Compare the use of the beginning complex sentence with the jerky beginning of

121

"Tale of a Monkey." Note also the use of such graphic verbs as "sneaked" and "crouched," as well as the use of conversation in an effective climax. Though this story does not compare with those written by other children in the group, either in imagination or in style, it does show for Ruth a real growth in conception of plot and suppleness of phrasing.

During the next year, experience with uncriticized personal writing helped considerably in freeing Ruth's imagination. Greater control of mechanics resulting from further practical writing gave her an increased confidence. She developed some power of invention but still needed an adult's approval. She asked if each detail of her story "would be all right." Given needed support, she was able without further help to carry out her plan effectively.

In the sixth grade she wrote with comparative ease in both the utilitarian and imaginative fields, though she occasionally asked for help that she did not really need but which gave her the assurance she still wanted. She accepted for herself high standards of clarity in informational writing, as can be seen in the following excerpts from a comprehensive report on tobacco. Ruth divided her material, culled from reading and conversations with a recent visitor to Cuba, into five sections: Growing, Curing, Tobacco Uses, Statistics, and, of course, References. "This is getting much too long," she complained on the seventh page of handwriting, "but it's all part of the report, and I don't see how I can leave any of it out." Only segments can be included here, since the final report was four full typewritten pages.

Tobacco

Growing

Tobacco grows mostly anywhere in the earth except where it does not rain often enough for the soil to be moistened. It takes a great amount of patience to take care of tobacco from when it is first planted in a seed bed. (The farmer has to plant the tobacco in a bed first because the tiny black seeds are so small that 60,000 of them make one tablespoon, enough to sow 100 square yards of seed bed) . . .

Curing

Curing is done when the tobacco leaves are fully grown and they are taken to a barn or put under a cheesecloth to be dried in the sun. Tobacco cured in a closed barn by means of hot air is called "flue cured." Tobacco cured in a curing shed is called "air cured." After tobacco is all cured sometimes the cured leaves are

shriveled up half their size and many times one third their regular
size . . .

Tobacco Uses

Tobacco is used for five or six purposes. They are snuff,
smoking, cigarettes, cigars, and chewing tobacco. . . .

Snuff

There is a certain kind of tobacco grown for snuff. It has a
very strong flavor. Snuff tobacco is ground up to a very fine
powder. It is then used by people who like to sneeze. They take a
pinch and place it in their nose and then sneeze. In the olden
days the men used to carry the snuff under their cuffs. They had
very small boxes and very elaborate ones. . . .

Cigars

[Note: The following is a description of how cigars are made
in Cuba, as described by a person who saw them made.]

There are four things that people do in a cigar factory. There
are girls that wear white gloves who take the largest tobacco
leaves and split them down the center vein. Then the split leaves
are given to a man who does the first step in sorting the tobacco.
He takes the split leaves and sorts them into about twelve
different piles according to their color. This man has to have
excellent eyesight. He must have the light coming from the
north. There are about 100 different colors and there is a very
slight difference between them. The lightest cigars are the
mildest . . .

The scope of information treated here and the detail included indicate the
thoroughness of Ruth's preparation before writing. She listed questions
before she started her reading of references and added to them in our
conferences. These questions shaped the general organization of her
paper, which seems to us admirably carried out for an eleven-year-old.
The detailed background, along with the control gained by frequently
talking over her ideas and findings with the whole group, enabled Ruth to
write with greater power.

Of course, increased maturity also accounts in part for her use of
more involved sentence structure. Elsewhere in her report she wrote,
"After the cigars are made they are taken to a man who sorts them into
piles according by their color." This complex sentence with two dependent
clauses was used naturally by a child who understood the relationships

existing before she tried to verbalize them. Note also that the sentences vary in length, construction, and order. One cannot help but observe the frequent bridging over from near-adult constructions to quite delightfully childlike expressions, as for example, "It is then used by people who like to sneeze." It suggests the amusement felt by Ruth and others of the group at what seemed to them phenomenal. Sneezing meant having a cold and staying in bed. Just imagine liking that! In contrast to this juvenile reaction to the use of snuff, the transitional sentences introducing the uses of tobacco are remarkable. Ruth presents a new phase of her subject and indicates five subordinate but pertinent topics in clean-cut fashion. Control of the subject matter is evident in her organization.

In the sixth grade the group was studying medieval life. Following several weeks of group study and building a common background, each child selected one phase of the study for individual pursuit. Ruth chose the daily life in the monasteries and, after general reading and discussion, made the following plan for her report: Daily Religious Life, The Rule, Work, Writing and Clothing.

Only the first two paragraphs of her report are included here, but these are enough to indicate the increasing smoothness of phraseology and more dignified style appropriate to her subject.

> Six times a day the monks gather for prayer and singing of psalms in the chapel. Again at midnight the bell called them from their hard couches to services. The monks who cultivated the field did not come to the chapel for every service but they would kneel on the ground and pray till the service was over.
>
> The "Rule" of the monastery at all times ordered that they should "speak slowly without laughter, humbly with gravity, with few and sensible words." At meals they sat silently while one monk (who was allowed to eat earlier) read from some religious book.
>
> Monks did more than just pray and have services all day. Each monk had his own task. Some worked in the kitchen, some in the monastery garden, some would tend to the cattle and sheep. Some gathered fuel, others tilled the fields, some cobbled shoes, others wove baskets until in a short time there came to be a thousand and one different occupations. The monks were assigned to different jobs by the head of the monastery to which they were best suited.

In spite of the misplaced clause in the final sentence of this excerpt, this is an excellent piece of paragraph construction for an eleven-year-old child. Note the transition sentence "Monks did more then just pray and have services all day," taking the reader from the first two paragraphs about religious services to the specialized tasks each monk performed for his monastery. Note also the variety of sentence length, the repetition for emphasis, and the economy with which the concluding idea is presented. Growing confidence is evident in content, phrase, and form.

By this time Ruth thoroughly enjoyed writing and wove her own friendly sense of humor into her stories in a truly effective manner. It seems scarcely possible that the same child who wrote with obvious fear and strain "Tale of a Monkey" could, less than three years later, write with keen enjoyment this gay and well-constructed story. Ruth laughed as whole-heartedly as any of the other children over the events of Mr. Martin's evening.

Cooking Difficulties

Mr. Martin, I must tell you, was not an expert cook. His wife and children had been invited to a dinner party but *of course* he wouldn't be invited. He sat perched in an easy chair with the evening paper in his hand, cigar in his mouth and radio on. The clock hands ran around till Mr. Martin became hungry. He strolled out to the kitchen wondering what to eat that was different; by this I mean besides mashed potatoes, lamb chops, and lima beans. He hastily pulled out the cook book. Finally his eyes sighted a picture that made his mouth water. The picture was of Devil's Food Cake. He started putting sugar and eggs in a bowl and began mixing them. The draft blew in from the window and the old wind puffed at the cook book and a few pages flopped over. Mr. Martin was too busily beating the eggs and sugar to notice the pages turn over. As his eye glanced back to see what was next to go in the bowl the next thing his eye saw was two cups of vinegar so in went the vinegar, wesson oil, salt, pepper. Then he put it all in a pan and put it in the oven. Mr. Martin turned the temperature gadget up to 520°. He then began to hear a funny noise. He hastened over to the oven; and there right before his eyes his supposedly devil's food cake was bubbling, fizzling, popling and doing everything. Mr. Martin got thoroughly disgusted; he stamped his foot, shut off the oven, turned off the lights. Mr. Martin then went down town to eat dinner at a restaurant, bought a box of cigars and went to a Mae West picture show.

What more typically human anticlimax could be imagined? The warm and humorous appreciation of simple, homey situations was as much a part of Ruth as of her story. Her perception of adult foibles and frustrations was both amazing and disconcerting. She maneuvered Mr. Martin into a ridiculous situation but with no cruelty in her treatment. Through graphic detail Ruth achieved a climax in which the oven's sound effects were exceeded only by Mr. Martin's noisy activities of retreat. Ruth maintained her characterization of a comfort-loving person from the first sentence to the last.

DANNY, GRADES TWO THROUGH SIX

Danny was the middle child in a lively, capable household. Shy and frail, he very early built for himself a protecting cocoon of silence and docility, within which he lived an exciting life of his own devising. Out of the abundance of interests to which he was constantly exposed, he took for himself only the things he wanted and moved along untouched by the rest. Thus with an intuitive wisdom he preserved and nurtured his unique self, although by the same process he developed an indifference to directed learning that made his academic progress slow.

When Danny first came to school, he rarely talked. If he had to communicate with adults, he hid his face in his hands, and mumbled so that his words were scarcely intelligible. Fortunately he found release in doing things. He was a busy child, cluttering up his room at home with roughly made toys or "inventions," and following at school some engrossing interest that was usually quite unlike what any other child was doing. It was not that Danny was uncooperative. On the contrary he displayed a friendly eagerness to help, but his vital activity—the kind that engaged his power—followed an independent course. And it was only as we examined his self-designed experiments that we began to appreciate his potential strength.

Through the early school years Danny continued to be a diffident, inarticulate child. Toward the close of the second grade, however, after he had been with the same teacher for almost two years, he felt enough confidence to dictate a few stories—some at home and others at school. One of these follows. In it he tells the story of his own craving. He is the weak and puny little rabbit that longs so passionately to be big and strong like the older ones in his family.

The Rabbit Who Liked Carrots

Once there was a little rabbit who liked carrots so much he ate them every day. One day he had some lettuce, but he wanted some carrots and he said he didn't have any for a long

126

time. One day his mother kept on giving him more carrots and more carrots and more carrots until he got sick. When he was well again he still wanted carrots so his mother told him where he could find them because she was tired of picking them for him. So he went there and ate up all the carrots and he didn't have any more. He wondered what to do.

One day he decided to go out and hunt for some more. On he went, and on and on and on till he came to another city where everything was very big and where he came upon some carrots and the carrots were very, very big. They were as tall as trees to him. Then he saw a man coming. The man, who was a very big man, asked him what he wanted. The rabbit told him he wanted the carrots so the man took out his knife and cut the littlest piece he could, but still it was bigger than the rabbit. So the rabbit said, "Give me the littlest knife you have in the city and maybe I can cut it." So the man gave him the knife, but when the rabbit got it he could hardly lift it. So the man helped him till he got the piece he wanted. He ate on and on till he grew very big like the other rabbits in the city.

He went home, but when he got to his house, he was too big to get in. So he went where the carrots were, but the carrots seemed so little to him that he could scarcely see them. Then he heard a voice. It was a fairy. He looked around a bit till he saw the fairy, who was very hard to see because it was so tiny. The fairy said he'd have to live in her house six weeks before he'd be small again. He couldn't fit in the castle so he stayed outside. The fairy took her wand and touched a place in the ground and there grew a big castle, big enough for him to get into. So he stayed in that castle six weeks and then went home where he lived happily ever after.

Over and over again we have had from young children similar stories or rhythmic chantings that were vigorous and sincere because they had been prompted by deep-seated personal impulses and desires. However, many forces operate to close the channels through which this original self emerges. With Danny, language expression was curtailed because his third year began with a new teacher. Again afraid, he slipped back into his sheltering cocoon. He followed what went on in the group as though he were an outsider, and in a detached, dutiful way did only what seemed to be required. Nothing broke through his defense until small groups began giving playlets. These he watched with obvious enjoyment. Gradually, very gradually, he began to take part. At first he was only a mover of scenery; later he performed small bits in pantomime, and finally, by the spring of his fourth year he was doing very short speaking parts with some degree of confidence. During this time he had told no stories, although in the last months of the fourth year he wrote two short ones.

This early history scarcely prepared us for what Danny did in his fifth year. Again he had a new teacher, and again he assumed his uncommunicative role. That fall the teacher began the writing periods by reading a variety of things, some from her files of fifth- and sixth-grade work and others from adult authors. The children were invited, though not urged, to contribute anything they had written. At first the offerings were disheartening. Little came and that little was lifeless and dull. Nevertheless, the contributions were read with as much enthusiasm as the teacher could muster. Then one morning one of the little bear stories was read aloud and the next day Danny handed in a tale of his own about them. Eyes lighted up as the teacher read the new version, and there was clamor to know who had written it. The hearty approval his story received worked a magical change in Danny. From that moment he began to grow visibly in poise and power. Although writing cost him great effort, every few days he produced a new story for our enjoyment. At length he persuaded his father to be his scribe, and the stories laboriously written at school were supplemented by those dictated at home. Experiences of the five bears were continued, and other series were invented. For many readings Danny held the class enthralled by the adventures of the Great Chimino, the second chapter of which follows. Even at this early stage he had learned, when ending one chapter, how to whet the appetite for the next.

The Adventures of Chimino, Chapter II

It was not long before Chimino met his first adventure. He came to the edge of a canyon completely made of glass. The sides were smooth so that he could not climb down and at the bottom there was a fiery dragon.

Chimino scratched his head and wondered how he could climb down. Finally he had an idea. He took one of his pills and then he let himself over the side of the canyon slowly. Then he kicked the glass with his foot and made a foothold. He did this several times until he finally came to the bottom. Then he traveled the best he could on the glass, but often slipped. Before long a fierce growl met him. He looked up and there was a fiery dragon.

Chimino took out his sword and hit the dragon with it. The

dragon was very angry at this so at once he jumped around, but slid on the glass and fell flat on his back. Then Chimino jumped on him, but the dragon jumped up and kicked Chimino. Before long it was a regular mix-up. Chimino and the dragon were slipping all around the canyon. The dragon shot fire on one side while Chimino sprang around to the other. Then the dragon would quickly jump around, while Chimino sprang over to the other side and the dragon slipped on his back. Then Chimino jumped on him and lashed him with his sword.

Before long Chimino won and at once continued his travels. In a short time he came to the other side. He climbed up in the same manner in which he had climbed down, although he slipped a few times and nearly lost his life.

When he got to the top he came to the same kind of forest that he did at first. Finally he got through to the other side, where he saw the wildest land he had ever seen in his life. It was all swamp and mushy, and there were a few trees that were very high and bigger than ordinary. All across the sky were black blotches. One seemed to get bigger and bigger. Suddenly an enormous black monster blotted out the whole sun. His huge hand quickly grasped Chimino and carried him away.

Although the Chimino stories gave full scope to Danny's love of invention, his bear stories were more revealing. The one that follows has an imagined setting—the old-fashioned school with the dunce cap, the answer book, the whippings—but it is peopled with characters from his own environment: the absentminded teacher, the boy who hid the chalk, the fair-minded, energetic mother, and even Danny himself. In the character of Bo he exposes his own reactions to life—his experimental attitude, his childlike reasoning, his immunity to punishment, and his open delight in getting ahead of adults.

It was Bo's second day at school. He had lately tried out some experiments, and he had found out that if you pushed pencils off people's desks, they got sent down to the principal to be whipped. And also he had found out that there was no school on Saturday or Sunday.

Now it happened that Bo was in school or rather in the dunce chair admiring the dunce hat that he was wearing. He had just lately tried to get out of school another way. Then he said to himself, "What good is it to get Roy sent down to the principal if I don't see him whipped?"

When the opportunity came to work on the auditorium lighting, he not only learned how to manipulate the switches, but he equipped his home puppet stage with as elaborate a system as he could manage. When the family got a new automobile, Danny, who so short a while before had sidestepped all speaking in public, begged for a chance to talk to the group. He told in detail how a gasoline engine works, and later came to school with an excellent illustrative model made from tin cans.

Because Danny put so much feeling and tireless effort into his work, one might expect his craftsmanship to be of superior quality, but that was not the case. Apparently he was so stirred by doing and discovering that he failed to see a result apart from his dreams. As a consequence he exhibited with proud satisfaction work that to us was crude and untidy. The glaring defects were not due to lack of interest or exertion; they were the reflection of Danny's immaturity. Until he had developed more manual skill and had gained the power to view his work more objectively, overemphasis on points of correctness could only confuse him. Therefore, in practical mechanics, we held him to standards as high as we thought he could reasonably accomplish, and we did not urge him beyond those. We believed that if we could help him to preserve that deep personal concern in what he did, he would master the necessary skills when he came to see the need and had acquired sufficient muscular control.

Undoubtedly the fifth grade was the turning point in Danny's school history, for it was then that he broke free from the fears that had restrained him. The early years of stubborn struggle had strengthened his courage, but the success of his storytelling gave the needed spur. During the sixth grade, he continued to develop along the lines already begun. So it is that whenever we think of Danny, our faith in the force of personal expression is renewed. To remember him literally sweating over his smudgy papers tells us how important creative effort was to him. To realize the change that was worked in Danny himself reveals how potent such effort can be in establishing self-faith and in releasing pent-up power.

JOANNE, GRADES THREE THROUGH SIX

On the playground Joanne was so rough-and-tumble that one would scarcely suspect the sensitive, fanciful nature her writing revealed. In the classroom she was the teacher's delight—and her despair. Her poetic imagination, her humor, her feeling for the dramatic, and her eager aliveness gave color and joy to the school day; but her spelling, her arithmetic, her penmanship, and her housekeeping refused to conform to accepted standards. Her whole nature intuitively resisted set pattern and

132

routine. Even though she well knew that six times two are twelve, she disliked having it be that *every* time. She could invent freely, abundantly, joyously; but she could not imitate. Copying was almost impossible for her to do correctly, and even a finished picture bore little resemblance to the initial sketch. Attempts to direct her creative work were fruitless. She promptly lost interest in the thing discussed and turned to something else. In this simple, effective way she maintained her creative integrity.

In the third-year group Joanne was the first to express herself poetically, and from the beginning her individual expression was fresh, rhythmical, and strong. The fun she had in voicing her ideas was so genuine that the desire to do likewise infected others. Her childish ponderings were transmuted into lyrics. "Me," dictated late in that third year, expressed in its rhythmic pattern, as clearly as in its words, the inadequacy a little girl can feel.

Me

When my mother plays on the piano
Her fingers dance like fairies
In the summer on the grass
Or like fireflies dancing at night.
But when I try to play
I put my fingers down on the keys
And the piano goes
Thump, bang, thump, ping.
It's like a giant stamping all over the land.

"Paper White Narcissus," dictated a year later, tells that there are fairy children, too, who cannot remember the practical and the mundane.

Paper White Narcissus

You know that flower called Paper White Narcissus
Well, the fairies use it for paper
To write their letters on,
And for their children who can't remember
What they have to get from the store—
A dozen ant eggs, or a pound of dandelion leaves,
That's what Paper White Narcissus are used for.

In the fifth year there was for Joanne, as well as for the rest of the group, a decided dropping off in poetical expression. The teacher, though sympathetic, was new, and so there was a slight constraint. There was more drive on academic work, and less opportunity for the teacher to be the scribe for the children's ideas. Perhaps, too, there were changes in the children themselves that led to different kinds of expression. The compact lyrical form may be more natural to the younger age. We do not know. Whatever the reason, Joanne turned to stories and to playing with the sounds of words. Often a tempting title was made up first, such as "Why Witches are Waterproof," or "The Short, Short Sink That Went to Heaven," and then a fitting story concocted. She struggled earnestly to be her own amanuensis, with results that were untidy, inaccurate, and often half-finished. Her clerical power could not keep pace with her flashing mind. But even under such difficulties she continued to experiment, to find joy in the doing, and to produce a few things that were truly good. Sometimes sound and rhythm engrossed her, quite to the exclusion of sense. In "The Haunted House" there are music and mood, but there is little logical meaning. Note, however, the directions she gave at the end for the reading.

The Haunted House

Once there was a house on the grey still ground;
Once there was a house all misty with fog.
Once there was a house and ghosts lived in it.
Once there was a house all boards a-shaking.
Once there was a house; nine grey old men lived in it.
(Fast, lightly) Down by the wayside, there's that house.
(Slowly) Witches are in it, but DON'T go there.

Consistently, everything that Joanne did revealed her as a free, intuitive worker. Her arithmetic, after the first few examples, never went in orderly rows, and her writing jumped from pigmy to giant in a single line. Her art work was distinguished by its spontaneity and its rhythmic movement and even her factual reports were transformed by her imagination into episodes that were vivid and alive. During her fifth year she made a study of ants, at the end of which she submitted the following resumé. It is not a report at all, but a fanciful incident focused dramatically on the queen and the royal eggs. In it, however, an abundance of information is evident, information that she had made truly her own. Since it was to be part of a class book, Joanne, with her teacher, edited her report to this extent.

My Trip Through the Ant Hill

"Oh, Mr. Guide," I said, "what is that tunnel and why is it so long?" "Well," said the guide, "it's this way. The queen of this state is laying eggs there and does not want to be disturbed." "Do you think she would mind me seeing her?" I said. "Well, I'll

see," said the guide; so he went to the door. "Knock, knock."
"Yes," came a voice. "What do you want?" "Well," said the
guide, "I have a visitor and she wants to see you." "Show her
in," said the voice again. The guide led me through many
passages till he came to a door. "Knock, knock." "Come in. I am
expecting you." The guide opened the door and bowed.
"Your—your—Majesty," blushed the guide, "here is your visitor." I had seen many things, but none so beautifully made. The
walls were solid and hard and shining dirt. All were even with no
faults anywhere. After a while the queen said, "Do you know
how I make my kingdom?" and she laughed, "I should say
queendom. Well," she went on, "I lay eggs and every once in a
while I lay a royal egg which is a male or prince or queen. The
male and queen are rare; but princes quite common." "Oh," I
said, "that's interesting. I always thought . . . Well I don't know
what I thought." "Well," she said, "you had better be going
because I have to lay my eggs." The guide took me out and said,
"Would you like to see our workers? You know," he said as he
went along, "we only have a few men and women to mate. Most
of our people are workers which are neither males or females."
"Oh," I said, "that seems impossible." "Well, it isn't," he said.

By this time we had reached a tunnel. An ant was guarding
it. "No one allowed!" he said excitedly. "No one allowed!
Danger of falling pebbles. No one allowed. It is a newly made
tunnel and we are making room for the royal eggs. No one
allowed!" And I saw a pile of white eggs or cocoons. I looked
closely and a black head peeked out of one. Then came the
body. Then we went on. Suddenly a great commotion fell over
the ant hill. All subjects were running to and fro. The new tunnel
was finished and eggs were being stored away. I asked my guide
what was happening and he said, "There is a war and we are
against the red ants. Most of our workers are fighting and not
many are left to do the storing of eggs." Soon the war was over
and it was victory for the Black Ants. "Well, I must be going
now," I said. And that ends my chapter and I hope you enjoyed
it.

The End

This is not a true story.

The same spring, caught up in the class enthusiasm for "The Five
Bears," Joanne wrote a story strongly marked by her individual traits. It
had no plot but was rather a series of lively pictures with touches of fun and

shrewd observations of human behavior. Part I—a sort of introduction—follow.

The Five Bears Have a Spring Festival
with Surprising Results

Part I

"Ma!" called Bo as he came down the path, "we're having a spring what-cha-ma-call-it, and I dress up as the Big Bad Wolf. Eenie, Teenie, and Tiny are the three pigs and Pug's the announcer. Sue's the Mother Pig. She has to fasten two pillows in front of her to make her fat and some string on for a tail, and you," he added, crossing his arms, "have to make us jackets."

"Well," said Mrs. Bear for the first time that she was able to speak, "well, that's nice."

"Ma! Ma! got to tell you sumpin'," yelled Teenie dashing down the path with the other three bears at his heels.

Then Bo said calmly, "I told it all."

"Oh!" Teenie's jaw dropped, "you would."

"No, he didn't," said Mother, "what is it?"

"Well," Teenie brightened up, "it's a festival—a spring festival. Nice?"

Although Joanne revealed originality and distinction in her writing, she was woefully inadequate in the skills. Through the fifth grade she evaded all our efforts to teach her. In her eyes, to spell and write correctly were hard work and useless. She was having fun playing with her mind, and she wasn't caring at all about appearances. Of course, we could have been insistent and perhaps thereby have made Joanne a better speller, but we might also have stopped all spontaneous outpouring. So, instead, we lowered the usual demands made in practical writing to match her undeveloped power and watched for opportunities to commend her slightest effort to improve her use of the prescribed skills. In her sixth school year our faith and forbearance were justified. Joanne was eleven when suddenly she came to care about her use of tool techniques, and she exerted enough well-directed effort to accomplish reasonable mastery of them. She always found it difficult to conform to set patterns, to discipline that pixie spirit within her. But she managed to write with acceptable correctness and with unabated satisfaction and joy.

ARTHUR, GRADES THREE THROUGH SIX

Because Arthur appeared to be always sweet-tempered and at ease, few people realized how much he was haunted by the fear of being inadequate. Lacking all inner assurance of power, he leaned heavily on the approval of others and worked as earnestly as he knew how to deserve it. On the playground his athletic ability combined with his strong desire to keep everybody happy made him a popular leader but in the classroom satisfaction did not come so easily. In his eagerness to do the expected thing he seized upon the forms, rather than the substance, of learning. Whatever the task, he set at it quickly and worked with dogged determination, though usually to the wrong purpose. In reading he aimed to call words and cover ground, in arithmetic to keep farthest ahead in assignments, and in practical writing to produce numbers of correct papers limited in vocabulary to the confines of his own scant spelling power. His workmanship was tidy, and he was always among the first to finish because neatness and speed were to him evidence of success.

For a long time we believed he could do no better. We respected his gallant though misdirected effort and accepted gratefully such meager accounts as the following:

An Experience

One time my Mother and brother and I was walking by a lake in California and I thought I saw a fish but it was a crab. I jumped in and I nearly drowned, but my brother got a stick and pulled me out.

Then one day when the class enthusiasm for telling "poetry ideas" ran high, Arthur's feeling was so stirred that it broke through the mask that had effectually concealed him. This time he had a real experience to tell, one that had touched him intimately. Without fear or hesitation he dictated:

Orchestra

When I blow the bugle
It's such a funny noise
And when I blow it for my father
He laughs at me.
And then when I grew up
I was in a big orchestra
And my father came to watch me
And he Didn't laugh

This and other dictations that followed exposed a sensitive, proud little boy who wanted too much to please people—not the shallow, unimaginative child we had thought him to be.

Arthur began the next year by writing an impressive number of letters to all of the friends he had made at camp—the counselor and caretakers as well as the boys. The following immature note is a fair sample of them all:

Dear Robert Dixon:

I hope you are not sick. And I hope you are feeling well because I am. Please write soon and tell me what grade you are in. I am in the fifth grade. I guess you are in the fourth grade.

Love from
Arthur

This was the only kind of voluntary writing he did for weeks and weeks. Eventually, however, he too began having such fun over the adventures of "The Five Bears" that again he forgot himself and made up a story called "The Pond," which surprised us by its length as well as its merit. It strongly reflected his happy life at camp, but his memories of the woods, the pond, and the games in the water have been converted by his imagination into a new story. In it he showed a power to handle language that we had never suspected. Note the effectiveness of the opening sentence, the suggestion of character, the movement, the action, and graphic quality of the whole. Some errors in form have been corrected for easier reading.

The Pond

On the steps of a shack on the edge of the woods were the five little bears. Their names were Eenie, Teenie, Tiny, Bo, and Pug. Teenie said, "Let's go swimming at the pond."

Bo said, "Where it is?"

Eenie said, "Don't you remember? It is about a half mile away."

"Come on," said Teenie.

"Let's go. What are we waiting for?" said Bo. So they started down the woods without telling their mother or anyone.

Teenie said, "Don't you think we better tell Father or Mother?"

"No," said Pug, who was very bad. "Why do Mother and Father Bear always have to know where we go?"

"Oh, well, let's go," said Bo, so off they went. Soon they came to the pond.

"Here it is," said Pug, "I will beat you in."

"Oh, yeah," said Teenie.

"You wait and see," said Pug. Off went Pug's pants and shirt and off went Teenie's dress and bonnet and there was a splash and then another.

"I beat you," said Teenie.

"So what?" said Pug. And then came three more splashes.

"Let's play tag," said Eenie.

"No," said Teenie, "let's play leap frog."

"O.K.," said the rest of the bears. The pond was four feet deep.

"I am scared," said Bo, "I want to be the first one because it is too deep in the middle."

"I am not scared," said Pug. "I will be the last one to be jumped over. Eenie, you be second. And Teenie, you be third; Tiny, you be fourth. And I will be last. Bo, you jump over Eenie and then over Teenie and then over Tiny. Last of all jump over me."

Over the first he went, then the second, then the third, and then the fourth, but where was Pug? Then they saw a lot of bubbles forming on top of the pond.

Bo said, "I bet he has drowned. How will we get him?"

"Eenie, you can swim under water. You get him," said Tiny. So under he went and brought Pug up.

"My, he looks fat," said Bo.

"He isn't fat," said Tiny.

"He drank a lot of water and he got blown up and can't talk," said Eenie.

"Let's sit up in the tree and put him under it to dry," said Tiny. So they did and while they were up there Eenie fell and landed right on Pug's stomach and all the water squirted out and he woke up.

"What happened?" said Pug.

"You blew up," said Teenie.

"What?" said Pug.

"You blew up," said Bo.

"Let's go home," said Tiny.

The End

Arthur was so lacking in self-faith that he dared not reach down into himself to discover and express his own thoughts and feelings. Therefore he fed his hunger for satisfaction with the social approval he received. All of his work was stereotyped. Only on these few occasions when a wave of feeling swept him out of his usual narrow channel of behavior did he reveal his potential power.

This case was especially meaningful to us because it showed us that we frequently may underestimate children's abilities. The customary school procedures seem to freeze them in the limiting patterns that they have already established. Undoubtedly, more learning experiences that are not set in conventional molds are needed to stimulate genuine personal interest. Only through such experiences can children free themselves so that they can begin to express their own possibilities.

LUCY, GRADES TWO THROUGH SIX

It is often surprising to see how clearly a child reveals the true self in writing. An adult might have known Lucy for some time without being aware of her unique qualities. She was an unobtrusive child, sensitive and shy without being aloof, and capable with none of the aggressive or irritating characteristics frequently implied by that word. Yet no one could have read what Lucy wrote and remained ignorant of the nature of her personality. Even her earliest stories exposed a power of sustained logical thinking, a love of fun, a rich, but realistic imagination, and an ability to lose herself in what that imagination created. Probably the fact that she was an only child kept at home frequently by slight illnesses fostered the development of these traits. Warmhearted and lonely, she found companionship in stories—usually stories she read, but sometimes those she invented. When she was working upon one of her own, she lingered over the fun of making it up, savoring each personality, each bit of adventure, each possibility for laughter. She never created rapidly in spontaneous outbursts. Stories did not pour forth from her as they did from Joanne or Danny. Instead, they were fashioned with leisurely and affectionate care. The ideas emerged slowly and lay for some time in her mind taking on shape and depth and color. Eventually she wrote them down. There was no need for haste because the story had been completely possessed and patterned before the writing began. Consequently her first drafts were reasonably correct and tidy. But they were still work sheets to Lucy, and she went over them thoughtfully, substituting a more exact word here or adding an enriching detail there. Such capacity for long-continued and painstaking effort is not usual for a child. It was, however, an essential feature of Lucy's personality and was evident in all that she did. Once in clay modeling she had worked for several successive periods on the figure of a dwarf. To the teacher it looked finished and so it was set on the shelf to dry, where Lucy found it, next art period. "Oh," she demurred, "I wasn't through. There were some little things I wanted to do to it." Thus she followed her own deliberate rhythm of working toward the high standards that she herself had set.

In the second grade Lucy wrote "The Story of a Car." It is long as second-grade stories go, and it shows thoughtful planning. Moreover, in spite of all the magical happenings, it is at heart a realistic story. Upon getting its wings the car does not go adventuring in the air, as a more fanciful child might have had it do, but instead it lands "plunk" in its own garage.

The Story of a Car

Once there was a doctor and he had a very nice car. One day the doctor had to see a sick person, so he jumped into the car and off he went. While he was inside, the car drove off. It went on and on. While the car was going down the road it met a kangaroo. The car stopped and asked the kangaroo to give him a pair of his hind legs. So he gave him a pair and the car went hopping off. Pretty soon it met a leopard. The car asked the leopard if he would give him some spots and he said "Yes." So the car said "Thank you" and went on. Pretty soon he met a bird. He asked the bird to give a pair of wings. The bird said he would so the car tried to fly, but the car was too heavy that the wings could not hold it up. So down the car came and plunk it was in its own garage.

All of Lucy's free writing was narrative. During the next two years, when most of the children in her group were interested in reporting their "poetry thoughts," she made no contribution. Finally, toward the close of the fourth grade, she began to write stories which were clearly an outgrowth of her reading. The idea, the phrases, perhaps even the design were unconsciously borrowed, but the power to imagine vividly was Lucy's own.

In fifth grade Lucy wrote "The Five Bears and William Whiskers," which shows a remarkable gain in the patience and the power necessary to record a complete story as she saw and felt it in her mind. In it there is a warm human quality and a sense of completeness that could come only with slow ripening. This was her single offering during the time that Danny produced thirty or more. While his active mind was bent on creating adventure after adventure for rather puppetlike characters, Lucy was cultivating such an intimacy with the people about whom she wrote that what happened grew naturally out of the kind of folks they were. Undoubtedly it was Danny's unflagging and sometimes strange invention that did

141

most to maintain the lively interest in the story-reading period during the fifth year, but it was Lucy's single story that sharpened the group's awareness for the more subtle qualities of characterization and style. A few corrections in punctuation have been added.

The Five Little Bears and William Whiskers

One sunny afternoon the five little bears were walking the ridge pole of their roof. Their cousin, Nellie Bear, had come over to visit them. She was such a golden brown little bear that even baby Bo admired her. Pug just loved to show Nellie how far he could walk on the ridge pole without tottering too much. He was just doing that now. His arms were wide apart and the leg he wasn't standing on was always swinging. The other five bears were sitting on chimneys swinging their short fluffy legs. But Nellie didn't look very happy. She kept glancing down at the ground and holding the edge of the chimney so tight that her knuckles showed white. Just then Bo said in his small voice:

"I'm hungry," and he began to whimper.

"Oh, all right," answered Pug. "We can take some fruit home from William Whiskers, the old billy goat gardener. He won't mind."

"You hope," put in Eenie.

"Let's go down the drainpipe," said Pug.

"O.K.," said Eenie. So the six little bears whizzed down the drainpipe. Splash!

"Oh, dear," said Nellie. All six little bears had landed in the rain barrel. "Oh dear," said Nellie again, "I'm wet."

"I think," said Eenie, who was always making wise cracks, "I think we slid down the wrong drainpipe."

"I wouldn't doubt it," said Tiny.

"Well," said Pug, "let's go to the orchard. We're men. We won't let a little water stop us, will we?"

"No," said Eenie, Teenie, Tiny, and Nellie together.

"No," said Bo last of all in his weak little voice.

So they all started out for the orchard single file, Bo taking up the rear as usual. They got to the orchard, but just as they were coming out with the fruit, down the path came old William Whiskers whistling a sailor tune. He had been a sailor a long time ago, and he had beautiful red and blue tattoos up and down his arms. The little bears dashed down the path past him and into the road still holding the apples and pears. William Whiskers stopped short and then ran after them, calling, "Ahoy, there—Ahoy, there! To the starboard! Port! Drop the anchor! Blast ye!"

"There's Father's car," yelled Pug. "Jump in!"

They did. Then Pug stepped on the starter. He thought he could drive, but five minutes' driving brought them to the brink of a lake. Plunk! The car was in it. Luckily it was an open car, and in a minute up popped Pug sitting on a cushion, and last of all Nellie and Bo clinging to each other.

"What do we do now?" said Eenie, blowing the water out of his nose.

"Nothing but wait," said Pug, hitting the side of his head to get the water out of his ears.

All of a sudden apples and pears began to pop up on every side.

"They look very nice in the water, don't they?" said Tiny.

"They'd look better in my stomach," said Bo.

"I could get them it I had my butterfly net," said Teenie. You see he was very interested in insects.

"My stomach doesn't feel good," said Nellie. "Boating never did agree with it."

"Mine doesn't feel top hole either," broke in Bo weakly.

Just then William Whiskers appeared. He began to laugh. He laughed and he laughed and he laughed.

"Oh, please get us out," said Nellie.

"On one condition," said William Whiskers.

"What is it?" said Pug.

"It is," said William Whiskers, "that you stay out of my orchard."

"We will," said Bo.

"Oh, sure we will," said the rest of the little bears. Then William Whiskers got a rope and threw it out to the bears. Then he put the other end around his horse and pulled. Soon they were on the bank of the lake.

"Oh, what a relief," said Nellie, with a deep sigh.

"And we promise we won't take any more fruit," said Pug.

Everybody was happy, especially William Whiskers. But one week after if you had looked at the spikes on top of the orchard gate, you would have seen little pieces of brown fur and little pieces of blue trousers that can come off nothing but little bears.

When Lucy had finished reading "William Whiskers," the response of the class was unique. Instead of the restless, excited approval that usually greeted the stories they liked, there was a pause and then a fervent, "Oh, that was good!" We talked a little then—a very little—about how clearly we had seen the funny, moving pictures. We spoke, too, of how the ending had pleased us because it was exactly what might be expected of those mischievous little bears. Besides, it tempted us to go on imagining what happened the next time they got caught.

This experience illustrates how we did most of our teaching of story writing. Lessons were never worked out in advance. Instead, we seized upon an effective use of a technique when it appeared. Then by appreciation—not by precept—we focused attention upon it, hoping thereby to infect the children with its worth. This does not mean that after the single instance of talking over "William Whiskers" the next crop of stories all had excellent endings and a wealth of concrete detail. Well-rooted growth comes slowly; hence we neither expected nor desired such miracles. Our purpose was, through repeated exposure, to lead the children to recognize and to appreciate some of the factors of good writing. We knew that each child would gradually appropriate the techniques for which he was ready.

In the early stages we chose basics in story structure, such as beginnings that evoked curiosity quickly, interesting inventions or surprise turnings, the sense of movement, and satisfying closings. Later we watched for the more mature techniques of lucid and convincing style. Natural audience reactions fortified our praise. In fact we believe that it was the audience situation—the age-old pleasure of telling one's tale directly to eager listeners—that inevitably drew forth the story qualities that grip and stir the imagination. Each child, being listener and writer in turn, became increasingly aware of what to do to hold his hearers in expectant attention to the end. It was out of their successes that story form naturally grew.

In the sixth grade Lucy wrote much more freely and abundantly. Her stories though perhaps not so compactly organized as the one about William Whiskers, grew richer in human insight and significant detail, as evidenced by the following excerpt from "The Hero." Through them all, too, ran an undercurrent of fun, as though she herself were highly amused by the way her characters behaved.

The Hero

Pug was on his bed pulling his shoes on and thinking very hard. "Gosh," he whispered, "I wonder what she's like. Maybe she's like Nellie's baby calf, but gee, I don't think I'd like that," he added, "or maybe like the puppies Roland Bear's dog had." Pug was thinking like this because his very own mother had had a baby. It was a girl. All he knew was that the five bears had to be very quiet, and he was very curious. Pug could hear Father Bear tiptoeing up the stairs. Father was trying to keep house. He pushed open Pug's door softly.

"Come down to breakfast," he hissed, and tiptoed out again.

Pug slid off the bed and followed the other bears downstairs. They had named the baby Daisy Mae. Father was doing the cooking. He had on a big checked apron and his hands were dripping with something. "Oh, can't someone help me?" he whispered almost in tears. "This is killing me. I hope we don't have any more children. Isn't six children enough?"

"I'll help," said Pug weakly. He brought in the food. The five bears grunted softly. Father Bear did not know how to cook.

"I don't think we're so hungry," hissed Bo.

Pug walked to school with half the school around him. "And," he continued, "I'm going to see her this afternoon."

"Gosh," said Roy Bear, "do you think she's real?"

"Well," answered Pug doubtfully, "I'm not so sure."

Pug was the center of attention at school. No one had ever had a baby sister before. Even the teacher was interested although Pug couldn't keep his mind on his work. "How's your mother?" she asked.

"O.K.," answered Pug. He was dreaming of little babies with wings on their backs.

The five little bears were standing outside Mother Bear's door. They were all very nervous although they tried not to show it. Pug was thinking, "What if she's awful funny looking after all I've told the kids at school."

"I'm not so sure I want to see her," murmured Bo.

"Oh, don't be so dumb!" whispered Pug, whose knees felt like water. Then the door opened. Pug said, "hello," to his Mother hastily, looking the other way at a crib in a dim corner of the room. He walked over to it and peeked in. There was the sweetest little brown ball that Pug had ever seen. "Oh—gee—gosh—oh my," he whispered. He was overcome with surprise. The other bears were watching the baby too. "Gee, could I touch her?" Pug asked. Mother Bear nodded. Hesitatingly Pug touched the soft little paw. He smiled down at the baby. The baby smiled back. Pug just stood there a while looking at the baby. Then he began to recover himself. He thought he must look very silly. Before he hadn't cared. Now he did. He saw Mother Bear smiling at him. "Pretty nice brat," he said, hastily trying to break the silence.

"I think she likes you best," Mother Bear answered. "She's smiling at you." Mother Bear tried to keep the amusement out of her voice. Pug blushed a deep red. Mother Bear could see his ears turning red.

"I think she's swell," cooed Bo. "Don't you, Tiny?"

"Uh, huh," answered Tiny, turning pink. He knew he was in bad with Pug for saying it.

"I agree," chorused the other two bears. They were a little scared too.

After they had gone outside Pug called a conference. "Now listen," he growled in his toughest voice, "I don't think I like her so much, but I'm older and I'm more careful so when she gets old enough and can go out I'm going to take her out, see! And understand first I don't like her. I just want to take her out."

Eenie murmured something like, "Oh yeah," but nobody heard him, which was lucky for him.

About the time she wrote "The Hero," Lucy's class was studying weather as part of their science program. The children had chosen to record their findings in booklets, an idea that the classroom teacher encouraged because she knew the problems in expression that they would encounter. After the science teacher demonstrated the making of a mercury barometer, they set to work readily enough, thinking it would be easy to write down what had happened. Soon, however, brows began to pucker, and one after another was unable to go on. Much of the difficulty lay, they concluded, in their lack of exact observation and understanding. So the demonstration was performed again, and points that had been vague were talked over. A second time they set to work at their writing, but they still found it an onerous task. Some gathered in small groups to read to one another and to ask for help on the parts that were not yet clear. Lucy's report done after the second demonstration showed her understanding of how the thermometer worked.

Making a Mercury Barometer

Mr. Allen filled a tube with mercury. The tube was about 36 inches long. One end of the tube was sealed as in picture A. No air was in the tube. Next Mr. Allen put some mercury in a bowl.

146

The bowl was about ⅓ full. Next he put his finger over the open end of the tube, turned it upside down, and put the open end into the bowl. It was quite difficult because the mercury tried to escape. No air got in because the end of the tube was in the mercury. Then the mercury escaped into the bowl as far as it could against the pressure of the air, as in picture B. No air could have gotten into the space at the top. So all that was in there was a vacuum. Mercury is very heavy. Vacuum has no power. When the tube was full, it was heavier than air. But when the four inches of mercury escaped, it was no longer heavier. The air and the mercury in the tube went down as far as it could against the pressure of the air. The air was pushing all around as in picture C, trying to get into the vacuum. In pushing down on the mercury in the bowl it held up the mercury in the tube.

The whole emphasis was on making the report as accurate as possible. Nothing was said about the abrupt beginning or the short, jerky sentences. Such awkward expression invariably occurs when children start writing in a new field. They feel the same lack of sureness that an artist feels when he undertakes to work in a new medium. Fluency of expression comes only after much experience in this different way of thinking, and writing at this point can serve best by revealing the inadequacies in that thinking. As the ideas and relationships become more familiar, sentence structure improves. This we know from experience.

Through six years we watched Lucy's growth with justifiable delight. From a shy little girl who flamed with embarrassment at the slightest provocation, she developed into a poised and able child. Many factors contributed to this wholesome change, not the least of which was the satisfaction and approval that came to her through her story writing. Because the stories she wrote were so intimate a creation, she felt their warm reception as a reception of herself. Slowly but steadily she grew in assurance and self-esteem. The rich quality of her writing gave impulse and direction to her group's writing improvement. We frankly admit that children like Lucy do our most fruitful teaching.

PAT, GRADES THREE THROUGH SIX

From the beginning a certain neat directness was characteristic of Pat and all his work. In science and arithmetic he showed remarkable precision even at eight years of age. Interestingly enough, his art work was superior and characterized by manifestations of this precision. His painting and clay modeling were distinguished by a strong sense of design and a dramatic use of color. In contrast to Ruth's uncertainty and fearfulness were Pat's clean-cut sense of direction and economical route to achievement. Though not outstanding in ability, his sureness of approach and his selection of significant detail gave power to everything he wrote. His thrifty style is evident in the following story, written at eight.

Little Rabbit

Once there was a little rabbit. One day he went down to the river to get a drink. On the way he met a fox. Now this was a very wicked fox. He had tried to catch little rabbit and now he had him. The fox sprang. Little rabbit tried to run, but the fox was too quick for him. The fox took little rabbit to his den. Then the fox tried to eat little rabbit. But when he had his hands on him little rabbit bit him. Then the fox screamed. So at last the fox let him go and never tried to catch him again.

This story had several errors in sentence structure and in spelling, which was Pat's Waterloo. However, the tale served its immediate purpose: the group was entertained, and Pat was pleased.

During the following year increasing experience in the practical phases of writing provided both the necessity and the opportunity for correcting mechanics. It was characteristic of Pat's whole makeup that he should assimilate most of these skills quickly and thoroughly. He did all the required writing with ease, but never produced an abundance of personal writing. Perhaps this was due in part to his ability to express himself effectively in art.

Pat was nine when he wrote "Mr. Ghost's Night Out." This story shows a decided growth in his particular narrative style and increased facility in the mechanics of writing. Several errors in spelling have been corrected.

Mr. Ghost's Night Out

One night Mr. Ghost sneaked out to play poker with the other ghosts. They played about two hours. Then Mr. Ghost looked at the clock. He snatched his hat from the post and ran home. But meanwhile Mrs. Ghost had found out he had gone and grabbed her rolling pin and started out to look for him. About halfway between the two houses they met. And in the dim light Mrs. Ghost saw a dark figure of Mr. Ghost. But she did not know who it was. A terrified look came over her face. She let out a scream and threw up her hands. The rolling pin went sailing into the bushes and away she went yelling and screaming blue murder. However she got home. Mr. Ghost ran home a different way. They got home at the same time. When Mr. Ghost came in Mrs. Ghost told all about what had happened and Mr. Ghost patted her on the back and said, "Don't worry. I'll protect you," and he took her off to bed.

Even though "Mr. Ghost's Night Out" is a much more ample tale than "Little Rabbit," its greater length is due to a larger concept of plot and not to superfluous detail. Note the incident in which "Mr. Ghost looked at the clock." Pat left interpretation to his audience but chose significant detail from which the reader can sketch the rest of the picture. Again, in the ending, Pat avoided the trivial, which clutters up much of children's writing.

Pat was especially adept at letter writing, for he enjoyed addressing his ideas to a particular audience. Here is a letter written when Pat was ten. Note the choice in telling detail and the richness of implication in its placement.

Dear Uncle John,

We had an art exhibit in school. We hung all our pictures we had made this year in our classroom or in the halls. Most of the children made clay models, too. These we put in glass cases in the halls or laid them on the ledges in our room. All the children in my class made a picture of either an imaginary or a real flower. The day after our mothers came we went around to the different groups to see the other classes' pictures. The sixth grade in my opinion had the best ideas but they didn't always have the best painting.

I hope that you are much better now and that you will soon be able to be out again.

Love,
Pat

Of course, this is a real letter of which the second draft was actually sent to Uncle John.

Writing, both practical and personal, increased rapidly in amount throughout the fifth and sixth grades. At first, Pat's power of selection when confronted with a wide and somewhat confusing array of material for a report produced an inadequate and telescopic jumble of undigested information.

Later reports, one on armor, for example, for which appropriate

149

references were available, show a reasonably thorough assimilation of facts and a more adequate presentation. A portion of this report is quoted here.

An armorer also made suits for knights to wear under their armor. To make a suit of mail the armorer took a small iron bar. This he heated and pounded until it was like a fine wire. Then he wound it around a small stake so that it took the shape of a circle. At that point he cut the wire into a link the ends of which he flattened and pierced and fastened together with a tiny nail. Often the nail was not larger than the head of a pin. When one link was fastened another was put through it and fastened in the same way. A shirt in a museum was estimated to have a hundred thousand links in it.

This paragraph contains facts garnered from three references, but Pat's increasing skill in selecting detail plus his realization of the dangers of telescoping material produced a clear and interesting picture.

One of the last stories Pat wrote in the sixth grade may well be contrasted with "Little Rabbit," for in it one can mark the same qualities, though strengthened and expanded, that were lightly indicated in that early story. Spelling errors have been corrected; otherwise it is exactly as Pat wrote it.

One day on the beach of Plome Island a white speck was sighted not far from land. As it came closer the bathers realized that it was a sea monster. From the water, women's screams pierced the air. For days no one ventured near the water until one day when there was no speck in sight, two men went in and swam out quite far. Then one of the men whose name was Joshua felt something very slimy against his legs. Now he was quite a show-off on shore with his loud bathing suit but in the water with this thing around his feet he sang a different tune. "Help," sputtered the unfortunate man, at the same time floundering wildly. His companion, seeing the antics of his friend, thought he was crazy and started swimming for shore as fast as he could. Meanwhile Joshua saw that the thing was slowly but surely coming to the surface of the water. When it came up far enough for him to see it plainly he found it was a dead shark. Seeing that it could do him no harm he turned it toward shore and was highly praised for his work. It was later found out that the "sea monster" was this dead shark because when a fish is dead it floats with its stomach up so that the white speck that was

150

supposed to be the sea monster was the dead shark Joshua found floating around beyond the breakers.

Pat's own neat way of telling a story remained unchanged during the three years since "Little Rabbit," but time brought growth and refinement of his style. Contrast, for instance, the characterizations "a very wicked fox" and "He was quite a show-off on shore with his loud bathing suit . . ." Both are quick, but the latter is subtle as well. The same direct, economical narration, the thrifty choice of detail, the same shorthand characterization will no doubt always distinguish Pat's writing, for they are as much a part of him as his straight back and steady blue eyes.

SARAH, GRADES THREE THROUGH SIX

Sarah was indeed a rare child. Seldom does one meet a person of so many dimensions. Physically large, often clumsy, interested and able in almost every field, whether artistic or academic, Sarah radiated a generous warmth that permeated all she did and fairly engulfed her friends and associates. She wrote copiously and well. She was gifted in music, studied both piano and violin, sang well, and had an unusually acute ear. Sarah's greatest love was for dramatics. She had an amazing insight into human nature and unusual power to create and interpret a wide variety of characters. Superior ability in art was but another part of this extraordinary constellation of talents.

Intellectually Sarah was also richly endowed, and she explored each new world of ideas as zestfully as she hurled herself into a game. This verve was coupled with almost irrepressible high spirits, which made Sarah an unusually delightful person. But sometimes her joyous headlong pace, joined with a complete disregard for the value of material things, wearied her teacher and companions. Sarah, for instance, had great difficulty learning to take care of her belongings or even to put her desk in order. Nevertheless, she welcomed severe correction with her usual generous spirit.

Though absent more than half of her third school year, Sarah was one of the first to turn from storytelling to story writing. Even at this early age she showed keen invention and a flair for the dramatic, as can be seen in the following story. We have added some of the quotation marks and corrected the paragraphing.

A Story

Once there was a poor little boy. His name was Bobby. Bobby wanted to go to the circus. But he didn't have any money.

151

His father was dead, he lived all alone with his mother. The circus had come to town that day and Bobby's heart was set on going. He had never been to one before. The boys on the block said it was wonderful. He asked his mother whether she would give him twenty-five cents to go to the circus.

"My son," she would say, weeping, "you ought to be glad you have bread and butter."

The next day Bobby went near the tents. He was just going to go in when a rough hand grabbed him. "Give me your money," said the man. And before Bobby could say "Jack Robinson," he landed neatly on the hard ground.

That night Bobby asked his mother whether he could get a job at the circus.

"Yes," was her reply.

The next morning Bobby got dressed and ran down to the circus grounds. Again the gruff man asked what he wanted there. "I want a job," Bobby replied.

"All right, what's your name?"

"My name is Bobby. What's yours?"

"My name is Bill. The manager is over there."

That afternoon Bobby White, for that was his name, came rushing home.

"Mother," he said, jumping and shouting, "I got a job at the circus and I can see the show free."

"But what do you do? How much pay do you get?" his puzzled mother asked.

"I carry water for the animals and I get twenty dollars a week."

Bobby went to the circus.

The dramatic quality of this situation and the method of its resolution are too obvious to need pointing out. Even at eight, Sarah enjoyed a cleverly turned phrase and graphic word, such as: "his puzzled mother asked" and " 'My son,' she would say weeping, 'you ought to be glad you have bread and butter.' "

At nine Sarah was writing copiously, and in addition to rich invention and dramatic quality other essentials of good writing began to appear. For example, contrast the structure of the first three sentences of Sarah's circus story with the first three sentences of "The Wormy Snake." Sarah was already alert to balance of sentence arrangement and quite unconsciously made use of a delightful cadence or euphonious quality in her choice of word and phrase. Note also Sarah's sly observation in the instance of Snapper's confession of what had not even been noticed by the unobservant school marm. Only two minor corrections in mechanics have been made.

The Wormy Snake

High in the tree-tops Miss Songster called all her pupils to singing class. One by one they came, Jenny Wren, Bob White, Jr., Cluck Cluck, Peep Peep, and many others. After all the rest were there, in walked Snapper.

"Snapper," said Miss Songster's sharp voice. "Why are you so late?"

"I—er—fell down."

"Well, never mind. I am going to call the cards."

Nobody liked singing lessons, especially the boys. But they couldn't play hookie because if anyone was absent Miss Songster would call up their mothers and ask them if their child was sick. If the mother said no, then when the children came home they would get a spanking.

But Snapper had a little scheme of his own. After the roll was called Miss Songster didn't pay any attention to the children. He sneaked out while she wasn't looking. When he was out of sight he thought he'd dig a worm. He did not have to dig because there was one right on the ground in front of him. It was a great big one, too. He tried to pick it up. It was too heavy. The animal turned around. Snapper saw what a mistake he had made. It was a Rattlesnake. Snapper had been strictly warned about snakes.

He flew back to the schoolhouse with unusual speed. Snapper confessed everything. Miss Songster was a bit puzzled. She had not yet noticed Snapper's absence and she was surprised he confessed.

Snapper is now the best singer in Birdland and he doesn't mistake snakes for worms.

During fifth grade when the group was hit by an epidemic of mystery stories, Sarah produced one as bloodcurdling and stereotyped as all the others but still marked by a rich flow of language and by varied techniques of characterization.

Sarah, like many other children, got positively gleeful from inventing preposterous names, as indicated in the following excerpt from a fifth-grade story:

153

pitcher which broke instantly. The princess suddenly turned into the fairy.

"For your meanness, I shall give you a gift. Whenever you speak a snake or a viper will come out of your mouth."

"Humph," said Fannie. A snake came out of her mouth and she went home. When she got there her mother said:

"Tell me what happened, sweet, and I'll count the jewels that come out of your mouth."

"It's all that miserable creature's fault," said Fannie (a lizard and a viper came out of her mouth), "and that horrible witch's!" And she told the whole story.

By the time she was through the kitchen floor was full of snakes and toads and lizards. The widow gave Janice a beating and turned her out of the house. Janice wandered into the woods and lay down and cried. Now the sovereign of the country who happened to be coming back from a fox hunt, saw this fair girl weeping on the ground and asked her what was wrong. Janice told him how her mother had turned her out (not sparing the jewels and flowers). The king was very angry and wanted the wicked mother and daughter executed but Janice, being very kind, would not have it. The king took her to his palace and there they were married and lived happily ever after.

Space prohibits the inclusion of any other fifth-grade writing, personal or practical. But Sarah, of course, did the expected amount of writing of letters, records, brief reports, and shared in the preparation of a science book about trees for a second grade in her school. The latter offered an excellent opportunity to practice simple, clear writing. And considerable practice was needed! The entire group profited from the discipline of exact expression and continuity of organization.

During the sixth grade momentum increased tremendously, partly because the prewriting stages of development had been richly explored. Though Sarah wrote frequently with a partner or two, only a few examples of her individual writing are shown here. When the sixth-grade group was making a series of industrial studies in geography, Sarah chose to study oranges and wrote an extended report noteworthy for its improvement in organization.

Another piece of work done by Sarah during her sixth year was entirely self-chosen. She had visited Austria at one time and had heard much about the days of the "dual monarchy," a phrase in which she took delight. With the class she keenly enjoyed hearing Kate Seredy's *White*

Stag and brought her own copy to school to hold and look at while the teacher finished reading the last chapters. When the class was studying medieval life, any reference to the Huns was sure to evoke some special response from Sarah. Her report was heartily enjoyed by the class. An excerpt follows.

The Huns

There are few certain facts known about the early Huns. In medieval books (which are very few) they were only spoken of unfavorably.

The Huns were very small in stature but their bones were strong. They also were very quick on their feet. These small men often had to endure unimaginable hardships. A Hun sometimes lived on his horse for days. This made him bow-legged. His broad face, large ears and slit-eyes half scared people out of their wits. He had no hair on his face except perhaps for a fierce mustache. When they were babies hot irons were applied to their faces and all the hair on cheek and chin was burned out. That accounts for all the scars on their faces in later years. Another custom of the Huns was to wash each new born babe out in the open air (regardless of winter or summer) and give it a bath every day for forty-two days (six weeks). These were to last it for the rest of its life. Cattle could not stand the rough life the Hun led so he had to keep sheep and horses. Sometimes he had camels. His food consisted of milk products (preferably mares' milk) and sometimes horses' blood. They also ate half raw meat which they warmed by putting it between their and their horse's body. . . .

References are duly quoted by pages so that notes can be rechecked if necessary, a technique highly respected by Sarah and the whole group. The last story written by Sarah in the sixth grade follows:

"I can't see," muttered Johnny Elephant, as he strutted before the reflecting walls of the mill-pond, "why all the girls of this village aren't in love with me. I being such a handsome young fellow."

So saying he reached into his back pocket, brought out his red bandana handkerchief and wiped his tusks. He then picked a white flower at the edge of the mill-pond and put it into the lapel of his little blue jacket. Then looking very important he put his hands into his pockets, held his head high and strutted down the road to Suzie May's house.

Splash! He had unexpectedly landed in a mudpuddle and a thin high-pitched voice was giggling from the house.

"Ha, ha! You—are funny," giggled Suzie May. . . .

In the rest of the story, Sarah developed the adventures of the young show-off elephant who finally ran away from home to make his fortune. She ended the story thus:

It must have been around twelve o'clock when he woke up and found two shining eyes staring at him out of the darkness.

"Oh," he moaned, as he cuddled closer to the tree. "I want my mother."

"Booo-o-oo," went the voice of the owl, who was the owner of the two staring eyes.

Johnny did not hesitate for a moment. He leaped up and ran as fast as he could.

The next day Johnny ate off the mantlepiece.

The discernment of human frailties so whimsically treated in the adventures of Johnny Elephant is another evidence of the flowering of unusual gifts. Furthermore, one sees real growth in ease and flexibility of structure, in economy and subtlety of implication. It is also obvious that the needed discipline in skills and techniques had in no wise crippled the free play of an active imagination. It seems essential to preserve in any child that spontaneity so necessary for later development. Therefore, it is a matter of signal importance that Sarah, like less able children in her group, retained a delightful unself-consciousness and a genuine zest to write simply for the joy of writing.

7

Writing, Reading, and Literature

The relationships of writing, reading, and literature would seem to be obvious, yet they are not easy to define. It is self-evident that without the written word there is nothing to read. Primitive beginnings of writing—crude markings to record the delivery of grain or the payment of taxes and similar transactions—attest to an ancient need for records. Use of symbols expanded from the making of records to the sending of important messages and eventually to expounding and to entertaining. Writing has come to embrace an almost limitless range of thought and feeling and bears witness to the grandeur of human possibility.

CULTURAL RELATIONSHIPS; JUVENILE EXPERIENCES

It is not surprising that children appear to learn to read most readily when they start with their own written messages. If they grow up in literate families, most children scribble words they can "read" or words they are sure a trusted adult can read. One youngster of four, using a typewriter on which he grouped random letters into spaces and lines that looked like words to him, was asked to read what he had said. "It's for Aunt Sue, so only she can read it," he replied. Quite a few children write lines of various designs and "read" stories as they look at their pages. To such children, reading and writing already seem a unified activity.

Observations of children's impulses to write lead many primary teachers to begin the teaching of reading from individual and group dictation. The words said and heard, the letter forms the children see taking shape, and their own words heard again are somehow connected with those, as yet, strange markings. Through such experiences children learn the seeming magic of reading. There is no question about meanings; the meanings were there before the symbols. Thus children repeat an ancient sequence by moving from reality to symbols and eventually to fluent literacy. This progression of learning activities is basic to the so-called Language Experience Approach to Reading Instruction.

The relationships among these three aspects of literacy—writing, reading, and literature—are far more pervasive than those dramatized in children's learning to read from their own dictation. The beginnings of literate behavior build upon a fund of stories and verse that children have already heard and seen. Storytelling, story reading, TV, radio, and recordings add to this store, so, too, does conversation. All these forms of exchange relate a speaker and an audience. Many adults are convinced that their background in casual reading, seeing plays, acting in plays, and studying literature all contribute to the clarity and effectiveness of their composition. There is as yet no research that verifies these contributions or defines them with precision. But that contributions do exist seems indisputable. Certainly an entirely illiterate person can not write the stories he can tell. A long tradition of oral literature precedes its written form in all cultures. One who has met many characters and episodes, who has followed many plots, who has preferences for certain styles and moods of writing has a reservoir from which to draw. Many authors attribute some of their achievement to wide and selective reading both in their young and adult years.

The power of myth and legend to influence our thinking and expression even centuries after these tales attained written form is evident in everyday language. A Herculean task (a very big job) Icarus's flight and fall (don't fly too high), King Midas and the evil of his golden touch (don't be greedy) are but three of thousands of allusions which traditional literature gives us to express and at the same time help to shape our thought. Cinderella's winning the prince even though she failed the twelve o'clock warning, Clever Hans outwitting the King's messengers, the rejected, sad old animals braying, crowing, and barking at the robbers all help to personalize the triumph of good over evil. So often has this theme appeared that it has crept into the very core of our thought and feeling and hence into the values of our society.

Children write many stories echoing this old theme. They vanquish the adults in their plot conflicts because they are the symbols of power. But the writers usually restore them to authority because they are indispensable even though they limit the actions of the young. Though this pattern of resolving story conflict may well be intuitive, it is reenforced by frequent appearance in both old and modern tales that children relish. This suggests one way that literature is absorbed and used though not as a model to be directly imitated.

A LANGUAGE-EXPERIENCE APPROACH TO BEGINNING READING

Some children have the good fortune to dictate messages, captions for pictures and stories in nursery school, kindergarten, and even at home. Other pupils, seeing this activity, can more easily reach out for the same satisfaction. Reading, talking, and listening occur naturally when the teacher reads messages back to the beginners to see if she wrote just what they wanted to say. Whether working with a group or individuals, teachers do this to link the words on paper with the writers' intent. Such opportunities build a foundation for pupils' own writing and for later focus on word recognition skills.

This procedure, used by some teachers over the last sixty or more years, has produced great gains for initiating instruction both in composing and in reading. Children cooperate with the teacher in reading sentences they have dictated. For them the meaning is clear because they know what they want to say. The beginner may rearrange a few words as he reads, but the teacher rereads thus recalling just what was said when dictating, at first moving a hand under the words while reading. Conversations about a visiting pet, about a new store in town, about a class walk to see autumn leaves, or about a science experiment with water and air pressure, or any interesting content lead to group discussion. Follow-up illustration, rereading, acting out a sentence, and finding repeated words are some of the steps that foreshadow the approach to word recognition skills.

From such experiences with content that has immediate significance, new learning tasks emerge. Following a dictation exercise, children can copy a sentence and illustrate it; they can perhaps find a word that begins with a given sound, and after showing that they discriminate between two different beginning consonant sounds, they can write that word several times. This blending of reading and writing is both a natural occurrence and a time-saver. Children who in kindergarten have used invented spelling and perhaps some conventional spelling can go forward independently. As charts, posters, captions on pictures and signs are posted, they use them to help spell words they want to write. They ask friends and the teacher for help. We now know that invented spelling is a constructive step toward eventual correct form and is to be encouraged. (Ch. 8 Research)

This urge to use a new skill is admirable, but it should not be interpreted as readiness for long, assigned writing tasks. Current research interest in young children's exploration of writing can easily be misinter-preted as a signal to assign five-to-seven-year-old youngsters to do a long daily writing task. Fatigue turns to resentment very easily. Negative attitudes as well as difficulties in correcting illegible letter forms in later grades compounds this waste of time.

It is more important to preserve fluency than to try to achieve rapid improvement of handwriting. Through dictation of real experiences and of "make-up" stories, through many opportunities for conversation, through telling imaginative tales, children enhance fluency of expression rather than endangering it by laborious writing sessions. In some situations, using a tape recorder can be a help. Typing the taped account at some convenient time should often follow if story invention, writing, and reading are the goals. Many oral experiences with storytelling can give much more exercise to imagination than the slow writing of beginners. And imagina-tion should be preserved at all costs—or nearly all costs! The greater story sense and feeling for sequence thus engendered are valuable in reading comprehension as the word and letter acuity supported by writing is valuable for word recognition.

TRANSITION TO BOOK READING

The transition from "experience reading" to book reading can be a natural one. Teachers read many stories to children; so does the librarian when children visit the school library media center. Children talk about these stories and play out some episodes they like. They look at many books in addition to those read to them. Often two children make up a story as they look at pictures together. This includes, for example, some dramatic responses such as imitating sounds of the fire hose, make-believe climbing a ladder, and then returning to narration as they turn the pages. Whatever the content, this combination of dramatizing and story telling assures the identification so essential to reading comprehension. As soon as some pupils are able to read their dictated accounts with minimum help, instruction can begin with selected easy books.

USING PRIMERS

Since most schools have preprimers of various editions from different companies, it is wise for the teacher to choose one with a content which appears to be of interest to the small group with whom she will begin. As with any new book, one should survey it briefly with the children, looking at pictures, talking about happenings, and then trying to predict what the first story will tell. With an able group, some may recognize a few words on the first page or two. The teacher need not hold back from supplying words freely as she and the children cooperate in reading a page. Then she can ask children to find one or two silent words, moving on quickly through the story in the same manner. It is important to have the group decide which of their predictions "worked." Besides engaging the readers' reactions, this technique helps to establish feeling for the unity of the story.

Many teachers find it helps to have the group dictate a few consecutive sentences about the story or its characters, emphasizing action rather than description. These sentences recorded by the teacher are read and re-read in the related discussion. After a group session, children may copy a sentence or two or make up a new one. Of course, those who have begun some independent writing profit more by inventing their own. In these experiences, pupils put the content of the primer into their own language.

To begin directed reading from books, it is sound practice to start with small groups of five or six. This allows the teacher to have the pupils close enough to see how they follow the pages being studied. She can, by reading upside down, usually tell if they are finding the words to be located and if they are searching in the right pictures for details being discussed. Observing closely how they work as individuals is of first importance in giving appropriate reenforcement and guidance. It is healthy curiosity, willingness to explore, and thoughtful questioning that directed reading must develop. The task is much larger and more basic than merely recognizing words. Even beginning reading must never be divorced from thinking.

It can take several weeks and in many cases several months to get all the children in a class started with books. Usually one waits for obvious signs of word recognition from earlier experience reading and related word study. To avoid pressure from both pupils and their parents, some teachers, after a few weeks, begin with preprimers as indicated but expect less. They provide only brief exercises in copying short sentences or labels from the pupils' own dictation. These immature children need to be included in the literature sharing, dramatization, and social conversations in which they talk with their peers and help to solve problems along with the more mature beginners.

BEGINNING WITH TRADE BOOKS

Rather than starting with preprimers, some teachers start with the easy-to-read books now so abundantly available in the school library media center. It is necessary to make sure in advance that the previous experience in

163

reading has established some of the vocabulary in the first few pages. Examining pictures, projecting possible events and conclusions, and then reading cooperatively for short periods are the steps usually of most help. Comment by teachers and pupils focuses on the story line and how projections or guesses worked out.

Pupils build confidence and skills by locating certain words they recognize from previous contacts. After a small group or two have read several books, an opportunity is at hand for reading aloud to another group or to the whole class. In some classes, a few children reach this stage of fluency by midyear or even earlier. Whenever this occurs, it should be a kind of celebration in an atmosphere that encourages others to seek the same pleasure.

STARTING INDIVIDUAL READING RECORDS

When children start reading books, even with a great deal of help, it is useful to begin their cumulative records. One way to encourge independence and pride is to ask the beginner to draw a picture on a card showing something that happened in the book or depicting one of the characters. The pupil then copies the title of the book on the card. Here again reading and writing support each other.

When several cards have been done, they can be kept together and filed under each child's name in a file box. As the year moves on, each should have a box or strong envelope for records. In later grades, this system can give way to more mature recordings. In second grade or third, many find it quite easy to record the title and author's name. Very soon they can record both beginning and finishing dates. But throughout upper grades, book records must continue to be brief. If children are required to write reactions to every book they read, they are very likely to curtail their reading. Appreciation of the extent and range of a child's reading can be shared in teacher-pupil conferences. The record is also useful when children recommend books to others and when looking back to point out contrasts and preferences in class discussions. Along with other data, such records are excellent sources for parent conferences. Moreover, they contribute to the professional evaluation of a child's reading range and interests as well as to appraisal of library media facilities and the total reading-literature program.

THE LITERATURE-READING PROGRAM

Two main streams make up the greater part of the literature program in elementary schools in which wide reading is an integral part of school life.

These two strands are the children's self-selected reading and the books the teacher and library media specialist present to them. In addition, the literature program includes adaptations of books on sound filmstrips; the plays the children adapt from books and stories; the professional and semiprofessional plays they see on television, film, and by live actors; the poetry readings they hear and take part in; and the authors they meet and listen to. In middle and upper grades, children's work in various subjects necessitates a great deal of reference reading. Encyclopedias and reference and text books are used in social studies and science. Reading in the school library media center and in the smaller classroom collection for the topic at hand is vital. Activities such as these support the total curriculum and instructional program. But the central core remains the children's personally chosen reading and the teacher's and librarian's roles in reenforcing opportunities to make choices and develop appreciation. Their leadership in recommending books that match certain interests, in reading aloud, in developing book talks and discussions of what is read, and in sharing some of their own enthusiasms are the dynamics of literature teaching to young children.

Though we have no research as to exactly how this regimen affects composition, it seems certain that the breadth and depth of literary experience work their influence on what and how children write. Though we need much more light on this intriguing question, we have some studies that add strength to the belief in a strong relationship. Cohen found that second-grade children who had heard and reacted to carefully selected books and stories showed significant improvement in vocabulary and increased reading comprehension.[1] Control groups which followed a more segmented, basal-reader approach made less progress in these essentials of reading. In her study, books were selected by adults knowledgeable about children's preferences, understandable language, and opportunities for identification. The fifty selected books were read to the children and were available in each of the classrooms in which the experiment was tried; they were also chosen for later browsing and individual reading by the children. In addition, the children responded by dramatization, much free talk about books, and some drawing of pictures of characters and their doings. Strickland found that using the same stories selected by Cohen, plus puppet playing of the stories involving some of the book language, resulted in kindergarten children's making measureable improvement in their use of oral standard English.[2] Older primary pupils made progress in appropriating correct language forms though their advance did not reach statistical significance.

Evertts found growth in syntax among pupils exposed to literature of high quality.[3] The extent to which new elements are internalized from

165

reading and from hearing both prose and poetry may determine their availability for use in writing. The reservoir of impressions, of plot and character, of wording and mood or sentence cadence seems *prima faciae* to constitute power accessible to the writer.

In support of this possibility is the observation by Dean Jones of UCLA, as quoted by Frank Mankeiwicz, that young people of an earlier generation who had read thousands and millions of English sentences, even though some of them were in "junk" literature, had learned ways of processing sentences that today's TV habitués have not internalized.[4] This deprivation may well be showing up in writing. Both High School and College teachers voice alarm over the poor quality of students' composition. Though quality of literature must not be ignored, there is much to be said also for sheer quantity of reading experience.

INTERESTS AND PATTERNS IN READING

Some records of children's reading in middle grades illustrate something of the diversity of individual pursuits. They show also great fluctuations in quantity throughout the school year and the influence of book popularity as well as the strength of individual choices. Illustrations from actual records may clarify this observation.

One boy in third grade read a total of forty-one books; in fourth he read twenty-two plus parts of nine reference books. Bobby's record shows a strong individuality well worth preserving. In third grade he read *Poppyseed Cakes, Ned And The Rustlers,* along with five others not read by any other boy. Though he read quite a few class favorites, he also read nine books in third grade not read by anyone in the class. In fourth grade, he read twenty-one books not read by any other boys, among them *Looking Ahead, Val Rides The Oregon Trail,* and *Stone Soup,* a book he had read in third grade. He also reread two Donald Duck books twice, first in January and again in May. This sequence of content shows much variety; so too does Bobby's time distribution.

BOBBY—NUMBER OF BOOKS READ PER MONTH

Third Grade				Fourth Grade			
Sept.	—6	Feb.	—0	Sept.	—5	Feb.	—4
Oct.	—4	Mar.	—4	Oct.	—4	Mar.	—2
Nov.	—7	May	—2	Nov.	—1	Apr.	—3
Dec.	—6	June	—0	Dec.	—0	May	—2
Jan.	—11			Jan.	—1	June	—0

Many conditions account for obvious differences in the amounts that Bobby read at different times. The pressure of class activities—such as an end-of-year play, finishing up a long written report—cuts down on time for reading. Getting ready for Christmas or other holidays, moving to another home, going on a trip or illness also influence available time at home and at school. Even though Bobby finished no entire book in some months, he took part in the ever-present incidental and casual reading that went on in classroom and library.

Length of books is yet another factor in this survey of one child's reading. So, too, is difficulty. Bobby's reading varied from the ease of *School Days In Disneyland* and *The Five Chinese Brothers* to *The Ranch Book* and *Enchanting Stories*. After *Freddy The Cowboy*, he read *Paddle To The Sea* and a sequence showing his historical interests: *Chief Black-hawk, Kit Carson* and *Davy Crockett*. *The Wizard Of Oz* was followed by *The Big Book Of Indians* and *Buffalo Bill*. Then again a change of pace: he went from *All About Oscar* and *Horton Hatches The Egg* to *Abraham Lincoln*, and *Stone Soup*. He concluded his reading in fourth grade with *Buccaneers And Pirates Of Our Coasts*, from which he selected a section of nine pages in which he was most interested.

Other records from the same class show clear-cut individual differences in selection, pace, and sequence. Some children follow a trail of reading about pirates or animals or mysteries, or as in the case of Harley, an historical involvement. In April and May of fourth grade he read as follows:

4/17	Boy of Old Virginia
4/22	David Farragut, Midshipman
4/28	Zachary Taylor
4/30	Andrew Jackson
5/11	Little Fox (stopped p. 40)
5/18	Anthony Wayne, Daring Boy

The decision not to finish a book is as legitimate for children as for adults. However, if not finishing becomes a pattern, then the teacher can help with selection of the next book. Checking on why a child thought the next one would be "good", speculating upon outcomes, talking with others who have read the same book all help to spur on the reluctant reader. Making an occasion of finishing a book by sharing some of its peak excitement with others helps to build enthusiasm.

Often children appear to change their interests with each succeeding book, yet a recurrent theme shows up in a year-long record. In third grade, Margie read fifty-two books including some as easy for her as *Curious George* and *Donald Duck and His Friends*. But she also read *Why the Chimes Rang*, *Stories of American Explorers* (60 pp.), and *Mary Poppins*. In fourth grade, she read twenty-eight books varying as widely as *Alice in*

Wonderland, The Secret Garden, The Wizard of Oz, and *The Twilight of Magic.* In addition, she read from nine references on deer, the animal she had chosen to write about in a class study of animals.

SHARING BOOK INTERESTS

There are many ways children can spread the contagion of their pleasure in certain books. The "classroom grapevine" may well be the most efficient communication system for influencing reading tastes. Strong leaders and well-liked children are likely to have their interests echoed among their friends. Many teachers plan at least one session a week in which pupils show the book from which they tell about an exciting, scary, or important event or character. This isn't always easy; children have a propensity for trying to tell a whole story with excessive detail. Presenting short and interesting highlights requires practice. It often helps for two children to rehearse together, one telling the other what he plans to say. Here they discover how to limit their comments.

Difficult as it is for children independently to create characters in their writing, it often seems they can limit themselves to a single person in a story more easily than to one piece of action. For some sharing sessions, a few pupils will have practiced reading an engaging section orally. They tell first some of the setting in which it occurs and then read a passage aloud to give the style and feeling of the book. This sharing results in many children's wanting to get the book at once to read for themselves. Signing up on a waiting list assures anticipation as well as fairness and furthers interest in that special piece of literature.

Making illustrated "ads" for a book is yet another way of encouraging book talk and book exchange. In addition, whenever possible at the end of an individual reading or library-media period, a few pupils tell some exciting or curious bit they have read and occasionally predict how they think the new book will turn out.

Besides advertising books to one another, children also recommend books to their teachers. No teacher is likely to read all of the books read by twenty-to-thirty pupils in middle and upper grades. But every teacher and administrator should know a great backlog of children's books and add to it constantly. "You gotta read this one, Miss K." is a familiar beginning for an avid narration of some character's great adventure. When the teacher reads a book that a child endorses and later expresses her enjoyment of it, another bond in literate human relations has been made.

A teacher's reading to the class is a powerful influence in children's literary growth. In primary grades, such sharing is a commonplace; in upper grades *it should be*. From book exploration with an entire class, there can be many rewards. Brief discussions of characters and how vividly they are shown through what they do and say along with their larger strengths and weaknesses, not only reveal how children perceive them but also with whom they identify. How authors build suspense, the authenticity of historical tales, the live and active "feeling" of a book that moves rapidly from episode to episode—these and other literary matters freely talked about build awareness of style and theme. Though few primary school children appear to seek meanings beyond the obvious happenings of an exciting story, the base for such powers of abstraction gradually evolves. One sixth grade responded to their teacher's effective reading and partial telling of *Johnny Tremaine* by finding other Revolutionary War stories and biographies. Comments on these readings brought them back to some responses to *Johnny Tremaine* with new insights and comparisons.

Adventure tales fill the need children have for the exciting and the dangerous. Sharing books of this kind can offer personal projection for the desire to be brave and strong. It is this sort of story that makes a good selection for class reading, but making such a choice is not easy. Books that combine action with vivid character development usually hold large-group attention. A great deal of conversation by book characters also helps. Sometimes the teacher can sample three or four books that she thinks would invite attention of most of the class. She reads and tells parts of the first chapter of each book on successive days, then has the children choose the one they want to hear.

Beyond the desirable values of enriching literary sensitivity, community of interests, and understandable allusions, oral reading does influence the choices of children's subsequent reading. One researcher found that fifth graders were affected positively by their teachers' oral reading of books they judged to have good literary qualities.[5] A procedure that helps children to choose good reading on their own is a powerful teaching tool. Moreover, such shared pleasure is also an economy for it saves time that might have been spent in writing unproductive book reviews. It would be difficult to find another technique that provides so many learnings both for teacher and children.

POETRY FOR CHILDREN

Poetry, like beauty, "is its own excuse for being." For children the joys of poetry are manifold; they are emotional, they are aesthetic, they are oral and aural. They help children to see new meanings in their familiar world. One sees such satisfactions when six-year-olds' faces light up as they chorus with the teacher as she reads:

The Meal

Timothy Tompkins had turnips and tea,
The turnips were tiny.
He ate at least three.
And then for dessert,
He had onions and ice.
He liked that so much
That he ordered it twice.
He had two cups of ketchup,
A prune, and a pickle.
"Delicious," said Timothy,
"Well worth a nickel."
He folded his napkin
And hastened to add
"It's one of the loveliest breakfasts I've had."[6]

To watch children edge closer and closer to teacher and book, the joint sources of the pleasure they feel, is to be assured that participating in poetry can be an all-over experience.

How to choose the poetry to present to children is now both harder and easier than in years gone by. It is easier because there is more child-appealing poetry than ever before; it is harder because there is so much from which to choose. Not only is the old, traditional verse generally available, but there is also an abundance of verse published in the last few decades. Much of the more recent poetry springs from ghettos and tenements, from discontent and anger. Examples appear in the collection *On City Streets* which presents the favorites of over a hundred city children. In another source young people show their love for the poetry that enhanced their own experience.

December

A little boy stood on the corner
And shoveled bits of dirty, soggy snow
Into the sewer—
With a jagged piece of tin.
He was helping spring come.

Sanderson Vanderbilt[7]

Though much of the poetry of this genre is stark and shows deep hurt, there are also poems that celebrate the beauties and the excitement of the city's seething life.

Today there is a huge array of anthologies in book stores and in libraries. Many are beautifully illustrated; only a few are relatively inexpensive. Among them, the searcher is sure to find a collection of humorous verse, a sure-fire attraction to children who have been "turned off" by poetry. Choices to present to a class must be geared to pupils' spontaneous interests, to their previous backgrounds and experience in poetry, or to what is going on in school or community. Over the year at different times, all of these choices are worthy. And once something of a reservoir of verse has been savored, children's choices should be respected for rereading. Their responses, revealed in brief comment, in their illustrations and independent rereading are often clues to what else should be tried. But teachers' choices are also important and open up different vistas. Often the new gains little favor at first, but occasional recall after weeks or months have gone by can bring a warmer reception and eventually build new tastes.

It is noteworthy that in our increasingly mechanized world, poetry has a greater audience than earlier. Poetry readings by adults now go on in many libraries and small auditoriums. Some magazines of general interest accept contributions for publication. Yet another evidence of the widened appreciation of poetry is the establishment by the National Council of Teachers of English of the first national award for poetry for children. Until this time, even though dozens of awards were given annually for different categories of prose for children, there was no such acknowledgement of the importance of poetry. The first award was given to David McCord in 1977, and subsequent awards have been given to Aileen Fisher, Karla Kuskin, Myra Cohn Livingstone, Eve Merriam, and John Ciardi. These winners have "contributed to excellence in poetry for children" which is the criterion for selection of the awardees.

CLASSROOM EXPERIENCES WITH POETRY

How best to share poetry with children has many answers. Most poems should be *heard* in an atmosphere conducive to acceptance. It is foolish to read poetry to a class that has just been reprimanded or faced with a serious problem. Choice of time is next in importance to choice of poem!

When children have settled in a comfortable listening attitude, the teacher may merely announce that she will read an old favorite or a new one about a recent storm or deep dense fog or other bit of weather drama. Or she may read one of the many poems about the circus, especially if the circus has recently been in town or in the news. A few comments about the poem from teacher or class may be followed by another poem in the same vein or one completely different. Perhaps another brief verse or two and a rereading of one that claimed considerable attention may be all for that day's introduction. Of course, if the teacher knows that the class has had many happy experiences with verse, a far different session would be planned. Leaving books open to attractive pages adds incentive to browse. Gradually building a shared repertoire with pleasant associations can lead to children's selecting and practicing oral reading of their favorites—again, only a few on any one day. Later they can plan their own poetry programs. A group may work on one to present to the whole class. The period should be very brief. Oral readings also can be planned with the library media specialist and given in the library, occasionally to a larger audience.

Children often repeat recurrent lines or phrases thus laying the foundation for choral reading. Development of choral rendition may take many forms: one group after another reads successive stanzas or other appropriate portion; one small group reads "solo" parts with all joining in for the last stanza; or two groups read alternate parts as the sense of the verse suggests. Picking out "light" voices for sections that seem to need such tone quality and "dark" voices for other moods adds variety in keeping with the thought, feeling, and rhythm of the lines. Many ways of experimenting should stay open, and children should have many opportunities to try out their ideas.

Two general problems need to be guarded against. One is that group oral reading tends to get slower and slower. Another is for voices to get lower and heavier. Obviously, a demonstration of appropriate tempo and of the deadening effect of lower, slower reading can lift the effort to a more musical effect. Simple choral reading in the classroom has many benefits, including some spontaneous memorization. Occasional programs for a larger audience can combine choral speaking of a short poem or two with simple dramatizations and group singing. These can often result in an aesthetic experience for both audience and performers.

The special pleasure shared poetry can bring to a group builds a sense of mutuality that enhances personal relationships as well as willingness to explore new horizons in verse. It would be difficult to say whether teacher or children reap the greater rewards.

Notes

1. Dorothy Cohen, "The Effect of a Special Program in Literature on the Vocabulary and Reading Achievement of Second Grade Children in Special Service Schools" (Ph.D. diss., New York University, 1966).

2. Dorothy Strickland, "The Effects of a Special Literature Program on the Oral Language Expansion of Linguistically Different Negro Kindergarten Children" (Ph.D. diss., New York University, 1971).

3. Eldonna L. Evertts, *Syntactical Analysis of Children's Composition, Nebraska Study of the Syntax of Children's Writing, 1964–1965*, vol. 1, 1967 (ERIC Document 013 814).

4. Frank Mankiewicz, *Remote Control* (New York: New York Times Books, 1978), pp. 170–171.

5. Beverly Sirota, "The Effect of a Planned Literature Program of Daily Oral Reading by the Teacher on the Voluntary Reading of Fifth Grade Children" (Ph.D. diss., New York University, 1971).

6. Karla Kuskin, "The Meal," *Dogs and Dragons, Trees and Dreams,* (New York: Harper and Row, 1980), p. 263.

7. Sanderson Vanderbilt, "December," in *Creative Youth,* ed. Hughes Mearns (Garden City, N.J.: Doubleday and Co., Inc., 1925).

Recent Research Related to Our Findings

More researchers are at work on the problems of children's written composition today than ever before. There is intense interest in how and why and when children learn to write. But it must also be recalled that before the present upsurge of interest only a little investigation had been done. Compared to the amount of research in children's reading, the history of research in children's writing is a very scanty account. A few of the studies which offer further clarification of our own findings are summarized here.

RECENT RESEARCH IN THE COMPOSING PROCESSES

Currently investigators are directing their attention to a systematic recording of what children *do* as they write. They note such activities as children's looking back over what they have started, crossing out words, asking for spelling help, reading a special bit of action to a friend, drawing a picture, questioning the teacher, and still other overt behaviors. Modern scholars also look at that elusive thing called atmosphere. Do children feel free to experiment and to choose what they write about? Do they sense that if they run out of ideas they can leave that story and begin another? Do they sometimes choose to write on their own when no assignment is given? Do they occasionally choose not to write, and can they do this without feelings of disapproval? To assess even informally the factor called classroom atmosphere is extremely difficult. To put such assessment into justifiable numerical terms is even harder. Some of the ways of solving these research problems are illustrated in the following reports of recent study.

One way of judging atmosphere is presented in a penetrating study by Graves using a formula that can be objectively applied to differentiate formal from informal classes.[1] Two classes of second graders were identified as formal and two as informal. Formal classes were those in which thirty percent or less of each day's activities were chosen by the pupils and in which teachers devoted no more than thirty percent of their time to groups of five or less. In informal classes, at least sixty percent of the day's activities were chosen by pupils, and teachers spent sixty percent or more of their time with groups of five or less. All four teachers were women with a minimum of six years of teaching experience. The schools were in residential communities in New York State; the neighborhoods were made up largely of blue-collar workers who had completed 12.2 years of school.

Two children were selected for special case studies from each of the four classrooms, but all children in all four classes were involved in the many writing activities that made up the study. All pupils kept folders of all their writings from December 1972 until April 1973. Observers filled out detailed observation forms for all children, recording what could be seen and heard from individuals as they wrote. In interviews, children reported what they thought about their own writing and what it takes to be a good writer. For the eight case studies, additional material included reports of parental interviews, tests, and educational histories.

To further the study of writing behavior, Graves recorded the frequency of writing, the frequency of unassigned writing, and the themes chosen by seven-year-olds. The case-study children were observed as they interacted with their peers; they were not aware of being singled out for special attention. Of the eight children thus observed in a classroom context, Michael was chosen for even more detailed reporting to round out a description of many events and conditions that affect writing.

Observers recorded how children got help in spelling—from resources in the room or from a neighbor. They noted conversations by writers and by whom initiated, whether by teacher or friend. How pupils reread and started writing again, what they did with completed compositions, and many other items of behavior went into the observation record. Analysis of writing content as well as externals of behavior illuminated some of the means the children used to get their ideas and feelings into written form.

Of the many conclusions to be gleaned from Graves's study, the following few seem of greatest value to teachers.

Informal environments give greater choice to children. When children are given the choice to write, they write more and in greater length than when specific assignments are given.

175

Results from informal environments demonstrate that children do not need direct motivation or supervision in order to write.[2]

Girls compose longer writings than do boys in either formal or informal environments. Boys from either environment write more in unassigned writing than do girls. Unassigned writing seems to provide an incentive for boys to write about subjects not normally provided in teacher assigned work. Teachers do not normally assign work that included themes from secondary and extended territory, the areas used by boys in unassigned writing.

Boys seldom use the first person form unless they are developmentally advanced. (Girls do more often.)[3]

Many forms of case study seem essential for research in writing and also for productive teaching of composition.

Graves's findings add new evidence for some of our own observations. We found no obvious differences in length between girls' and boys' personal writing, possibly because we never gave assignments to write poems or stories. Further, even in whole-class informational writing projects, every pupil chose the special interest that he found within the general science or social studies area. A wide range of choices for factual writing is necessary; in imaginative narrative, complete freedom is even more essential. Both experience and controlled research merge their findings in this regard.

A DIFFERENT RESEARCH APPROACH TO WRITING

Another way to investigate writing behavior is to ask children what they do, how they get ready to put their thoughts on paper, and how they work after getting started. Sawkins's study is a detailed report of what fifth graders *said* they did when they wrote.[4] She interviewed children using carefully detailed procedures to assure consistency from child to child. She asked pupils what they thought about before they wrote and as they wrote, what problems they had, how much they used an outline or notes, if they proofread and rewrote. The papers of thirty boys and thirty girls were judged using the Diedrich Scale. The fifteen best and fifteen poorest papers were selected. The children who wrote these papers were then compared as to their approaches and their performance when interviewed. Analysis of responses showed that both good and poor writers worked in much the same ways. Girls received higher scores than boys generally and responded in more detail in interviews, but the differences between boys and girls were not statistically significant.

Interesting conclusions appeared from what the children said they thought about when composing. Some of the inferences arose from a closely controlled situation in which all the class wrote the same assignment. For example, pupils told Sawkins they thought about the content both before they wrote and while doing so, but they made no notes or outline before starting the composition. When writing a story, they said they had little in mind as they started, but ideas came as they wrote. According to their interviews, not many gave much thought to choice of words.

More children were concerned with spelling than with which words to use although some did give examples of choosing words to set a certain mood. A few drew pictures to help them see what they wanted to say. It is also curious that most of these fifth graders did not know when they started how they would end their stories, a statement made also by many professionals about their writing. Though attention to content was evident from the interviews, the children's overwhelming concern was for correct use of mechanics.

In our own critical examination of what "worked" with children—an inquiry that focused on what kept the children wanting to write and what resulted in clear content and in honest individual expression—we found it useful to children to make plans for factual exposition and to make memos for letters that had to inform someone of exact events or conditions. (Chapter 3, Practical Writing)

How much this directed learning influenced children's imaginative writing in subtle ways we can not know. However, it was our strong belief that directed planning of informational writing, all the while respecting and prizing individuality of style, strengthened the clarity of their imaginative tales. We also observed a gradual increase in control of mechanics in their personal writing. Conversely, the spontaneity and freedom enjoyed in imaginative expression added color to their reporting of information.

ANOTHER APPROACH TO WRITING PROCESSES

The preceding two studies (Graves, Sawkins) used two different ways of approaching the query as to what goes on when children compose. Still another research procedure merits attention. Tovatt and Miller, working with ninth grades in Muncie, Indiana, used tape recorders to help children retain their composing thoughts as they wrote.[5] Teachers demonstrated the technique, dictating to the tape recorder, pausing when necessary to sense a flow of ideas, slowing or pausing in dictation to let pencil catch up with voice, playing back what had been written, and changing the written form as needed while listening. There was a control group of 30 children with test-determined range of abilities equal to those of the experimental group (stratified random sampling) and used to conventional procedures in English teaching. Gains made by the experimental group, using tape recorders to assist writing, were greater than those in the control group but not to the point of statistical significance. Tests of positive attitudes toward English instruction showed no difference between the two groups.

The Tovatt and Miller inquiry sought to get at a phenomenon of composing that has teased the curiosity of many a teacher and writer. How do phrases and sentences take shape in the mind so they can be put onto paper? Some adults think they almost hear a kind of "inner voice" as they seek to write an idea, perhaps an idea held only nebulously in or near consciousness. James Britton put the import of this complex act into clear focus.[6] Britton said, "We continue to cherish our hunch that 'shaping at the point of utterance' may be a crucial aspect of the writing process in a great many kinds of writing."[7]

The recorder seems a rapid easy device to catch the evanescent thought. On the contrary however, it may be more an intrusion than an aid. Tovatt and Miller found no evidence of significant improvement in writing nor were positive attitudes toward instruction strengthened by use of the recorder. We may not know for years to come whether one "hears" a vague sequence of words or at times only one salient word or whether one "feels" a kind of conflict embraced in the desire to transmute the vague into the particular, to bring unfocused verbal awareness to clarity. Perhaps neurological techniques not yet available will eventually inform our ignorance. What we can be fairly sure of is that individuals differ vastly in their coping with the task of written composing. We are on safe ground in making arrangements in which children often share information and books with one another, where teachers consult with children as to intended meaning, and where in many other ways, children learn to help themselves. These kinds of mutuality appear to flourish in classrooms where writing is done for genuine and often tangible purposes as well as for reflection, for explorations in imagination, for sheer fun, and for entirely private self-discovery.

SUMMARY OF RESEARCH IN WRITING PROCESSES

Walter Petty offers lucid interpretation of the values and difficulties of both traditional and new research procedures along with a summary of some of the studies done largely under his guidance.[8] Those systematic inquiries broke new ground in the search for understanding of what goes on in the young child when he writes. Two of those studies (Graves, Sawkins) have already been reported in this chapter. Petty contrasts the research procedures of analyzing the products of children's composing (the written papers) with techniques aimed at observing children as they write. He points up the observation that children do not spontaneously make notes before writing, but he considers that they need help in this preparatory phase. He notes Graves's conclusion that boys write more than girls when choosing their own subjects (voluntary writing) and that they explore in "extended territory" (beyond home and school) more than girls do.

Of the difficulty of written composition, Petty cites particularly penetrating wisdom.

> While written composition may be intimately related to oral composition—and I would argue that it is—it is also uniquely different and particularly tough. . . . I simply want to stress that children struggle with the transition from the basically overt language of speech to the essentially covert activity of writing.[9]

He further differentiates between the external activity that can be seen, heard, and recorded and that activity which goes on within.

> A second fundamental consideration is whether the meaning of the term *composing process* as it is used in much of the literature is the same as the behavioral process engaged in by an individual as he or she writes. . . . or even by those behaviors observable in oral composition.[10]

Petty's summation of essentials from research and generalizations derived from long experience point to a strong necessity to fortify individuality in ways of working, in writing style, and in choice of content. To write about something for which one has no concern results in bland statements, not vigorous composition. The latter takes energy. Not only opportunity but also warm encouragement need to be given to voluntary writing in a climate that welcomes many different products of children's literacy.

MEASURES OF MATURITY IN CHILDREN'S WRITTEN COMPOSITION

Until recently, most studies of child composing have looked into matters that could be seen on paper and counted. These have included the total number of words the pupil wrote, the number of different words, the length of sentences, and the proportion of dependent clauses to the number of independent clauses. These assays have presented the common finding that length of writing, length of sentences, and the number of dependent clauses all increase with age and maturity. One of the difficulties in the examination of sentence control, however, is that it is often very hard to know what a pupil *intended* as a sentence. Children often *read* their own writing voicing sentences quite appropriately, albeit their pages might be devoid of punctuation or show only a quixotic sprinkling of capitals and periods. One technique of solving the problem of sentence structure has presented a useful measure of maturity while ignoring the confusing signals of capitalization and terminal punctuation.

Rather than length of sentence as a measure, Hunt tackled the problem by inventing the "minimal terminal unit", generally referred to as the TU.[11] Hunt defined the terminal unit as "one main clause plus all the subordinate clauses attached to or imbedded within."[12] A TU may have no such clauses or it may have several. Example: [On my way to school I lost a book,] [it was a very valuable book.] The brackets show two independent clauses, each of which, of course, could stand alone, hence two TUs. A TU may have one or more dependent clauses or it may have none. "I lost a book that my grandmother gave me when I was six years old." Although this example contains two dependent clauses, it is one TU.

Hunt compared the writing of fourth-, eighth-, and twelfth-grade children, finding that the TU does indeed increase in length over time. The writing samples for this analysis were a thousand words accumulated in sequence in classrooms. Whatever the assignments, whenever each of the seventy-four pupils in the study had accumulated a thousand written words, those papers were turned over to the investigator. Obviously this would take longer for fourth than for twelfth-grade pupils. Student IQ scores were all below 110. The mean lengths of TU per grade were: Gr.4—5.6, Gr.8—11.5, Gr.12—14.4.[13]

Other kinds of grammatical analysis applied to children's writing revealed a great diversity of characteristics other than length. One of the important searches was for the proportion of subordinate clauses to total clauses. This resulted in an improvement upon an earlier formula which had served in establishing the use of subordination as an index of maturity in thinking-expression. The new approach made use of the TU rather than the total sentence. Hunt found the proportion of subordinate clauses to increase with age as did the length of main clauses also.

Teachers are concerned with children's tendency to string many short sentences together with *ands*. Indeed, at the extreme, occasional papers have been found written as only one "sentence" containing as many as a dozen main clauses. Hunt found that the number of TUs per sentence decreases as children move through the grades: Gr.4—1.60, Gr.8—1.37,

Gr.12—1.17.[14] Both the increased use of subordination and the lesser use of short main clause connected with many "ands" contribute to a more pleasing style and often to increased clarity. For statistical analysis of overall progress in large surveys and in certain acute problems, investigators need to use such sophisticated measures of progress. For most teachers and curriculum directors, however, observations of these changes in sentence writing, along with noting variety and clarity of communication, are sufficient.

One frequent interpretation of the increasing length of TU is the assumption that long sentences are always and intrinsically better than short ones. Merely teaching children to write long sentences, or long words, results in artificiality and monotony. To write with vigor and honesty as one thinks and feels, to hear and to read a variety of literature, all contribute to growing power to use the conventional structures of our written language with individual style.

GROWTH IN SPELLING

Children's spelling is a matter of great concern to the community, and indeed, it looms large as a hurdle to children themselves. Even in a congenial atmosphere where they are told that "spelling won't count", or where they are told to begin a word with the first letter they know and get help later, many middle graders forego using the word they originally wanted. Neither does the dictionary offer real help for it usually takes children a long time to find a word they can't spell—even to find words they can spell! During the search they forget their train of thought and give up looking for the word. Some understanding of developmental levels of spelling growth must underlie a sound spelling program in elementary schools.

By first grade, most children from even modestly literate homes have moved through the more primitive stage of scribbling and of "drawing" some letters they have seen. Whether or not they think of these letters as words is not possible to determine, though it seems apparent that many do. By four or five, some children have acquired the ability to initiate writing words beginning with one or more appropriate letters. Growing up with books, signs, posters, and other print, including captions and ads on television, many choose enough of the salient letters to make their words readable by others.[15] Researchers have shown how much young children learn about spelling from their chance encounters with print.

Although many children have made a good start on the English alphabetic system, there are many others who, in first and second grades, have developed almost no knowledge of sound-letter-word relationships. Those for whom English is a second language and those who hear and see little reading and writing at home need time to develop a fundamental awareness of print-reading-sounds-words. The stages through which pre-school children grow from a dawning consciousness that symbols stand for words toward considerable uniformity in conventional spelling have been established by Gentry.[16] He defines four stages: (1) Deviant, in which the child uses a random ordering of letters and other symbols, (2) prephonetic, in which he uses one, two, and three letters representing some sounds in the word, (3) phonetic, in which he uses all sound features that he hears, and (4) transitional, in which he uses vowels in every syllable and some spelling patterns along with nonstandard spelling.

Wood showed the admirable logic in generalizations children make about the correspondence of certain letters with the sounds they hear and say in familiar words.[17] These studies help teachers understand some of the difficulties in pupils who have not made the expected progressions formulated by Gentry when confronted with writing tasks. Problems in copying a sentence or even their own names illustrate the difficulties these immature youngsters face in perceiving words in print.

These observations point to the wisdom of taking down the messages the less developed pupil wants to dictate and helping to read what has been said once it is written. Illustrating the message or caption often leads to spontaneous copying or using some of the letters or words in the designs. And for all children, dictating to the teacher followed by hearing and seeing the words they have said, contributes to eventual spelling maturity as well as to story sense and imagination. Using a tape recorder when there is time to type the dictated message later has some of the same value. Further, this rapid recording of an ephemeral story helps to develop the fluency so needed for further growth in literacy.

Research by Horn and Rinsland in written vocabulary usage has determined those words most frequently used by adults and children.[18, 19] Subsequent studies of words used in common written discourse have made very few additions to these words of highest frequency. Many of the words used by adults are also used frequently by children. Indeed, the degree of overlap is very considerable. Words from the above frequency studies are generally included in spelling text books, though different authors assign the same words to different grades for introductory study. In addition to a basic list of some three thousand words deemed essential to most nontechnical writing, children need words peculiar to social studies, science, other school subjects, and school-community activities.

For more than a decade, the hottest debate has blazed around the issue as to whether children learn spelling better by rote or by rule!

Generalizations by Hanna and others about sound-letter correspondence (phoneme-grapheme correspondence) have recently been declared much more dependable than scholars had previously believed.[20] From this report and others, the conclusion has gained currency that children should discover patterns of sound-letter relationship and apply the logic of such observation to learning to spell.

Horn disagreed strongly with the notion that children could proceed from sounds and patterns to appropriate spelling and thereby gain sufficient control to spell a considerable number of words accurately in writing.[21] Many published spelling systems and many teachers follow Horn's principles resulting in orderly weekly plans for testing-studying-retesting to assure automatic control. He formulated basic psychological generalizations leading to the now familiar study steps, the use of a few rules as aids to seeing patterns and word relationships along with periodic testing, review, and retesting.

To date no long-term comprehensive experimental study has compared pupils taught by the two different approaches. It is hard to keep different methods "pure" in school situations, but until such a controlled study occurs the debate will continue.

Since weekly spelling lists are still widely used for study and testing, insight into the contributions from the entire curriculum should guide the amounts and kinds of practice required of children. Hodges summarizes these curricular sources that need consideration in the total school spelling program.

—a substantial amount of knowledge is learned during the school years in situations outside of formal instruction, much of an individual's knowledge about spelling—that is, knowledge about English orthography and other writing conventions—is learned throughout life by an interaction with written language wherever it is encountered. Every teacher is, in a practical sense, a teacher of spelling.[22]

Yet another contribution to children's mastery of a working spelling vocabulary arises from their own writing, especially their editing of many of their written compositions. Growing out of *The First Grade Reading Studies* in the 1960s were several investigations carried on locally for a second and even for a third year. One was a comparison of an eclectic Language Arts Approach—also called Language Experience Approach or LEA—with a Basic Reading Approach or BRA. Many learnings were tested in these centers. Marian Stauffer found that in classrooms where teachers had more than one year of experience with the integrated approach, the children learned to read as well as or better than did those taught by

Compartmentalized Basic Reading Approach.[23] The LEA children also became better spellers.

Of great interest was the finding that on measures evaluating samples of children's writing, including diversity, story content, and mechanics the LEA children did better to a statistically significant degree.[23] Stauffer commented on the superiority of spelling which was included in the mechanics test in spite of the fact that the teachers were asked to encourage writing but not to emphasize correct letter order, punctuation, capitalization and the like. Teachers of the LEA "experimentals" had had one previous year of teaching in this integrated approach and in both groups were experienced professionals. The advantages of much writing of an original sort and much sharing and enjoying what the children had written, both as to content and mechanics, are worthy of note.

Another much longer study of the effects of an integrated, eclectic language arts program was carried out by Russell G. Stauffer and others throughout a span of six years.[24] An experimental group of 159 children was compared with a control group of 175 children using Basal Readers and their English and spelling programs as in previous years. Groups were equated as closely as possible as to intelligence and other selected factors. All children were tested annually by a complete battery of tests. After six years, the Integrated Language Arts group showed up favorably in most areas—though not to a statistically significant extent. As to spelling, sixth-grade boys spelled a little less well than control boys, but experimental girls spelled significantly better than did control girls.

A random selection of thirty children from each group was used for the time-consuming task of analyzing a writing sample. In two tests, experimentals exceeded controls by significant amounts: the total number of running words and and the total number of different words. This greater variety and number of words written are strong indications of writing power but such writing entails greater spelling risks. The more one writes the greater the risk of spelling some words wrong. And though length is no guarantee of excellence in writing, the greater number of different words bespeaks at least a greater variety of concepts and potentially of styles.

The problems of teaching spelling are many and the foregoing research reports point to no foolproof recipes. Several principles seem to emerge. Programs that include real needs and opportunities for informational reporting to a known and inquiring audience also present the need for editing first drafts. Teachers of all subjects and pupils share the responsibility for correct spelling. Such purposeful correction makes a real contribution to spelling achievement. But complete success for all learners is not guaranteed by any one program.

A second principle appears to be that children can build many accurate perceptions of words by observing spelling patterns and regularities that texts and teachers help them to discover and by direct instruction. Interest in words and their rich and diverse meanings is a frequent product of this kind of activity. Further, orderly word-list study may very well be a valuable adjunct for most children and an absolute necessity for others. Reviewing through testing and individualizing the study of needed words is an economy too great to be overlooked. Some children enjoy and look forward to weekly word-list procedures. They need not be a burden and must never be a punishment. Viewed in the broad context of language enrichment and purposeful public writing, learning to spell can assume a respected but not autocratic role in children's lives.

An extremely important principle of teaching and learning is that children's concepts available for writing should never be limited to the words they can spell. To do so, is to put brakes on intellectual growth. Editing of drafts before making a good copy for public use must enable even pupils with inferior spelling achievement to enjoy the fruits of labor that serves warmly felt purposes and brings pride to the writer. Such satisfactions build motivation for new and ongoing learning.

The investigations we have reported, though few in number, throw light on some of the discrete areas included in our long-term study. They demonstrate the importance of elements that mesh in the complex art of written composing: classroom atmosphere (Graves); vocabulary and integrated curriculum (Stauffer, M. and R. G.); sentence structure (Hunt); what children think about as they write (Sawkins); growth in spelling (Read, Hanna, Horn, Hodges, Wood); and the importance of voluntary writing (Graves). Other researchers have also dealt with these and other components.

We were deeply concerned in building self-confidence, and above all, with fostering the *desire* to write. It is axiomatic that if children write only when forced to, growth suffers, perhaps terminally. The role of children's literature and dramatization we found to be exhilarating. Thus the classroom climate, human relations, diverse and stimulating experiences, a high regard for literacy both for that of adults and of the very young—these and still other factors all operate in nurturing excellence in writing. Future researchers have much to build upon and many problems yet to solve.

Notes

1. Donald H. Graves, "Children's Writing: Research Directions and Hypotheses Based upon an Examination of the Writing Processes of Seven-Year-Old Children" (Ph.D. diss., State University of New York at Buffalo, 1973).

2. Ibid., 211.

3. Ibid., 211–212.

4. M. W. Sawkins, "The Oral Responses of Fifth-Grade Children to Questions Concerning their Written Expression" (Ph.D. diss., State University of New York at Buffalo, 1970).

5. Anthony Tovatt and E. L. Miller, "The Sound of Writing," *Research in the Teaching of English* 1 (1967), 176–189.

6. James Britton, "The Composing Process and the Functions of Writing," in *Research on Composing—Points of Departure,* ed. Charles R. Cooper and Lee Odell, (Urbana, Ill., National Council of Teachers of English, 1978), p. 24.

7. Ibid.

8. Walter T. Petty, "The Writing of Young Children," in *Research on Composing—Points of Departure,* ed. Charles R. Cooper and Lee Odell (Urbana, Ill., National Council of Teachers of English, 1978), 76.

9. Ibid.

10. Ibid.

11. Kellogg Y. Hunt, "Grammatical Structures Written at Three Grade Levels," *Research Report* 3 (Champaign, Ill.: National Council of Teachers of English, 1964), 49.

12. Ibid., 21.

13. Ibid., 23.

14. Ibid., 39.

15. Charles Read, *Children's Categorization of Speech Sounds in English* (Urbana, Ill., National Council of Teachers of English, 1975).

16. Richard J. Gentry, "Learning to Spell Developmentally," *The Reading Teacher* 34 (January 1981), 378–381.

17. Margo Wood, "Invented Spelling," *Language Arts* 59 (October 1982), 707–717.

18. Ernest Horn, *A Basic Writing Vocabulary, Ten Thousand Words Most Commonly Used in Writing* (Iowa City, Iowa, College of Education, University of Iowa, 1926).

19. Henry D. Rinsland, *Basic Vocabulary of Elementary School Children* (New York, Macmillan, 1945).

20. Paul R. Hanna, Jean S. Hanna, and Richard E. Hodges, *Spelling Structures and Strategies* (Boston, Houghton-Mifflin, 1971).

21. Thomas D. Horn, Research on Handwriting and Spelling, (Champaign, Ill.: National Council of Teachers of English. 1966)

22. Richard E. Hodges, "Research Update on the Development of Spelling," *Language Arts* 59 (1982), 289.

23. Marian A. Stauffer, "Comparative Effect of a Language Arts Approach and a Basic Reading Approach in First Grade Reading Achievement" in *Action Research in LEA Instructional Procedures,* comp. Russell G. Stauffer (Newark, Del., University of Delaware, 1976), 220-221.

24. Russell G. Stauffer, "Effectiveness of a Language Arts and Basic Reading Approach to First Grade Reading Instruction Extended into Sixth Grade" in *Action Research in LEA Instructional Procedures,* comp. Russell G. Stauffer (Newark, Del., University of Delaware, 1976), 183-188.

Story Supplement

We have found it helpful to have on hand a stockpile of children's stories to be used for various purposes. Such a collection is not an accumulation of the best stories but rather a cross section, including some that are meager, some that are full of active aggression, and some that start with verve but are unfinished. We have found we could never have too many stories on hand, for what catches on with one group may fail with another.

From this collection we draw stories to read during the warming-up process with a new group, or when a class is caught on a plateau of writing and needs a lift to a new level, or just for fun because children take such delight in them. Always we read for stimulation and enjoyment, *never* to make overt comparison or to present models to be copied.

The stories that follow are kinds we have found useful; they may serve as the beginning of a working collection. Some may seem immature to adults, but they satisfy children whose sense of story is as yet comparatively undeveloped.

A Naughty Bird

Once there was a little chickadee who was a very naughty little bird. His grandmother, Speckleface, always told him not to get up too early because he went to Farmer Pickle's house and started to sing and wake him up. He threw his shoe so hard that he hit the fire box and set off the alarm. Then the fire engine came, and the little chickadee flew off and never came back again.

187

A Monkey without a Tail

There was once a monkey that had no tail. His name was Burk and he lived in a forest.

He asked his mother, "Where can I get a tail?"

His mother said, "Go to Mr. Owl. He will tell you where to get one."

"Thank you," said Burk, and he went to Mr. Owl as fast as he could go.

Mr. Owl said, "Go to the Wishing Well and wish."

So Burk went to the Wishing Well. When Burk got there he wished. Then he waited and waited. Then Burk began to worry, but a low voice said, "What you are supposed to do now is to go home."

So Burk went home. He wanted to have a tail so he obeyed the voice. That night a little fairy came and gave Burk a tail.

In the morning Burk didn't see his tail, but his mother said, "Burk, I told you Mr. Owl would tell you where to get a tail."

Burk said, "Where is it? I didn't see it."

"Here it is."

Burk was so happy he forgot where he got his tail. He began to ask his mother, but then he remembered that Mr. Owl had told him to go to the Wishing Well. Then he stopped thinking. He went to Mr. Owl and said, "Thank you."

So Burk lived happily ever after.

A second-grade girl

A Girl That Makes Men into Foxes

Once there was a mean old girl. She liked to make men into foxes. Every man she sees she makes into foxes. She saw the biggest man and she made him into a little fox. Then she saw another man, and she made him into a fox. Then she met a boy and he killed the old girl and all the men came back to be men again.

A second-grade boy

The Cave

Once there was a cave. It was a big one. It looks like someone has been living in it. Somebody like a bear could live in it. Maybe a lion could live in it. Maybe one of those could live in the cave in the woods.

Then one day a little boy came to the cave. He walked right

into the cave, and he was never seen again. Then one day a man looked all over for the cave but he could not find the cave. Then the next day a man was taking a walk, and right before him was the cave. So the next day he went to the newspaper place. He told the newspaper people that he had found a lost cave. The newspaper people had the story in the newspaper.

The next day hundreds of people got around the cave. Then the cave disappeared just like that. Then all the people sued the man. The man did not have enough money to give everyone. Each day the man got a penny he had to give it to someone. Every day he got any money he had to give it to someone. Two weeks from then his aunt sent him some money but he had to give that money away, too. The next day he wrote a letter to send him some more money, so his aunt did send him some more money and he had to give that away, too, to some people. Soon he had enough money to pay all the people. And he could buy food for himself. He had so much money that he was rich and he never was poor again.

The End

A second-grade girl

The Lion That Took Over The Town

One time there was a town that was quiet. Then the zoo bought a lion. He was king of the beasts. Then the lion broke loose. Everyone hid.

Then one man said to another, "What should we do? The police have hidden, so we should hide, too." So they did.

The lion saw where the two men hid. Then the lion went to the place where the two men hid. Then the lion opened his mouth. The two men thought they were dead ducks, and they were right. The lion did eat them up.

The town did not want to see the men die. A man said, "We should fire a cannon ball."

So they did, but they missed the lion and hit a tree.

Then a man said, "Let's get a machine gun." And so they did. And this time they got him, but the people did not believe he was dead. But a man went by the lion, and lion did not do anything. Then the people believed he was dead. Then everyone got out of their hiding places and went home.

A second-grade boy

189

Jimmie's Stick

Jimmie had a little stick that was magic. And one day Jimmie wanted a dime.

He said, "Hocus pocus, let me have a dime."

And that second he had a dime. And he said it over and over again. And he got more and more money so that he can have ice cream and soda and candy and cake and all good things to eat. And he lived happy ever after.

A third-grade boy

There was a little bear. He did not have a name. People called him names, and he punched them and sometimes he cried. And he tried and tried to get a name. But he cannot. So he sat down and he was thinking for days and soon he came to a name. It was "Fire."

And a fox asked him, "What is your name?"

He said, "Fire."

The fox said, "I can't hear you."

So he called out, "Fire."

So all the animals in the jungle came and wanted to put out the fire.

His mother told four animals to come to the house. So they came. They sat down thinking. The four of them had a name and all of them had the same. The mother bear said to one, "Have you got a name?"

He said, "Bee."

"No, no," said the mother bear. "That ain't a name." So little bear started to cry.

Mother Bear said, "Little bear, do not cry. You can go out if you like.

"I do not want to go out. All the animals will call me names." So he named himself "Monkey."

So the same fox asked him, "Have you got a name?"

He said, "Yes, I have."

So the fox said, "What is it?"

He said, "Monkey."

So the fox called out, "Foxes, come here. This little bear's name is 'Monkey.' "

So all the foxes called out, "Oh, look at the monkey."

So he went home and told his mother and she named him "Tim" and he lived happy ever after.

An eight-year-old boy*

Buttercup Wilkins was a yellow cat, a really nice cat, but no one liked her. The other cats felt very uppity about her and never asked her to play with them. But Buttercup Wilkins didn't mind. She had fun by herself.

One day Priscilla Moore, a black cat with white paws, made some duckleberry jam. Duckleberry jam is very extra-special good and she decided to have a party about it.

She said to the other cats, "Will you come to my house and play cards and have some of my duckleberry jam?"

They said, "Yes, but don't ask that Buttercup Wilkins."

"I won't," said Priscilla. "Come tomorrow at three."

But they didn't know that Buttercup Wilkins was hiding in the bushes beside them.

So the next afternoon Buttercup Wilkins watched the other cats go into the party. Then she slipped gently through the door into the pantry where the jam was. Without making a sound she quietly pawed out and ate every bit of that jam. She even put her nose in each jar and licked it shining.

Then Buttercup Wilkins slowly licked the jam from her face and paws. She carefully closed the door of the jam closet and, wearing a smile at the edge of her whiskers, she slipped past all the mean chattering cats whose noses were all so uppity they did not even see her.

A third-grade girl

Uncle Black Bear's Birthday Party

Griz, the bear was just getting ready to go to his Uncle Black Bear's birthday party. He had his necktie on and his new suit. Away they went in their car.

When they got there, Aunt Black Bear was cooking some bacon. Now it happened to be that Griz liked greasy things, and

---

*The boy who wrote this at the end of the third grade was burdened with the name "Bodo." His original copy consists of but two run-on sentences. As he read the tale his voice indicated the punctuation used here.

when he saw the bacon he dove for the pot. His paws, his head, his face all went into the pot. It knocked Aunt Black Bear over and the fork that you turn the bacon with went flying.

Just then Uncle Black Bear came in. "What is going on?" he said. "It sounds like a rumpus. And what's all that bacon around the floor? Griz, come here!"

Uncle Black Bear put Griz over his knee and you know the rest. So Griz went in and sat down and began to eat. Uncle Black Bear was furious all through supper because Griz had spoiled all his bacon.

So Griz is a spoiled little bear. When Griz got home his mother put him to bed right away.

Boy, end of third grade

Mud and Tud

Mud and Tud were two ducks that lived in Mrs. Hakelman's house in the ice box. They liked the cold spots. Mr. Hakelman is mayor of the town and is going to give a ball. Mrs. Hakelman has had to bake some cakes. She has laid them in the ice box on the second shelf down.

It happened to be that Mud and Tud were on the top shelf. Mud was holding Tud's hand. All of a sudden Mud slipped and they both went down. They landed right beside a huge cake which towered above them. It had three layers. Mud and Tud started to eat their way in. Luck was with them. The icing dripped down to cover the hole.

Mrs. Hakelman came home about four o-clock. "A-a-a-a-h, my cakes seem to be ready. Now to take them to the ball. Oh cook, oh cook! Oh, there you are. Take these cakes to the car."

Part Two: At the Ball

The thirteenth piece of cake was passed to Mrs. Bradley, the fattest lady in town. All of a sudden out jumped Mud and Tud. Mrs. Bradley SCREAMED.

A third-grade boy

The Adventures of the Princess Kitty

Once upon a time there was a kitten and she was a princess kitten, but she did not act like one except in public and even in public her mother had a time with her.

One day there was to be a festival. The king and queen were to be there and also the princess. Just before the kittens started to show their fine arts, the princess kitten slipped away to play baseball with the boys. The queen, her mother, had a time getting the princess back into her silk gown and getting back before the festival started. She was embarrassed and the king gave the queen a dirty look.

One day the queen and the king were giving a royal picnic. Everyone was to be there and so was the princess.

"She is a headache," said the people.

One lady was afraid that the princess might bury her little baby, but they dared not let the king know about this.

Everything went all right until the grand march began. The queen was in a daze about the princess so she slipped out of the march and ran to the water's edge to look for her. There in the middle of the water she found the princess swimming about gaily in the pond. The queen was so surprised she fell right into the pool and caught onto the princess and yelled, "Save me, save me!"

The poor king was shivering like a leaf . . . stepping along out of step in the march.

A third-grade girl

Taffy Tugboat

Taffy Tugboat was in the dock when an ocean liner came in to dock in some fog and bumped Taffy Tugboat 'way under the dock. Taffy Tugboat was stuck. Taffy Tugboat tooted his whistle but nobody came to help him.

Now Taffy Tugboat was in a mess. He tugged and pulled but he could not get out. What would his master say? He would be very angry if he was not there to take him out to the big boats to pull them in.

He had to get out from under that dock. All of a sudden he heard two men coming over the dock. He tooted his whistle. The two men heard him. They were scared. They ran to the police. They said a big monster was under the dock in a very big rage and if he wasn't caught he would try to control the whole city.

The whole police department went to the dock very quietly and started to shoot at the dock. Taffy Tugboat was in a mess.

All of a sudden the shooting stopped. A man said he thought

what they were shooting at was not a monster. It was his tugboat and it *was his boat*. It was Taffy Tugboat.

A third-grade boy

Fuzzy Gets in Trouble

Bang! Bang! Bang! There was an awful racket coming from the cellar. "Ow-w, my thumb!" Fuzzy and Billy Rabbit were making a wagon.

"Whew, thank goodness, that's done! Now let's play in it."

"Yes, let's coast down the hill by Mr. Snobbottom's house."

"O.K., but we won't be able to make any noise," said Fuzzy.

"Why not?"

"Because he'll bawl us out."

"Yeah, I guess so."

"Well, come on," said Fuzzy, pulling the wagon out of the yard. "Whee-e, boy is this fun? Hey, Billy, I can't steer."

"Help, we're going right into Mr. Snobbottom's yard," yelled Billy.

"Yes, and the drive's just been cemented."

"Get out of my new driveway," bawled Mr. Snobbottom.

"We can't," wailed Fuzzy.

"Why not?" yelled Mr. Snobbottom.

"Because we're stuck in the cement."

"Well, get out anyway. Walk off. You can get the wagon later," he yelled, "but get off my new driveway!"

"O.K.," said Billy, climbing out of the wagon. Fuzzy climbed out too.

"HELP!" yelled Fuzzy.

"Help!" echoed Billy.

"Oh, I can't walk. I'm cemented in," wailed Fuzzy.

"So'm I," cried Billy.

Then the front door opened and Mr. Snobbottom waddled out of the house, for he was very fat. "Well, why don't you take off your shoes?"

"O.K. Now we're stuck again."

"Well, take off your socks."

"I can't because they're wet," said Billy.

"Oh, I'll get them off for you," said Mr. Snobbottom, walking onto the cement. He had gone a few steps when he let out a yell. "HELP! I'm stuck too!" Then he forgot all about being scared and started bawling Fuzzy and Billy out. "I'll get the police on you if I have to use hounds."

"First you'll have to get a tow truck," said Fuzzy under his breath.

Now really Fuzzy and Billy were on a dry part of the driveway, but Mr. Snobbottom wasn't. So Fuzzy and Billy just walked away laughing.

BUT (a small word with a big meaning) the next day Mother Rabbit opened the door on a much battered-up cross man. "Mrs. Rabbit, I demand to take your son to the police."

"Why—what do you mean?" asked Mother Rabbit, a bit astonished.

"Just what I said," and he told the story.

Bang! The front door slammed in his face. He was so astonished he lay down and died; so that was the end of Mr. Snobbottom.

The End

A fourth-grade boy

Clean Hands and a Pure Heart

Tommy Rabbit tried to sit down at the table without being noticed by his mother. But she saw him all right.

"Let me see them," she said.

Tommy showed her his right hand which was pretty clean.

"Now the other," she said.

He had to show her his left hand which had a big ink spot on it.

"Now, Tommy Rabbit," said his Mother, "you know better than to come to the table with hands like that, especially today when all the mothers are going to school for a program. You go right upstairs and wash them again."

Tommy went upstairs grumbling to himself about how silly grownups were about clean hands. While he was upstairs he got an idea. That bad little rabbit tip-toed into his mother's room and there was her hat and her gloves laid out for the program at school. Very quietly Tommy put a lot of black powder from his chemistry set into each glove. Then he washed his hands and went downstairs.

After lunch Mrs. Rabbit put on her hat and pulled on her gloves and started off with Tommy. While they were walking along, Tommy picked up some stones and a piece of dirty string and in no time his hands were dirty again. Of course, Mrs. Rabbit had to notice that.

"Tommy," she said, "you will be the death of me. Look at your hands."

"Oh, well, Mother," said Tommy, "boys always have dirty hands."

"No," said Mrs. Rabbit, "your father never had dirty hands and anyway I always say, 'Clean hands and a pure heart.' I am very careful to see that my hands are always clean." When she said this Tommy began to cough and look up at the sky.

When they got to school, Miss Fluffy, the teacher, came out to meet all the mothers. Mrs. Rabbit pulled off her glove as she shook hands with Miss Fluffy. Of course her hand was black with powder and in a minute so was Miss Fluffy's. Neither of them noticed it because they were so busy shaking hands with the other mothers.

Suddenly Mrs. Rabbit looked down at her black paws.

"Oh, my heavens," she said and fainted.

When she came to, Tommy said, "You had better go right upstairs and wash your hands, Mother. How about clean hands and a pure heart?"

And from that day Mrs. Rabbit was never quite so fussy about Tommy's dirty hands.

A fourth-grade boy

Griz and Fuzz Go to the Woods

Mrs. Bear was packing the camping bag for Griz and Fuzz. "Just think," said Griz, "tomorrow we go camping in the woods."

Twelve hours later they were in the car heading for Joe's Woods. "Bye, now," said Mrs. Bear, as Griz and Fuzz left the car.

"Hey, look!" said Griz, "it's a snake."

"N-n-n-now don't panic," said Fuzz, as he shivered. "Just don't move."

"Hey," said Griz, "it was only a king-sized earthworm."

As you can see, the boys didn't know much about the woods. It was getting near evening when Fuzz thought it wise to set up camp. In the middle of the night he heard something go "whoo-oo." He woke up Griz. "Hear that," he whispered in Griz's ear.

Griz looked outside the tent and in an uninterested way said, "It is only the wind in the trees." And he fell back to sleep, too.

In the morning they had a breakfast of eggs and bacon. They were off in less than an hour. An hour later Griz was tired and he sat down on a rock. All of a sudden the rock moved. Griz jumped about six feet in the air and ran into the bushes. Fuzz laughed 'till his face was red because the rock was a turtle. Griz came out of the bushes mad as a volcano, but he decided he wouldn't do anything about it. Where there were turtles there's almost got to be water.

They decided to look around. They found a nice big pond and went swimming. Next thing you knew, a fish caught Griz's toe. Five minutes later they were on the bank with the First Aid Kit their mother had put in the camping bag and a fish.

"Oh, that smarts," said Griz, as the iodine was being applied.

"Put on your shoe and let's get moving," said Fuzz.

"How much farther do we have to go?" asked Griz.

"About ten miles."

"Oh, no! After what happened today, I don't know if I can survive."

"Don't worry. Somehow I think you can."

That night they had trouble with the mosquitoes. They didn't get much sleep. In the morning they slept late. It was ten when they woke up. That day they saw a real snake and thought it was a worm and had almost got bitten.

Two days later they met their mother at the end of the woods. "Well, boys, how did it go in the woods?" "Awful!" was the only word they could say.

A fourth-grade boy

Mother's Day

It was Mother's Day in Bearville and the Five Bears were looking in the dictionary to see if they could find something to give Mother Bear for a Mother's Day present.

Just then Bo interrupted, "Why don't we earn some money and get her that perfume she wanted."

"Oh, you mean that stuff that smells like gas poisoning?" said Pug.

"Well, I guess that's what you call it."

"O.K. We'll go to the grocery store and see if we can deliver groceries."

"Let's go!"

At the Grocery Store

"Hey, Mister," said Eenie, "we want a job."

"O.K. Here, take these to Mrs. Bottom-Puss at 44 Killiver Lane.

At Mrs. R.F.D.'S House

"Come in, you darling boys. It was so nice of you to bring my groceries. Here you can each have a candy bar."

Just then the clock struck six.

"Oh! We better go home. We were meant to be home a long time ago!"

At home a robber was stealing Mother Bear's best china. Just then the Five Bears walked in. Pug grabbed his B-B gun and shot the robber.

"My heroes!" said Mother Bear. And Pug got rewarded.

A fourth-grade girl

Wham! went the door of the Bear home. "Ma," cried Pug and Bo together. "Ma, can we have the living room for our club?"

"Well—" said Mother Bear.

"*Please*, Mom."

"Well—all right."

"Yippy," cried Bo and Pug. "Let's tell the gang."

Next day the five bears were decorating the living room. Pug and Bo were giving orders. In two more days the living room was a sight. The wallpaper had been peeled off and in its place were crayon Indians drawn by Bo. The drapes had been pulled together and the room was very dark. The carpets had been rolled up and sheets had been put in their place. All the tables and chairs in the house were put in rows and Eenie was getting the gang together.

All this time Father Bear was away (Thank goodness!). But the *day* the first meeting was to be held was the day Father was to come home. Father opened the door of his home to find the living room in the sight it was. Father grabbed all five bears but Mother Bear saved the bears from a sore seat that night by telling Father. *And* Father saved the bears from another sore seat.

198

Because if Mother had heard what kind of a club the Bears were running, she should have spanked them.
P.S. The bears were talking about cookies and cake and ice cream. (at the club meeting) They were going to take them from Mother Bear. She was making them for the County Bazaar.

A fourth-grade girl

Starry Light-up

Now Starry Light-Up was a little star that lived in the town, Invisaville. One night, he and his brother, Mego, were shining down on a meadow when Starry spoke up and said, "I wonder if Mom and Pop are awake, yet."

"No, I doubt it. They never are awake this early. Then why don't we go to the moon?"

"Excellent idea," exclaimed Mego, "but what about Mom and Pop?"

"Oh, they'll never guess we went there."

So, off they flew, gaining more speed as they flew. And in a woosh they were on the moon.

"Wow, it's windy," Starry said.

He was only one foot three inches high and weighed only seven pounds, which was underweight for a star of seven years. So he was blown into a gravity pit which held three times as much gravity as there is in the earth. (The moon really doesn't have that much gravity.) What will Starry do? Mego has fallen into one, too. Fortunately, Starry knew how to use wind. He blew as hard as he could upward. He started falling up. It was working. Soon he was out and told Mego to do the same. Both boys had starchutes. They were like parachutes. But it was so windy that the starchutes blew away and they forgot all about them.

For an hour or two they were hunting for rocks to take home when suddenly, from out of the rocks, came something. Starry shouted to Mego, the expert on Nature, but it was only a rock lizard which were very common. Then Starry noticed that they had no starchutes and told that to Mego. They decided to shoot. This was very difficult, and they hit Earth. Mom and Pop were still asleep. It must have been strange to see stars in the daytime. They had to shoot again. This time they hit Rockway, a village far from Invisaville. Again they shot and landed right on their house on the chimney and slid right down with a big thump. All this awoke Mom and Pop. If you ever see marks of a shooting star in the daytime, you'll know it's Starry and Mego.

A fourth-grade girl

Bip and Burp, Two Kids

It was Saturday. Bip's and Burp's mother was having the painters over. At 10:30 the painters came. Their mother went into the kitchen to start lunch. They saw an empty ladder with a pail of paint on it. They climbed up and started to slop the paint on the wall. Suddenly their mother came barging out of the kitchen. The pail of paint lost balance and dropped on their mother's head. For the next few minutes the only thing that was heard was "glub" coming from the pail and the bumping of knees coming from Bip and Burp.

Bip and Burp ran upstairs. Their mother came tearing after them. For the next hour and a half there was a spilling of paint and the falling of ladders. Luckily the furniture had been moved into the garage!

Finally their mother saw a white flag sticking out the keyhole of an old closet. Bip and Bup knew it was the end. Or was it?

They saw their mother's old wedding dress and a lot of other stuff. They tied it all together and climbed out the closet window, but their mother had been looking through the key hole and saw it all. She caught them as they were coming down. I suppose you know what happened then.

A fourth-grade girl

Starring Horny Hornet
in
Relative Trouble

One day Horny Hornet was flying along and all of a sudden to his surprise it was his cousin, Wilbur Warbler, who probably ran away from home because his mother never let him out of the house.

Horny was suprised. "Hey—what are you doing here?"

"Yipes!" Wilbur turned around and flew as fast as he could. Something white fell from his tail feathers.

Wilbur was wanted by the police because he ran away from

home. Horny buzzed as fast as he could and "Ouch!" Wilbur zoomed—crash!—right through his bedroom window.

Horny got a beautiful wool stinger-cover for a reward.

A fourth-grade boy

Danny Woodchuck

Once upon a time there lived a little woodchuck named Danny. It was winter, and all little woodchucks were very fast asleep and the winds were cold and sent a whisk of winter cold through Danny's door and made him shiver in his winter blankets.

Funny enough, he started to yawn and woke up and stared all around him because a witch in his dream was about to eat him up. But remembering his house he laughed, but the cold wind broke his laugh and he remembered it was winter and crawled to the door. Sure enough, there was snow on the earth everywhere.

He said, "I have never seen snow. It looks like white frosting"—and so he ate some birch bark, jumped in some clothes, and went out the door.

Before you knew it, he bumped into Mr. Squirrel and WHOOOOOOOOOOO SMACK! A landslide of snow came down on him.

Finally he got out and walked home and from that day on he had to take sleeping pills!

A fourth-grade boy

Mac-the-Worm Stories

One day Mac got tired of mowing the lawn, and so, after ten hours of sweating he said, "I will build a robot."

And as you came by his apple-born house, you would hear a rat-a-tat-tat and a bang-bang.

That afternoon Mac came out with a robot who could cut the grass for him. At three o'clock he took it for a trial run. B-r-r-r-r-rm! Crash, boom! The race is on. Z-z-z-z-z-z. It went right through the hedge. Pow—right through Mr. Talk-a-lot's apple. Z-z-z-z-z-z. It crashed right into a police car.

Just then a policeman came out and said, "Get this contraption out of here."

Poor Mac had to got go to prison for the rest of his life, but that's not the end of his stories 'cause there's another old worm in prison named Charlie Hill and every day Mac dictates to him.

The End

One fine morning, Mac said to himself, "I need a vacation." So Mac-the-Worm called the airport. Yes, there was a plane leaving for Florida in just six hours. Mac packed in a hurry. When he got to the airport, some men took his baggage. Then he plopped down on a seat to rest.

After four hours there was a great commotion. It startled Mac. Mac got up and went to the window of the plane. Then someone shouted, "Plane buzzards! Plane Buzzards!"

Now if you don't know what plane buzzards are, you rightly now should know. They're giant ropelike birds. Then Mac heard, "Get the guns! Get the guns!"

Pow, pow, pow, pow! BANG!

"Bye, bye, Bud—er—I mean Buzzards," said Mac.

But one of the bullets had hit the only good propeller. Mac cleared his throat, and said, "Er—bye-bye to me, with tears!"

Mac jumped off the falling plane, but he forgot he had a parachute on. Mac was relieved. But he also saw an island below. Then Mac saw a cannibal. When he landed, lots of cannibals were around. Poor Mac!

Mac got taken to a big pot. "Not me," he grunted. "Worm stew!"

But the cannibals let him go. Mac saw a boat with a motor. He ran, jumped in the boat, and put-putted away. Soon he saw a tugboat coming.

The captain said, "I'll take you ashore, young fella."

So Mac got home and said, "I lost my clothes, but I had an exciting trip." And he fell fast asleep.

The End

A fourth-grade boy

Mrs. Twiddle-Works was a lady who twiddled with her work. Stinky, Inky, and Flinky-Dink were three little mice. They lived in her sewing box. They would get her yarn all mixed up. They would have yellow, green, brown, blue all mixed up.

One day, Mrs. Twiddle-Works went out shopping. Stinky,

Inky, and Flinky-Dink were all left alone. They said, "Let's go out and hunt for some food."

Stinky started out, but his foot was caught in some yarn. He got out and went in the kitchen and got some cheese, but when he got back to the sewing box there was a long string of yarn from the sewing basket to the kitchen.

Mrs. Twiddle-Works came in and saw the string. She was very surprised. She ran up the stairs to see where the string came from. Stinky, Inky, and Flinky-Dink heard her coming so they went to the bottom of the basket and they got there just as Mrs. Twiddle-Works arrived.

She was very much surprised to see three mice jump out. "Land sakes," said Mrs. Twiddle-Works, "of all things! Is that who's been eating my cheese? Well, Well, Well!"

Inky had found a hole in Mr. Twiddle-Works's closet. Stinky went into Mrs. Twiddle-Works's closet and into a pair of shoes. Flinky-Dink had found a hole in the floor.

Mrs. Twiddle-Works went and called up Mr. Twiddle-Works and she said, "I think that we will have to move into an apartment because there are mice living in the house."

And Mr. Twiddle-Works said, "All right." So they moved.

Inky, Stinky, and Flinky-Dink lived in the house for a long time. Mrs. Twiddle-Works had left ten pounds of cheese on the table.

A fourth-grade girl

Don and Miss Tippy Toes

Once upon a time there lived a little girl mouse and a little boy mouse. They had to go to Miss Tippy Toes's ballet class and they hated it. Well, Pamela Mouse liked it a little bit. Today they had to go for their lessons.

"Children," Mother Mouse called. "Time for ballet class. You must hurry."

"I'm ready," called Pamela.

"Just a minute," called Don, as he struggled to get into his leotard.

Soon they were at Miss Tippy Toes's house.

"Little higher leg, Janet. Stick in your stomach, Jane. Perfect, Pamela. Don, you know that it's your left leg, not your right."

Don was the only boy and all the girls giggled as Miss Tippy Toes changed legs.

"Now girls and boy, we will perform our little dance number. Music . . . one, two, three, four." Miss Tippy Toes started to sing and everybody plugged their ears.

Soon ballet class ended and Don headed for the door. "Wait a minute," said Miss Tippy Toes. "You're going to have to stay after and learn our little number."

It was five o'clock before he got out. He was about to go out the door, but then he turned to Miss Tippy Toes and said, "I QUIT!"

A fourth-grade girl

Wash Day

"Children," said Mother Bear, "today is Monday and a holiday from school—and now," she said in a low tone with a little gleam in her eye, "you can do some washing. Wash day, you know—YOUR WASH DAY."

The five bears slowly, inch by inch, got up from the dinner table, but in the wink of an eye Mother Bear caught them by their big floppy ears and dropped them one by one ker-splash into the tub.

A fifth-grade boy

"Children, I have a treat for you," said Miss Flower, the bears' teacher, "a special treat."

"What is it?" asked the class in chorus. "Is it ice cream and cake?"

"Oh no, much better than that," said the teacher, "Miss Brown—she is one of the teachers in a western university—she has come to see how boys and girls act."

Miss Brown smiled and began to speak. "I love to come and visit schools and see the boys and girls. You remind me of my childhood. I teach older boys and girls, but they are almost grownup while you are just beginning life. How I envy Miss Flower, your beloved teacher, for she has you with her every day."

Miss Flower was very jealous of Miss Brown, but she hid her own feeling and offered Miss Brown her chair. She didn't know that Pug had put a tack in the chair. Miss Brown sat down. Miss Brown got up rather fast and started for the door.

"I never did like children," she said as she started through the door.

"You shouldn't have done that, children," said Miss Flower, but she gave them each ten cents to buy a Good Humor with.

A fifth-grade girl

The five little bears were in school one afternoon. "Now," said the teacher, "I will tell you something. On your way home will you hunt for signs of spring?"

Pug shot a bean out of his beanshooter.

"Ouch! Oh-h-h!" said the teacher.

"That's a sign of spring," said Pug.

"You're dismissed," the teacher said.

"Good!" said all the bears except Bo.

The next day the bears went to school bright and early. But Pug decided to play hooky. He sneaked away from the other bears.

"I hope," said Bo, "that we won't be late."

"Come on. Let's run or we will be," said the other bears.

When they got to school the teacher asked if they had seen any signs of spring. Teenie raised his hand and said, "I was digging and I found a worm and it was growing pink."

"No, Teenie-a-I-er-a don't think that's a very good sign of spring," said the teacher.

"You don't say so," said Teenie. "Why, where is Pug?"

The teacher said surprised, "Huh?"

The bears said, "I guess he must have played hooky, don't you?"

"Yes I do," said the teacher. "Eenie, Teenie, Tiny, and Bo, go out and find Pug."

"All right," they said. They went outdoors and saw a truck.

"I'll tell you what let's do," Eenie said. "Let's get up in the truck and ride all over town and maybe we will find Pug."

They got up in the truck and lay down as flat as they could. Bo whimpered a little after they were on the way. "Oh, stop your crying and look," said Eenie.

They finally saw a little ash can walking around on two brown fat, chubby bear legs.

"I think that I see Pug," said Eenie.

"Where?" the other bears said.

"Over there," he pointed to the ash can.

The bears tumbled out of the truck. "Oh dear—oh dear—oh dear!" they said. They ran over to Pug. "Hey, you've got to go home."

They pulled off the ash can. Pug did not want to go home. The four little bears pulled and pulled. They got Pug home. About an hour later Pug was rubbing his seat. The other little bears were eating a nice piece of cherry pie. "Um-m-m—" they were saying when they got to bed.

A fifth-grade boy

Pug Shows Off Daisy May

The bears were coming home from school. Pug was running so fast that the other bears had a hard time keeping up with him. Now this was very unusual for Pug for he always dallied on the way, stopping at the baseball field to bat a few balls. But today he hurried; no one knew why. But Eenie suspected that he had a date with Susie Bear.

When they got home Pug ran up to Mother Bear's room. The other bears followed him because they wanted to know where he was going. When they got up to the room Pug was talking breathlessly.

"There's a new girl in school called Elizabeth Ann, and I am going over to see her this afternoon, and bring Daisy May for she wants me to."

"Well, all right," said Mother Bear. "Wrap her up warmly in a blanket and you will have to dress her."

"So he is going over to see Elizabeth Ann," thought Bo, "and show her Daisy May, and I wanted to. Well, I'll fix him." Then Bo said in a very sweet voice, "Let me dress her for you."

"Oh, all right. Put on her best dress and her best coat and hat and put her in her new carriage and put on her new blanket."

With these instructions Pug straightened his tie and combed his hair while Bo went to fix Daisy May. Ten minutes later Bo wheeled Daisy May's carriage into the living room where Pug was.

"Don't pull the hood up," said Bo, "for she is asleep."

"All right," said Pug. Taking the handle of the carriage in one hand and his father's cane in the other he started over to Elizabeth's. When he got there Elizabeth ran down to meet him.

"Oh, let me see Daisy May!"

"Why, Pug, you deceitful thing. Don't you think I can tell the difference between a person and a doll? You are teasing, you mean thing!" With that she went into the house and Pug was left with the doll.

That night at supper, Bo had a black eye and Pug had a warm seat.

A fifth-grade boy

The Five Bears Start an Orchestra

One day the five bears decided to start an orchestra. Bo was to play the drum. He couldn't quite reach the top, but he had talent. They discovered it one time when Pug was fighting Bo, and Bo started pounding on his back. Tiny played the tuba. He did it 'cause it hid him, and if he struck a sour note, nobody would know who did it. Teenie played the flute 'cause he knew Joy Bear was coming, and she could see him easily with the flute. Eenie played the violin. When he was small he had swallowed a toy whistle; so he said he wouldn't mind the squeaks. Pug had the bass violin 'cause he liked to take up a lot of room to be noticed.

One day their school decided to put on an amateur hour, and the bears decided to enter their orchestra. Finally the great day arrived and they were very much excited. They just got there in time.

"Ladies and gentlemen, and contestants, we present to you tonight Major Blows, who is to judge our contest. The first contestants are Eenie, Teenie, Tiny, Bo, and Pug Bear, who have an orchestra."

They all took their places and began. Bo and Pug started a piece called "Thunder," while the rest played a piece called "Twinkling Stars." The discord was enough to blow everybody out of the auditorium. They finally finished quickly and took their seats. At the end everyone was supposed to clap for the best, but when the orchestra went on the stage, nobody made a sound.

"Aw gee," said Pug, "nobody appreciates good music."

A fifth-grade girl

Tall, Middle-size, and Small

Once upon a time in a little house lived three otters. They lived with their mother and father (of course). The tallest otter's

207

name was Tall; the middlesized otter's name was Middle-Size; the little wee otter's name was—What do you think it was?—Small!

One day Tall, Middle-Size, and Small said to their mother, "Mother," said Tall.

"Mother," said Middle-Size.

"Mama," said Small in his small wee voice.

"Mother," they said all together, "Mother, we are going to do something, but we can't think what it is. What are we going to do?" they asked.

"Why don't you know? You are going to the fair with your father and me."

"Oh, yes, yes, yes! Now we know," they cried.

"Now we know! Now we know! Now we know!" repeated Small.

"Oh, shut up," said Tall, "or it will be the worse for you." Small began to whimper but brightened up at the promise of an ice cream from his mother.

"You spoil him," said Tall who was just like his father.

"What's that about spoiling somebody?" came a cheery voice.

"Oh, nothing," said Tall grumpily. "She's just spoiling Small just 'cause he's the littlest."

"Well, Oscar, after all he IS the littlest and—" said Mrs. Otter.

"I know, Ophelia," said Mr. Otter, "but you shouldn't baby him."

"Well, why shouldn't I? After all, he's our smallest child—".

"Well, why don't you do something about it? Why don't you give birth to another baby otter? That's an idea!"

"That's an idea! I'll do it. I'll have another baby."

"She'll have another baby," echoed Small.

"Oh, hush up," said Tall.

Chapter Two: The Baby's Arrival

When it came, it was a girl and on the day of its arrival the mother called the children into her room. When all were assembled (even the father), the mother said, "Now children, what shall we call the baby?" Silence . . . "Well?"

"We're thinking." More silence.

Then from Tall, "We could call it Ophelia after you, Mother."

"And call her Ophy for short," put in Middle-Size and then he giggled. "Can you tell why?"

Then Small said, "We could call her Small Junior after *me*."

"Who would want to name anything after *you*? You're the smallest." Tall is speaking.

"I'm the smallest," echoed Small regretfully.

But then Mother said, "Not any more, sugar plum. That little girl in the cradle is the smallest now. But come, can't anybody think of a better name than Ophelia or Small Junior? Papa, can you think of anything?"

"Why not call her Tiny? That's a good name."

"Yes, yes," said everybody, "let's call her Tiny."

"Let's call her Tiny," echoed Small but nobody said, "Hush up," this time.

Chapter Three: Going to the Fair

Coming to the fair had to be delayed a few weeks 'til the baby should be able to sit up in the baby carriage. But animals grow very fast and Tiny was no exception. So in a few weeks Tiny could walk, a little wobbly perhaps, but still she could walk.

So one sunny morning they started out for the fair. As soon as Tiny was tired, Mr. Otter picked her up and carried her. It was plain that Tiny was Mr. Otter's favorite for nobody likes to have all boys however nice they may be. After all, one likes to have at least one of a different sex.

Finally they reached the fairgrounds. Small shrieked with delight when he saw the Ferris wheel. Tall and Middle-Size acted more grown-up than Small but they were pleased nevertheless. Tiny could not go on the Ferris wheel as she was still a baby, but she did not seem to know what she was missing and gurgled and cooed all the time.

When Tall, Middle-Sized, and Small came down from the Ferris wheel, they all went to the merry-go-round. Small and Tiny wanted to try it immediately but Tall and Middle-Size said, "Ach, such babies to ride on a merry-go-round."

But Small and Tiny didn't mind. Indeed, Tiny *could not* understand a word they said as she was only a few weeks old.

All afternoon they gorged themselves on hot dogs and soda pop and ice creams—that is, all except Tiny. *Her* diet was limited to one ice cream and a glass of orange juice.

What a happy afternoon they had! And when it was all over and they were riding home in the wagon, Small said, "Gee, we had fun!"

The End

A fifth-grade girl

Small Gets a Haircut

"Why does everything have to happen to me?" Small sighed. "Huh! I don't need a haircut anyway. Women are so silly, always thinking little boys need haircuts. Well, here I am. Should I go in or should I stay out? Oh, I might as well go in—but—Oh, I'll go in."

He walked slowly into George Goat's barbershop. "I want a crow-cut," he announced.

"Don't you mean a crew cut?" asked the attendant.

"No," said Small, "I mean a crow cut. Just like the crows wear."

The attendant finally got Small settled in the barber's chair. "Now you say you want a crew cut," he began.

"A crow cut," said Small firmly.

"But—but there isn't any such thing as a crow cut," said the bewildered attendant.

"I don't care," said Small; "I want one anyway."

The attendant said he'd try and was just about to put the sheet about Small's neck when Small suddenly said, "I don't need a bib. Watcha putting a bib on me for?"

The attendant's pride was hurt. "Young man," he said sternly, "this is not a bib. It is merely a sheet to keep the hair off your clean suit—"

"Tain't clean," said Small sullenly.

"So you won't get it dirty," continued the attendant.

"Don't care if I do get it dirty," pouted Small.

"Now will you sit still?" asked the attendant impatiently, after a vain attempt to cut Small's hair straight.

"Why?" asked Small impishly.

"Because," said the attendant, "if you don't I won't be able to cut your hair straight and then you won't look nice."

"Don't wanna look nice," said Small. "Wanna go home."

"Go home then," said the angry attendant.

"All right, I will," and Small stomped out of the barber shop, the soap suds all over his head.

A fifth-grade boy

The Five Bears Go Daisy Picking

"Oh gee," said Bo, "I wish there were something to do."

"You can come and look at the postman with me," said Pug, who was perched in the window and staring at the postman. "He's coming up our front walk now."

Ding, ding. The doorbell rang.

"I hope he has something for us," said Eenie as he ran over to the door.

"Here's a letter for ye boys," said the postman as he busily chewed his tobacco.

"Looks like it's from Sue Bear's house. Hey, look, it's an invitation to a-a-a-aoh-h—" Eenie collapsed.

"Read it, Pug," said Bo excitedly. "What's it say?"

"We're invited to a—oh, my gosh—to a daisy-picking party."

"Oh-h they all moaned, "I've got a stomach ache," and they all dashed upstairs, that is all but Bo. He stopped to look at the invitation.

"Golly, of all the stupid things to ask he-men like us to go to. I—Gee, what's this? Refreshments will be served. Golly, I'm going."

A sixth-grade girl

Eau de Cologne

"One more tack," said Pug to Bo. "When we get this sign up our luck begins."

Pug was pasting a sign on the door. It read:

Classical Beauty Parlor

Mud Packs   Hand Permanents

Manicures

Haircuts   Back Massage

Children Only 3¢ to 13¢

The five bears had decided that they would have a beauty parlor and get rich. They had fixed up the attic. In it was a bucket of mud, a bucket full of water, four chairs, Eenie's toy cash-register bank, which was on top of the bookcase which had three or four magazines on it, a copy of Red Riding Hood, Grimm's Fairy Tales with three pages out, a funny page from the Saturday paper, a Big-Little book, and a cupboard, which contained miscellaneous things such as water paints and bobby pins. The last had come from Mother's room, and there was a table with a vase which had some withered daisies which Bo had contributed. The beauty specialists were in the attic when the bell rang. Pug opened it with a bow. There stood Ann Bear.

"Are you the manager of the beauty parlor?" she said.

"Yes," said Pug, guessing that he was.

"Well," said Ann Bear, "I want a mud pack, please. Where shall I go?"

"Er—uh, right upstairs. Follow me," said Pug. "Here we are," he said as they came to the attic. "Sit right down, please. Hey, Teenie, how do you give a mud pack, anyhow?"

"I don't know," answered Teenie.

"Well, I guess you just put mud on a person's face. Yeah— well here I go. Now, Madam," said Pug, "please sit back."

He picked up a rag, dipped it in the mud, and washed Ann's face with it.

"There," said Pug. "Four cents please."

"But you're not finished," said Ann Bear, "you have to wash it off."

"Why," said Pug, "our sign didn't say so. It says MUD PACKS. It didn't say a thing about washing it off, but since you're so unhappy about it I will take it off for one cent."

"Oh, all right," said Ann, who had been wondering what she was going to do. Pug got another rag, dipped it in the water, and washed it off. Pug thought it was a perfect job, but he did not see how Ann's yellow fur was still striped with brown.

"Well," said Ann, "here's your five cents. Goodbye."

As soon as Ann had gone Eenie said, "Pug, it's my turn now."

"O.K.," said Pug, "you can take care of the next customer, but," he warned, "do it good."

Eenie had just mumbled something under his breath about he wasn't so hot when the doorbell rang. Eenie slid down the bannisters and opened the door. "Why," he said, "it's Louise Bear."

"Yes," said Louise Bear, "I have come to have a hand permanent."

"O.K.," said Eenie; "follow me."

"All right," said Louise Bear.

"Er," said Eenie as they got up to the attic, "would you pay me in advance, please?"

"I suppose so," said Louise Bear, "how much?"

"Three cents," said Eenie, "for the rubber bands, two cents for the trouble, one cent for doing it. That adds up to um—er—let me see—three cents and two cents makes five cents plus two cents more makes seven cents exactly."

"Very well," said Louise Bear, "where shall I sit?"

"Over there," said Eenie, thinking that the water pail was a chair.

Louise Bear sat down, "Oh," she cried, "my new dress! Give me back my money!"

"Now, now," said Eenie, "you know it was just a mistake."

"Wasn't," yelled Louise Bear. "I'm going to tell my mummy." And she ran home.

"You're not so good," said Bo timidly. "Let me try."

"Oh, all right. See what you can do," said Eenie.

"Oh goody," said Bo. "Just watch me."

Just then Mother Bear, who did not know what the bears were doing, led the real-estate man upstairs to the attic. He had come to see about repairs and Mother was saying to him, "And the attic needs repainting."

She opened the door of the attic.

"So," said the real-estate man, "this is the way you take care of your house. The company shall hear of this." And the man started to go out the door.

"Wait, Sir," said Bo. "Would you like a haircut?"

"How much?" said the man.

"Three cents, Sir," said Bo.

"O.K. Clip away," said the real-estate man softening.

Mother Bear was so grateful to Bo for saving the day that she called up the drugstore and ordered five chocolate ice cream cones for the bears. Meanwhile Bo started cutting. Cut-cut, cut, cut.

"Are you finished?" said the man after a while when Bo stopped.

"Yes," said Bo, innocently, "there isn't a hair left on you."

"What?" yelled the man.

"I said," said Bo, "that there's not a hair left on you by this time."

Bo Bear, Eenie, Teenie, Tiny and Pug were laughing so hard they were crying.

"Well," said the man cooling off, "since you are so sorry I shall not report this."

That night Mother Bear was so mad about the attic not being painted that she took the five bears to the drugstore and got them five sodas each.

A sixth-grade boy

Five Brave Knights

Once upon a time Pug said, "I am going to read my new book."

"I will read it with you," said Bo.

"So will I," said each of the other three bears.

They all ran into Pug's room. Pug said, "I am in Chapter Fifteen." So he began to read: "The knight vowed to kill the giant, and so he went to the giant and cut him with his sword."

"He did not," said Bo. "He killed him with his sword."

"Well, that's what the book says," responded Pug.

"I have an idea," said Eenie suddenly. "I saw five suits of armor down in the living room. We can each wear one and then we will go out and slay a giant." And they all ran down into the living room.

"Help me into this suit of armor," said Eenie. The other bears helped him squeeze into it. Then they got into suits too, all except Bo. Bo went over to examine Eenie's suit.

"You look nice," said Bo, lifting up the armored arm. Suddenly he lost his grip. The heavily armored arm crashed down on Bo's head. A huge crash echoed through the house. The other bears were so scared that they jumped right out of their armor and sailed six feet into the air. They came crashing down to the ground, and their suits of armor fell on top of them, breaking all to pieces. Tiny stuck his head out of the pile of broken armor.

"What happened?" he asked.

"Bo got squashed," said Pug carelessly.

"Well, then we'd better unsquash him," said Tiny.

"I don't know how to do that," said Pug, and so they put Bo in his room and started on their adventures. Before long they heard a great crashing noise.

"It's a giant," whispered Eenie fearfully.

"I'll get him," said Pug, and he ran up and stuck the sword into the giant's leg.

"Ow!" yelled the giant, so loud that it seemed to make the whole village shake.

"I will kill him now," said Pug, and he started to climb up the giant's leg.

"So will we," said all the other bears, and they followed Pug up the giant's leg.

"Get off!" screamed the giant, and he kicked his leg so hard that Pug lost his grip and found himself flying through the air. Luckily he landed in the giant's hair and yelled, "Come on, you fellows," to the others.

Meanwhile Bo, back in the house, was very much disappointed because he could not go along with the rest.

"Oh dear me," he said, "if I weren't squashed I could go along with the rest of them." Then suddenly he had an idea. "If you hammer down a person," he said to himself, "he would be squashed, and so it is very reasonable to suppose that if you hammer up on a person he would be unsquashed." So at once he ran down to get the hammer, and he unsquashed himself as far as he could. Then he ran out to where the other bears were fighting with the giant.

"Now I will show them," said Bo, and he began to climb up the giant's leg. Now Bo was a very bad climber, and every time he climbed up the leg he slipped down again. This tickled the giant so much that he began to laugh. He laughed till he sneezed and he sneezed till he fell over backwards. Then the five bears all ran up and down his stomach and made the giant laugh himself to death. Bo was so happy that he sang this song all the way home.

> Who slew the giant?
> Five brave knights;
> But it was really I
> I killed the giant.

> A sixth-grade boy

Verse Supplement

Just as hearing children's stories often starts a wave of story writing so, too, does listening to verse composed by other children serve as a touchstone for poetry making. We find it productive to have a collection of children's poems to read aloud. We use them to provide contagion for poetic expression—sometimes to set a mood, to show how differently people feel about the same thing, often to build confidence, but never as models to be imitated or copied.

For these reasons we present here a supplement of verse by children seven- to ten-years old. It is not children's "best"; rather it represents a broad spectrum of their writing and dictation. We purposely have included poems that illustrate unevenness of quality. The brief flash of individuality along with the matrix of pedestrian language in which it is imbedded, serves to fortify another beginner's belief in himself. Many are about weather and other natural phenomena. We do this to show how different children respond to the same theme. We offer also some examples which show merit in the elements that are the essence of poetry.

There are four blue eggs in the brown nest;
The mother robin gentles her red feathers
Down over them
And never makes a sound.
Then suddenly there are four baby birds
Squawking with surprise
To see the great brown world of the nest.
And the mother bird

Stands on the edge of the nest
And sings to everyone,
"Look, Look,
The world is full of baby birds."

*   *   *

Who scratched the sky?
Last night some clumsy giant cat
Roared over the edge of night,
And blackly reached his giant paw
To scratch with gold the sky.

*   *   *

Froggy

Froggy,
Why do you have
Such a big Adam's apple?
How is it to be bothered
By all the fish?
Don't you ever get tired
Jumping around?
How is it to be in shallow water
All the time
Under the beautiful shade
Of the trees?
And, by the way,
Are you going to be home
Tomorrow?

*   *   *

Oh, Moon above me,
Where do you go
When you are gone?
Do you go visiting?
Make the next person
On your visiting list
Be me!

*   *   *

Clouds

Clouds are like a white, lovely pillow
Where you can lay your head down
For a hundred years.
Every minute a baby cloud is born.
Sometimes the clouds aren't so lovely;
Sometimes they fight
And all the rain falls,
But it quenches the flowers' thirst.

* * *

How to Make a Poem

Don't say "pretty" or "nice",
That's not very good,
It doesn't have a color in it.
Don't say "pretty" or "nice"—
It's no good at all,
Just like a flower when it's dead.
It isn't like a paint picture
Because *it* runs down the paper;
It's like a story
That's a short one;
The words are a good kind of words—
Ones that you know about.
It isn't anyone else's poem;
It's yours!

* * *

The Seasons

When spring comes I'm ever so glad,
It's not because it's spring or I can pick flowers,
But it is that summer's coming soon
And my birthday's in summer, too.
That makes it very nice:
I can go swimming, and have picnics,
And romp in the woods.

I like winter, too,
Because it's almost Christmas
And Halloween comes around.
I play in the snow and have such a jolly time.

It's just like a ball of string
That keeps unwinding all the time
And winding back again.

*   *   *

The Halloween Night

The two pumpkins sit on the back fence,
And their fire is shooting up.
And the cats are sneaking behind them;
And the witches
Are riding
In mid-air,
As the light
Of the pumpkin's candle
Touches the tree above it.

The tree throws back its branches with anger,
And the wind comes along
And scolds the pumpkins
And blows them out.
The witch is very annoyed,
And rides furiously away with the wind carrying her.
She casts a magic spell on the wind and it dies away.

*   *   *

Over by the sweet lily pond
Where the frogs
Do their little dance
And sing their merry little tune,—
Over by the sweet lily pond
All of a sudden
A big blow
Comes to their little home
And they jump up
And skip into the water.

Then sunshine comes
Through the shadows of their rooms,
And they pop up
And sing
Their merry little tunes,
Down by the sweet lily pond.

*   *   *

The lily of the valley
Looks like an old fashioned lamp.
I wonder if it ever
Would light up in the dark.
If it would,
I would pick one
So it would guide me home.

*   *   *

The Star's Mother

In morning when the sun rises
All the little star children
Twinkle themselves to sleep.
The mother moon watches over them
So they will not wake up.
They sleep so soundly in the blue sky
That they sink into their cloudy pillows
And you can't see them.

*   *   *

Was it the wind?
NO!
Creeping, creeping,
Though you could hear nothing
Save the low steady growl
Of the giant's cat.
Like a wild bear
He was purring contentedly
As though he had his fill of milk.
Putting his head against the furnace

He meowed once,
Yawned, showing his teeth
Like the fangs of a hungry wolf.
He put his head on his paw,
Stopped his purring,
Curled his tail around his legs,
And went to sleep.

*   *   *

One day I was walking along
In the city;
The streets were black,
The people weren't gay
As they are in the country.

In the country
You see men
Driving cows home,
But in the city
There are no cows
To be driven home,
Or no cows to be milked.

I like the country
Better than the city
Where the hills
Stretch far and clear.
Nothing can stop them
Since nothing's strong enough
Except an earthquake.

*   *   *

Another World

Once I saw an army of ants marching,—
They marched and disappeared
Through the blades of grass,
And then appeared again.
Then I saw them disappear
Down a hole.
I saw another army

March into that same hole.
Ants seem to have
A world of their own;
I wonder if
I'll ever see them again.

* * *

Make Believe

The clock is chatting all the time.
He never can close his mouth;
His tongue is going back and forth
Because he's out of breath
From talking so much.

* * *

Leaves look like an army
Going to war;
Leaves look like fighter planes
Flying in formation.

* * *

What is gloom?
Gloom is a sticky, messy day,
Gloom is a disappointment
Gloom is a misunderstanding.

* * *

The water comes tumbling down
The stone wall.
When it meets with the river
They turn together;
The river runs to the ocean.
The Baby Waterfall, Mother River,
    and Father Ocean
Join together.

* * *

The trees look like an upside-down broom
Sweeping the sky;
They sway back and forth
Just like a real broom,
And clean all the dust
Off the clouds.

*   *   *

Leaves have beautiful talents—
When they fall
They make me
Think of a bird
Diving down to earth.
Then they blow in the wind;
They look like clowns
Doing somersaults.
Birds make patterns;
Rivers have a twisty-turn flow;
The world seems like a circus.

*   *   *

When the moon is happy
It is very, very small;
But, when it's sad
It's very big,
And the shadows
You see on it
Are the tears.

*   *   *

A lot of things can happen
On a bright spring day:
Birds will be flying
Above you,
Maybe you'll even see
A little field mouse,

Or a chipmunk
Running around,
Enjoying the springtime
As we do.
The grass will be light green,
Ducks will be swimming happily
In the pond they like so much.
A lot of things can happen
On a bright spring day—
More than I have told you.

*   *   *

A best friend
Is someone you can love
All your life—
A friend to play with
And to do what is fun;
It may be dolls,
Or riding a bike;
It may even be baseball
If that is what you like.
But best of all, I think,
Is to sit on a leafy branch
Where no one can see you,
And talk and plan the things
You are going to do
In the summer to come.

*   *   *

The Trees

Whenever I'm in trouble and talk to myself out loud,
The trees nod their heads to and fro,
They know what is troubling me;
They hold out their arms
As if to make a bed for me.

*   *   *

Shooting Stars

Shooting stars
Are the divers of the skies,
They go with fleetness
Across the heavens,
They come in a sudden
And leave so fast—
Shooting stars
Are the divers of the skies.

*   *   *

Snowflakes

Snowflakes marching down, down, down—
They make such a pretty sight
I even see little fairies
Sitting on them
Holding reins to drive them down.
But when they get near the bottom
The little fairies jump off
And catch the snowflakes
So they will not come down
With a bump!

*   *   *

Peace

Peace is the glory of a nation
Standing for its rights,
It is the unison of the world
Clamped together to stay.
We praise Peace
The most of anything
On the earth . . .
Peace is something to keep.

Bibliography

Arnstein, Flora J. *Poetry in the Elementary Classroom.* New York: Apple-
ton-Century-Crofts, 1962.
Arnstein treats both our traditional heritage and children's ways of
composing poetry. She gives ample help for beginning teachers and
for experienced ones who have long enjoyed initiating children into
the deep satisfaction of writing and responding to verse. This slim
volume is both lyrical and practical. This is a publication of the
National Council of Teachers of English.
Betzner, Jean. *Content and Form of Original Compositions, Dictated by
Children Five to Eight Years Old.* New York: Teachers College,
Columbia University, 1930.
An important finding of this study was that young children compose
longer more complex dictated accounts than when they write. The
intellectual opportunities and the language growth available in oral
dictation were clearly demonstrated in this early investigation.
Burrows, Alvina Treut, ed. *Children's Writing: Research in Composition
and Related Skills.* Champaign, IL: National Conference on Research
in English, 1960.
Each of six leaders in the language arts presents the outstanding
research and its role in teaching the skills needed in written composition. Interpretation is both succinct and helpful to classroom teachers.
————, *Teaching Children in the Middle Grades.* D. C. Heath and Co.,
Lexington, MA: 1952.
Five case studies and three chapters describing three classes at work

in many related pursuits illustrate principles of children's learning. Other chapters on the content curriculum and language learning round out a successful program for middle grades.

———, *Teaching Composition: What Research Says to the Teacher,* no. 18. Washington, D.C.: National Education Association, American Educational Research Association, 1959, revised 1963.

Both the research related to teaching composition in elementary grades and its current applications are presented along with its suggestions for helping children achieve greater enjoyment and effectiveness.

———, Dianne Monson, and Russell G. Stauffer. *New Horizons in the Language Arts.* New York: Harper & Row, Publishers, 1972.

The authors stress the importance of oral language in the electronic era and relate it to the other arts of language. They give specifics of method in meeting children's needs and in leading children toward society's increasing demands for literacy. There are many examples illustrating children's work and their experiences in literature; all contribute to optimum growth and deep satisfaction in learning.

Clegg, A. B. *The Excitement of Writing.* London: Chatto and Windus, 1964.

Writings from schools in West Riding, England, represent the work of children from Infant Schools through Junior and Secondary Schools. Children from poor mining communities, encouraged to write freely in a stimulating school program, produce clear vivid accounts with a minimum of exercises. Distinctions are made between personal and recording (factual) writing. Interpretive commentary adds to the value of the collection of writing.

Cooper, Charles R., and Lee Odell. *Research on Composing—Points of Departure.* Urbana, IL: National Council of Teachers of English, 1978.

The Buffalo Conference on Researching Composing (1975) pooled its reports in this NCTE publication. Emphasizing studies in children's processes and behavior while writing, this volume contrasts with previous conventional research which has focused on products. Chapters on young children point up many possibilities and problems in researching their composing.

Cullinan, Bernice, Mary K. Karrer, and Arlene Pillar. *Literature and the Child.* New York: Harcourt Brace Jovanovich, 1981.

This beautifully designed and illustrated reference is a joy just to thumb through and to skim here and there. And careful reading reveals a scholarly study of the broad expanse of children's literature from its historic origins to its twentieth-century flowering. Analysis of literary values is balanced by wise teaching ideas and suggestions for activities involving varied arts and experiments. Bibliography, lists, information about authors and various indices add to the usability of this encyclopedic work.

DeStefano, Johanna, and Sharon E. Fox, eds. *Language and the Language Arts*. Boston: Little, Brown and Co., 1974.

This book is really by about sixty authors, each an authority in some specialty. Every section of each chapter is preceded by a brief introduction that puts it into context. Each section is reprinted from a longer work by that author. Thus the reader gains access to a broad field and can go further into each source.

Ferebee, June D. "Learning Form Through Creative Expression." *Elementary English* 27 (February, 1950): 73–78.

Miss Ferebee demonstrated how children's spontaneous writing lead to their acquiring essential narrative techniques. The teacher's welcome and friendly class listening assure satisfaction and motivate pupils to write again and again. Minimal pointing up of a telling phrase or bit of gripping suspense and other qualities lead to exceptional writing power.

———, and Doris C. Jackson. "Working with Children in Creative Writing." *Journal of the Childhood Education Association* 17, no. 6 (February, 1941): 258–262.

After many trials and much patient searching, two teachers found ways to support children's efforts in self-expression no matter how poor. Then writing and storytelling both improved; so too did attitudes and behavior. Philosophy, its illustration in action, and children's responses are all included in this classroom account.

Gardner, Howard. *Art, Mind and Brain—A Cognitive Approach to Creativity*. New York: Basic Books, 1982.

Biographical sketches of leaders in modern psychology emphasize their contribution to understanding of creativity. The artistic development of children is presented in relation to their intellectual maturation.

Goodman, Yetta M., Myna M. Haussler, and Dorothy S. Strickland, eds. *Oral and Written Language Development Research: Impact on the Schools*. Champaign, IL: National Council of Teachers of English; Newark, Del.: International Reading Association, 1978–79.

A series of four conferences sponsored by IRA and NCTE is here presented. Eleven main speeches, the reactions of two national leaders in language arts instruction, and an extended bibliography

(1976–1980) point to changes in teaching-learning that should occur in the 80s and 90s.

Graves, Donald H. *Writing: Teachers and Children at Work.* Exeter, N. H.: Heineman Educational Books, 1982.

This record of teachers working with elementary school children concentrates on their factual reporting and gives many techniques for children's exploring communities for firsthand information. Teachers trace growth in many individuals' expository writing. The author also presents personal progressions in his own writing processes.

Haley-James, Shirley M., ed., *Perspectives on Writing in Grades 1–8.* Urbana, IL: National Council of Teachers of English, 1981.

Leading professional opinion and recommendations precede description of what happens in classrooms as discovered by an investigating committee. Accounts of some highly successful programs offer many suggestions for local adaptation. Needed directions in research are contrasted with older studies. Committee positions on writing are clarified in both beginning and ending chapters.

Jackson, Doris C. "Poetry Making with Children." *Elementary English Review* 20 (April, 1943): 129–134.

The teacher gives many examples of her pupils' original verse and follows with detailed accounts of how they came to be. First attempts with a new class and results of experiments over weeks and months are carefully presented.

King, Martha L., and V. Rentel. "Toward a Theory of Early Writing Development." *Research in the Teaching of English* 13, no. 3 (October 1979): 243–253.

This article begins with the question, "How do children learn to write?" The authors answer the question from careful scrutiny of recent research. A set of theories develops explaining how story sense grows, how writing builds upon and differs from talking emphasizing the values of early learnings heretofore unnoticed.

Kuskin, Karla. *Near the Window Tree: Poems and Notes.* New York: Harper and Row, publishers, 1975.

Kuskin begins this small collection of some of her poems with an introduction she says children may skip! But teachers will find in it the shortest, clearest, friendliest approach to poetry making with children. A preamble to each poem tells a bit of how that poem came about. Both comment and verse are sheer delight.

LaBrant, Lou. *Study of Certain Language Developments in Grades IV–XII.* Worcester, MA: Clark University Press, 1933.

This early study of sentence structure in child writing reported growth in use of dependent clauses even when mental age was held constant. Social maturity rather than mental age alone appeared to account for increased complexity of sentence structure.

Langer, Suzanne K. *Feeling and Form: A Theory of Art—Developed from Philosophy in a New Key.* New York: Charles Scribner's Sons, 1953.
The author states the main purpose of her book as that of establishing an intellectual framework for a philosophy of art. The relationship and the differences between prose and poesis and the distinct functions of language are particularly valuable for teachers of writing.

Loban, Walter D. *The Language of Elementary School Children. A Study of the Use and Control of Language Effectiveness in Communication, and the Relations among Speaking, Reading, Writing, and Listening,* Report no. 1. Champaign, IL: National Council of Teachers of English, 1963.
Researchers studied 338 children and followed them over 11 years. Report no. 1 is the elementary section of the total coverage. Oral language was analyzed by showing the phonological units segmented into communication units. Important conclusions are vigorously stated.

Lundsteen, Sarah W., ed. *Help for the Teacher of Written Composition.* Urbana, IL: ERIC Clearinghouse on Reading and Communication Skills, 1976. The authors summarize pertinent research and organize findings around such topics as developmental trends, the relation of literature to writing, the nature of motivation to write. Research in the thorny matter of evaluation is briefly presented and includes statistical techniques and developmental guides.

———. *Children Learn to Communicate.* Englewood Cliffs, NJ: Prentice-Hall, Inc., 1976.
Lundsteen shows the relationships among all aspects of language arts and presents many class activities with brief interpretation of their basic psychology. Each of these related arts of language is also given its special treatment. A comprehensive view of pupils' growth in communicative power, this text bases its activities and expectation on broad knowledge of child development.

Mearns, Hughes. *Creative Power.* 2d ed. New York: Dover Publications, 1958.
———. *Creative Youth.* Garden City, NY: Doubleday & Co., 1929.
These two books tell the story of Mearns's teaching high school youth, how he encouraged their honest, unique expression by accepting whatever they wrote without negative response, how he surrounded them with literature and encouraged freedom of discussion

233

and of taste. His work in the 1920–1940 period influenced many schools and contributed to a new era of education in Amercia.

Moffet, James. *Teaching the Universe of Discourse.* Boston: Houghton Mifflin Company, 1968.

An understanding of Moffett's views of the many diverse kinds of discourse should preclude conventional classroom writing-for-the-teacher as sole audience! Useful also is his reduction of grammar's claims for its contribution. Examples from literature illustrate his chief tenets. "Learning to write by writing," the last chapter, applies largely to secondary schools.

Newkirk, Thomas, and Nancy Atwell, eds. *Understanding Writing—Ways of Observing, Learning, and Teaching.* Chelmsford, MA: Northeast Regional Exchange, 1982.

Many teachers record their success in encouraging children's writing. Emphasis appears to be on a daily stint of writing, pupils conferring with one another, and much, much revision. Developmental stages in individuals' progress are clearly defined.

O'Donnell, Roy C., William J. Griffin, and Raymond C. Norris. *Syntax of Kindergarten and Elementary School Children: A Transformational Analysis,* Research Report no. 8. Champaign, IL: National Council of Teachers of English, Research of Teachers of English, 1967.

Excellent summary of earlier studies of syntax in speaking and writing reveals their emphases and procedures and their relative merits. The authors present detailed evidence in charts, diagrams, and explanations of juvenile changes in syntax in grades kindergarten thru seven, showing when greatest growth occurs and raising important questions about teaching.

Petty, Walter T., and Julie M. Jensen. *Developing Children's Language.* Boston: Allyn and Bacon, 1980.

Broadening teachers' views of language and of many necessary teaching activities are among the first values of this professional reference. Specific classroom procedures, practical guides, and lucid undergirding of theory enlighten the whole. Oral language, writing, dramatics, literature, spelling—all these and more are included in this very comprehensive treatment.

————, and Patrick J. Finn, eds. *The Writing Processes of Students. Report of the Annual Conference on Language Arts.* Buffalo, NY: State University of New York, Department of Elementary and Remedial Education, 1975.

Dr. James Squire leads off this report with a stimulating view of the teaching of writing in English and American schools, a view that is both realistic and philosophical. Eleven reports from leaders with varying experiences in researching and teaching composition present their insights with vigor and clarity.

Robinson, H. Alan, ed. *Reading and Writing Instruction in the United States: Historic Trends.* International Reading Association, Urbana, IL: ERIC Clearinghouse on Reading and Communication Skills, 1977.

Five leaders present their perspectives on how reading and writing have been taught and researched in such a way as to help innovators avoid pitfalls of the past and clarify goals and methods for new departures.

Strickland, Ruth G. *The Language Arts in the Elementary School.* Lexington, MA: D. C. Heath & Co., 1969.

This comprehensive view of language arts teaching and learning is both scholarly and practical. No panaceas are offered; no "fashions" are promoted. Pros and cons of divergent points of view are enriched with psychological and linguistic insights. The broad range of knowledge gained from research and successful teaching that illuminates this third edition of a successful reference remains timely and professionally sound for decades to come.

Stauffer, Russell G. *The Language-Experience Approach to the Teaching of Reading.* New York: Harper & Row Publishers, 1970.

Teaching beginning reading from children's dictated messages, reports, stories, and later from their beginning writing is not only sound theory, but it is also economical in practice. Stauffer presents ways and means of classroom procedures and many examples of children's work. Theoretical foundations in psychology and linguistics buttress the presentation of methods.

————, comp. *Action Research in Language-Experience-Approach Instructional Procedures.* Newark, Del.: University of Delaware, 1976.

Stauffer's introduction traces basic philosophical insights from Descartes to Dewey and beyond, thus presenting a sound basis for his seven convictions as to the nature of reading and learning to read. Chapter one reports a comparison between LEA and Basic Reader Approaches in Grade 1. Following chapters report similar statistical comparisons through 6th grade. Studies of children's oral language, writing, reading, and spelling complete the volume.

Tway, Eileen, ed. *Reading Ladders for Human Relations,* 6th ed. Washington, D.C.: American Council on Education; Urbana, IL: National Council of Teachers of English, 1981.

Five "ladders" leading toward maturity begin with "Growing into

Self" and conclude with "Coping in a Changing World." Introductory sections explain how the many books for each human relations problem were chosen for age groups from preschool to young adults. Many hundreds of books are briefly summarized in this indispensable guide.

————. "Teacher Responses to Children's Writing," *Language Arts,* 57, no. 7 (Oct. 1980): 763–772.

Tway cites direct dialogue with children as they wrote in some sessions, and she summarizes other sessions. She noted ten pupils' spontaneous use of literary elements found in their reading and highlighted in their discussions.

————. *Time for Writing in the Elementary School.* Urbana, IL. National Council of Teachers of English, and ERIC, Clearing House on Reading and Communication Skills, 1984.

Case studies record observations of and conversations with three seventh graders and contain helpful notes on writing processes. Many apply to younger, middle-school pupils. All point up need to mull over, think about, and do seemingly unrelated things as part of the composing process.

Index